FLY FISHING
TACTICS
FOR
BROWN TROUT

FLY FISHING TACTICS FOR BROWN TROUT

GEOFFREY BUCKNALL

SWAN·HILL
PRESS

First published in the UK in 2000
by Swan Hill Press, an imprint of Airlife Publishing Ltd

British Library Cataloguing-in-Publication Data
   A catalogue record for this book
   is available from the British Library

ISBN 1 84037 101 3

Typeset by Rowland Phototypesetting Limited, Bury St Edmunds, Suffolk
Printed in England by The Bath Press Ltd., Bath

Swan Hill Press
an imprint of Airlife Publishing Ltd
101 Longden Road, Shrewsbury, SY3 9EB, England
E-mail: airlife@airlifebooks.com
Website: www.airlifebooks.com

To good friends in hard times – Annie Douglas, and the late
Maisie and Jack Curd. They dressed the most beautiful flies you
ever saw, or ever will see. I shall not forget them.

Acknowledgments

I have some difficulty with acknowledgments, being an anti-social angler who prefers to fish either alone or with a companion or two. I have mostly had to develop my own tactical ideas without help.

I must thank Aideen Canning for drawing up my flies with her usual expertise.

Of course I owe a posthumous debt to the late Oliver Kite for his practical dry flies. A similar debt is owed to Charles Ritz, an unacknowledged genius upon whose revolutionary casting ideas I developed my own. Ken Walker, of Bruce & Walker, admirably developed the ultra-light line blanks I use – I hasten to confirm that I have no commercial connection with this firm. And there are ideas developed from long-dead masters of the past: 'Lemon Grey' for wet fly dressing styles, W. C. Stewart for the upstream wet-fly technique, and in my early days a phone call to John Veniard resolved fly dressing problems.

I am indebted to numerous editors of game fishing magazines over the years to allow me space to discuss my methods: Ian Wood and Roy Eaton in the early years, then Jerry Hughes, Brian Harris and more recently Crawford Little and Mark Bowler. In taking up my author's pen again, after many years, the encouragement of the late Alastair Simpson, my book publisher, will be sadly missed.

These are all friends, but of course one tests tactical ideas against those who disagree: quite a few over the years, I dare not name them, but where would fly fishing be without 'friendly fire'? And who knows when to duck?

GEOFFREY BUCKNALL
Bromley
England

Contents

Introduction

Nice to meet you, Mr Fario

This book deals with tactics to catch brown trout, wild ones by preference, but always native to this country.

The natural history of the brown trout has been thoroughly recorded in a book by Frost & Brown in Collins' *New Naturalist* series. It has one important lesson for fly fishers, which I will expand in later chapters, which is that during its first four years of life the brown trout recognises its food by its activity. It is the behaviour pattern of an insect, for instance, which triggers the predatory response of the fish, and the structure of the artificial fly and the way it is fished must take this into account.

So if I have one small quibble with the text book, it is that I would prefer the word 'behaviour' to 'activity'. Being dead, for example is not a form of activity, it is a form of behaviour, and chalk stream trout lock on to the spent drake mayfly to the exclusion of hatching duns or still active female spinners returning to the water to lay their eggs. The word 'spent' indicates either a dying or dead state. It is important to understand this, for although we enjoy reading and discussing the controversy between Halford and Skues in days gone by, and I have been as guilty as any, in a practical sense it is unimportant. The feeding response of the trout is far more simple, and even though we dress our sport in mystique and mystery, raising it to a high pinnacle of intellectual skill which salmon fishing lacks, this basic principle is plain common sense.

An illustration is the way a chalk stream trout anticipates a hatching dun. When the fly is still some feet away the fish is alerted by the dimples of light made in the surface film by the legs of the fly. In a split second the fish quivers, moving slightly to gauge the exact direction of the fly. Once committed, the rise to the dun will be swift and precise because that behaviour pattern has been impressed by repetition to become a conditioned reflex. I use terms such as 'impressed' or 'locked on' to describe such feeding behaviour which has been conditioned by the repetition of the same visual image. Therefore, in this situation the fly dresser is wise not to over-hackle his dry fly, for a mistake in structure is more likely to bring about refusal than attention to a perfect match in colour.

Compare that action to the fish taking a spent gnat. Here the legs of the fly do not dimple the water, the wings support the dead fly, they are outstretched on the surface film. Unlike the dun, hastening to harden its wings and take off, this fly has nowhere to go. The approach of the trout is leisurely, it has all the time in the world to snaffle the fly and it's not unusual to see the fish take a turn downstream, side by side with the fly, then to mop it up in a casual way. These two well recognised examples prove that *behaviour* is the recognition signal.

This is why the fly dresser would wisely choose a stiff, bright hackle for his dun imitation, but a short, soft one for the spent gnat so that its copy would be supported by the hackle point wings, or other structure tied in the 'spent' fashion. A further lesson learnt from observation of the behaviour of the spent gnat would tell the angler that he should not lift off his artificial as soon as it has floated past the target fish, for it may well pursue the fly downstream. It often does so.

It is not my purpose to reiterate the information given in scientific text books, though we can learn much from them. It is interesting, though to discuss significant aspects of the wild trout's life.

The general picture today is that the species is more and more being forced into the remotest parts of this land. The rainbow trout is the predominant species favoured by both angler and fishery manager. The reasons are obvious. It is cheaper to rear and buy if only because of its faster growth rate. Although the brown trout has a longer life span and breeds far more successfully in Britain, it is also strangely less hardy in the period immediately after stocking. The brown trout has a higher percentage of mortality for new stock. Nor is its longevity entirely useful for angling, for after the fourth year its feeding habits change, it becomes partly a scavenger and feeder on other fish. Sometimes it becomes ugly, having a head like a bull terrier, sabre teeth and lank body. This gives rise to anglers giving it a special name, the *ferox*. It is a normal brown trout, nonetheless.

You will now know that my 'fly' philosophy is based on that famous phrase, that 'in the first four years of their lives trout recognise their food by its behaviour'. This conditioning of the fish to accept their food in this way is called 'imprinting'. There follows from it an interesting controversy.

To what extent does 'imprinting' develop into distinctive 'strains' of trout, such as the *ferox*, *gillaroo* and the *sonaghan* which have distinctive colouration and physical characteristics? It is also claimed that there are distinctive DNA fingerprints in these fish. This leads to the supposition that they have separate spawning times and places, and from that it is postulated that they at least constitute a separate 'strain', or even a distinctive species or sub-species.

Against this it is claimed that if these fish are intermingled with 'normal' trout, they spawn with them and produce a normal progeny which are not mules. Is it then proven that there are two separate strains of cannibal trout, one feeding on, and following char, the other simply an old fish which becomes a cannibal? Further reading is provided by Ron Greer in his book *Ferox Trout and the Arctic Char* (Swan Hill).

Unless proven otherwise, and I have a flexible mind, my opinion is that the factors are environmental. We know the conditioned wide colour variations in trout and an exclusive feeding behaviour must also be reflected in physical characteristics. This is why I have applied the term 'ferox' loosely to all large cannibal trout with distinctive feeding behaviour, as this falls within an acceptable angling definition. I am not yet convinced that a case has been made out for these fish being genetically modified to constitute a sub-species, and this term 'strain' is vague and ill-defined. Until the case is made, I remain within the realm of angling practicality.

This habit of the trout changing feeding habits and appearance is strange. My guess is that many older trout lose visual acuity because of parasitism in the eye, the so-called flukes. We have the mysterious gillaroo of Irish loughs, quite distinctive in colour, lying mostly in deep water to feed on snails. Occasionally taken on fly, the angler feels the snail-shells crunching beneath his fingers, he decries the poor fighting quality of the orange-bellied fish. I smiled to see an angler on lough Conn, weighing in after a competition. One of these fish was pinned up by its tail onto the score board when a stream of snails poured out of its mouth, obviously reducing its weight.

A similar phenomenon was experienced in Blagdon reservoir when trout which fed almost exclusively on snails and corixidae developed thicker stomach walls. All these fish were brown trout. Their appearance was changed by specialised feeding, though to argue that they had branched away from the usual evolutionary chain into a sub-species is a controversy which anglers have enjoyed for ages. One commentator opined that about 10% of Blagdon trout changed to this exclusive pattern of feeding behaviour.

A change in feeding behaviour of an organism has been the basis of a Darwinian theory: i.e. when two species feed in the same way on the same food items in the same environment, then the weaker must change or die. An example in Hanningfield reservoir many years ago was the explosion of bottom-feeding perch forcing the trout to become surface feeders to the delight of the fly fishermen, but when a disease exterminated the perch, the trout reverted to the richer lake floor for their sustenance. The sinking line and lure then became the intelligent tactic during daylight hours. This is another example of intelligent observation of feeding behaviour being the key to tactical choice.

What is a sub-species or special strain of trout? The famous Loch Levens are a case in point, being almost of a herring-silver and said to be bonnier fighters than their neighbours. Whilst researching another book I came across the report of the stocking of Loch Watten in Caithness with the 'Leven strain' in the early years of this century, and to this day Watten fish are distinctive in colour from those in neighbouring lochs like Calder, which have the typical dark sepia of moorland trout. I leave the scientists to argue over what determines a distinct sub-species whilst I discuss 'behaviour' in angling terminology, noting, though, that a persistent feeding pattern gives rise to our own vocabulary; words like *ferox, sonaghan, dollaghan, bull* and *slob estuarine trout* being applied because the habit is reflected in the appearance of the fish, and is instantly recognisable. Are these characteristics hereditary? It could be proven either way experimentally, but I do not need to know. Whilst investigating trout parasites in the far North it was mildly surprising to see that the growth rate of trout in Calder Loch unusually accelerated after the fourth year of life. Average weights of fish there are small, and one senses that in that fifth year the trout turned towards preying on the smaller fish almost exclusively. Similarly, older trout in the High Pennine unstocked reservoir at Cow Green preyed extensively on bullheads and trout fingerings.

A favoured explanation is that fish find food on the usual predatory basis of the best return for energy expended, and that this may be the explanation for the change in habit. My belief, I repeat, is that eye flukes may have an impact, diminishing the vision as they accumulate, making bigger targets, the equivalent of our own large-print books in libraries. One authority has it that when there are fourteen or more such flukes in a trout's eye, then it is virtually blind.

As with all fish populations, average weights are related to the number of mouths to feed from the existing food supply. Nature does not scorn a stunted population, say in a hungry beck, for the small fish grow slowly but reach sexual maturity whilst still small, and this is all that nature needs. It is not what the angler requires however and his purpose should be to improve the average growth weights by improving the food supply and, perhaps, reducing the fish population.

The angler imagines nature to be some legal force which adjusts everything in the environment, if only it were left alone. He talks about 'the balance of nature', a happy concept which does not exist in reality.

This is nowhere more true than in the problem of fish parasites. Taking human worms as an example, a Roman Citizen would have had no problem in regarding them as part of nature, for he would see them in every body orifice, even the eyelids. We would regard human tape worms as unnatural, a disease to be remedied. The parasites which alarm anglers are intestinal worms simply because they are visible when the fish is cleaned. They would miss probably the liver, heart and tiny eye flukes which are more widespread, and which bring about blindness in a fish.

I was instrumental in asking the Salmon & Trout Association's Charitable Trust to finance a research project into brown trout parasites in ten lochs in Sutherland and Caithness where I feared the parasite burden was harming the condition of the fish. If the levels of parasite were considered as normal, would this have increased as more and more marine bird hosts were forced to feed on inland freshwater fish because of shortage of food in the sea? And then does this become the norm we call Nature?

I mention this, for if you are used to preparing sanitised rainbow trout for the table which have been carefully reared in a fish farm, the first time you clean a wild loch trout you will find live parasitic worms squirming about in your sink. They do not affect the eating quality of the fish, though one rarer species, if the fish is not properly cooked, can possibly harm a human who is in low physical condition. Worms found in muscle tissue may well be trying to leave the trout when it is dead, much like a guest escaping from a rotten hotel. The answer is to clean wild brown trout soon after capture, but do not return the offal to the water! Or leave it for host birds. Alternatively, get them into the freezer quickly.

In passing, the report sadly concluded that nothing could be done to reduce the parasitism without harming the ecology. We cannot shoot the bird hosts, can we? The danger is that in concentrating on stocked, cash-crop fisheries we may neglect our indigenous wild brown trout populations.

There are two avenues for investigation. The first is to include a parasite killing agent into trout food for trout farms and small fisheries. Of course, we need to find an agent which is non-toxic to mammals and birds. The other is that some fisheries have large populations of smaller fish. They could do with intensive seine netting and trapping to reduce the population dramatically. Not only should this improve the quality of the fishing, but the faster growth rate could lead to a lower level of parasite infestation. The problem is that wild lakes and lochs are not truly commercial, other than to enhance tourism in the district, so the interest and investment is unlikely to be found. You cannot see the problem being discussed on local Tourist Boards, can you, even though fishing brings in much revenue, including wilderness areas?

It is of interest, though of little practical use, to discuss the many issues of trouts' senses. Simple observation tells us much. We can read learned debates on their vision, the famous 'trout window' for example, but observation tells us that a fly line passing high over the head of a fish is far more likely to spook the fish than one moving just a foot or two over it, as in side casting. The way in which they see colour has always absorbed angling scribes, and we know from experience and history of the strange colour shift which makes orange important in copying the Blue Winged Olive Duns and the female March Browns. Like insects, it is probably demonstrable that fish have a different vision spectrum to ourselves. Skues was preoccupied with why trout refuse certain insects altogether. He even chewed up various insects. 'They all taste the same,' he declared. 'Bloody awful!' On the Test I saw the large yellow duns of summer pass unmolested over fish, and I've never seen a trout take a Yellow Sally stone fly whilst pond skaters are quite imperturbable in their presence.

Why? We simply don't know. It may be that mysterious 'race history' or more simply the result of a one-off sampling. Taste would seem to be the logical factor.

Although, dear reader, you will discover new and novel tactical ideas in this book, there is also a basically traditional philosophy of the fly itself. The reason for this is simple. If a fly pattern has caught fish for over a hundred years, it has passed the only test which makes sense. There is a deeper reasoning behind this, for the emphasis is on catching wild fish in wild places, where wind and water conjoin to emphasise the 'behaviour' approach, rather than strict imitation. There will be exceptions, but as a general rule, taking, say a Scottish loch fisherman with his Grouse & Claret, he is not an unthinking automaton. He knows the lesson of this book, that the water around the fly is as important as the fly itself. That water is a moving, living entity, quite unlike the small, sheltered area of a commercial put-and-take fishery. Consider the difference between a Chironomid pupa hatching in the placid surface of the latter fishery with the same insect breaking through the waves of a wind-whipped loch, and then you realise the difference between the use of a Footballer type nymph (or its modern derivative) fished in the surface film, and a hackled Black Pennell, say, worked across the wave-tops of the turbulent loch.

So, if I had to emblazon one slogan over the top of the brown trout angler's fly dressing bench, it would be this: *trout recognise their food by its behaviour*. And now read on.

Geoffrey Bucknall
Bromley
England

The love of the wilderness – a scene in Caithness

Part One
General Considerations

Fishing the white water of a cauld on the River Teviot.

A New Philosophy

The purpose of this book is to introduce a new philosophy into fly fishing for brown trout, and to couple it with various tactics for catching this species, with emphasis on wild fish. Many years ago I introduced a new fly casting philosophy into bank fishing for still water trout. This was an option to the prevailing and popular methods outlined by Tom Ivens in his classic book, *Still Water Fly Fishing*. Like myself, Tom was primarily a bank angler, so his need was for distance casting, and the basis of his personal approach was a long, butt actioned rod with an easy action. His rod design was accomplished by the fine rod building firm of Walker Bampton. It so happened that my own enthusiasm for reservoir bank fishing was dampened by a fresh, raw duodenal ulcer, and this compelled me to search for a less demanding way of achieving distance. My search took me to bass fishermen in Alabama who had adopted a scaled-down tournament technique to achieve the same object, that is the shooting head, balanced to a shorter and lighter rod, for those split-cane days, with a double-haul casting method.

When I had developed the system in Britain to my own satisfaction I wrote it up in my book, *Fly Fishing Tactics on Still Water*. It was eagerly seized upon by those who, like myself, had modest physique and found that Tom Ivens's 'Iron Murderer' nearly murdered them. This is another story of another time, but, coincidentally, the basic philosophy of this book also arose from a physical disability – tennis elbow – and it required both a new tackle system as well as changes to fly casting method. It seemed sensible to extend the range of my 'tactics' books to accommodate the new ideas.

I should explain the personal development of my fly fishing from out of which the new philosophy sprang. My earliest days were passed in stream fishing in the Weald of Kent where I lived as a youngster, and I graduated to reservoir trout fishing when the great Weirwood reservoir opened for fly fishers in 1958. Some years later the opportunity came to fish the famous River Test, and my horizons widened further into migratory fish. As the years passed I became gradually disenchanted with the increasing artificiality of my southern fly fishing. Stocking was increased in reservoirs to meet the demand of competition fly fishing, in which I had no interest, and the smaller 'put-and-take' fisheries were forced to follow suit. This was based on the introduction of the rainbow trout which was cheaper to buy and easier to catch, so much so that a scientific study on the 770 acre reservoir at Bewl Water concluded that the average life span of a stocked rainbow trout between introduction and capture was 16 days. This is not long enough for the fish to lose the imprint of the fish farm and the artificial feeding. I began to yearn for the challenging conditions of my boyhood stream where the stocking was of fingerling brown trout only.

Definitions of 'wild brown trout' vary. Pedants would claim that it applies only to a population spawned in the natural environment. My own definition is more liberal; I apply it to fish which have been in the fishery long enough to acquire a natural feeding habit and a wariness of man and other predators. The evolution of a fly fisherman was neatly described by Grey of Fallodon. At first the angler wants to catch as many trout as possible, and I vividly remember my friends and I competing for the earliest thousand fish in a season. Later he goes on to target the biggest fish, and this took me to Blagdon and Two Lakes. Finally, he strives to catch the most difficult and challenging fish. At first the River Test satisfied my quest for these, the stream having its share of overhanging bushes and branches as well as lies protected by drag to the dry fly.

As years went by fishery managements on chalk streams also made concessions to the prevailing competitive mood. Rainbow trout were introduced. The 'dry-fly only' rule was relaxed, and the stretch which I fished, once having a natural wildness, was cleared of obstacles to easy fishing. Grass and bankside vegetation were cut down, trees pruned back and the weed cutting became ruthless. This coincided with the 'national mood' to make fly fishing easier, for society was also discarding ancient values and adopting a harder market philosophy. It was natural that this hard, competitive mood would invade sport, so much so that anglers came to believe that their ticket money entitled them to a relatively easy limit catch each time they went out. This introduced the dreaded disease of 'limititis'.

This is not simply a stroll around the houses, for I now reach the starting point, the competitive pressure on fisheries had to satisfy the demand by the public to catch bigger and bigger fish. Luckily for them it is easy to raise rainbow trout to immense weights. There were extravagant claims for these portly fish, one of which, I recall, was that they were a superstrain of trout which made better use of the food supply. I riposted that if you caught Billy Bunter guzzling cream buns in the larder would he be a 'superstrain of human being making better use of the food supply'? Of course it was always nonsense, which tempted me to remind anglers of the discredited theories of T. D. Lysenko, that characteristics acquired in an organism's lifetime could be transmitted to the next generation. This concept ruled out entirely the existence of the gene and its application on a wide scale in the Soviet Union caused havoc to food production.

At first sight the development was tolerable if it meant that urban anglers were enjoying themselves. I was mildly amused to see that a sport which was once an escape from the stresses of modern life had changed to one which was based on those anxieties. There was, though, a material change in tackle philosophy, for both the hauling out of the big trout from confined spaces as well as the 'time is money' way of dragging in fish quickly in competitions, meant that rods became more powerful, lines heavier.

Then two things coincided in my own fishing life. I was losing interest in the competitive scene, dominated as it was by this artificiality, and I also had a sharp attack of tennis elbow.

Commenting to the lady assistant in my city tackle shop that I would have to give up casting for a while, she pointed out to me a short rod on the rack which only needed a size 2 line to load it. I was fishing the River Anton at that time where an eight footer was perfect. I used the rod for that summer, and apart from being frustrated at not being able to stop a three pounder from ploughing through weed-beds I came to love the light line fishing. I had also started to read that famous treatise on upstream wet fly fishing on northern rivers, *The Practical Angler* by W. C. Stewart. The three things were churning around in my mind. I made certain decisions. The first was to give up my rod on the Test and Anton. The second was to turn to the rain-fed rivers in the North. The last, which was to come later as a result of my experiences on the northern streams, was either to find or to develop a longer rod to take an ultra-light line.

Let me expand on this last decision, with one proviso. The problem in writing any text book on fly fishing is that our equipment evolves at an alarming rate. Our tackle trade is a fashion business, it has to build-in obsolescence this year to make way for new products next year, very much like cars or ladies' clothes. Although I have to guard against this in my writing, there are some age-old truths which hold good in tackle choice. There are also wonder materials which no one will know about in a few years time.

Although Stewart wrote his book over 150 years ago, it was a revolutionary concept in its time, for until then anglers of those border rivers fished down and across the current. If you pick up a standard text book for beginners this method is described as about the easiest way for a novice, since the flow straightens out a badly thrown line and it virtually fishes the flies. It is not entirely fair, an experienced downstream fisher can raise his game to a high level of expertise, and accuracy and line management are conducive to success, but that's another matter. In Stewart's time, the limitations of tackle were such that when the rivers became low and bright in mid-summer most anglers gave up fishing. The *Fishing Gazette* recorded the great debt that northern anglers owed to Stewart if only because he opened up summer fishing to them. It went further than that, though, for this famous angler also cited the four common sense advantages of upstream work. They were, and still are:

1. That the angler approaches from the fishes' blind spot.
2. That given reasonable care, he is less likely to spook fish as water disturbance is carried away downstream of the quarry.

3. That striking into the fish is more efficient than pulling the flies away from the fish as in downstream fishing.
4. That the flies approach the fish in a more natural way than when swinging across the current as in downstream work.

I would add my own fifth advantage, that a fish struck downstream will sometimes kick or leap immediately the iron goes home, and with the force of the current, it comes free. My records show that more fish are lost when fishing downstream, than when fishing up, with the current working for you.

To suit his technique, Stewart proposed a long rod and a short line, these things being relative so to speak. I shall return to Stewart's ideas later. I shall also explain the problems I first encountered when applying his ideas for the first time, when it became immediately clear to me that the heavy line I had been using before the tennis elbow period was unsuitable. At that time the popular size was an AFTM 7. I had come to the conclusion that I needed a rod length in excess of nine feet which would be loaded with lines, say of sizes 2 to 4. A hopeful sign was that rod makers were designing rods to take a wider size range, of two or even three sizes, thanks to new carbon material from the aerospace industry.

The downside of my search through the trade catalogues available to me as a tackle dealer was that no one was making such a rod. This set me on the trail of rod design.

The carbon tube on which fishing rods are made is called 'a blank' in the trade and it goes without saying that this blank is the heart of the fly rod. It can be made to a chosen length, weight and action to suit both the fisherman's need and the market place. Basically, a blank is made by wrapping a carbon 'cloth' around a tapered steel mandrel, then cooking it in an oven. The mandrel is then pulled out of the cured blank and Bob is almost your uncle . . . but not quite; it must be cut to length, the joints, either overlapping or spigot type, arranged, and, usually the product is then ground to a flat surface so that the cosmetic varnish may be applied for display purposes.

How is the carbon material rolled around the mandrel? This is done by a rolling table, two surfaces pressing on the material as it wraps around the mandrel. In passing, by balancing a blank over the forefinger, and in gently turning it, two apparent 'flats' are revealed. Some fastidious anglers believe that the line guides should always be aligned with one of these spines for extra strength, and Scandinavian customers who came to my shop usually tested a rod in this way prior to buying. I am not sure if it is an important factor in heavier blanks, but I am certain it is an important point in my ultra-light line designs.

I approached British blank makers to see if they could make an ultra-light line tube to my longer requirement. I had one advantage insofar as a new technique of manufacture had come out of the aerospace industry. Earlier and cheaper 'cloth' had been made from a unidirectional carbon strand, and when rolled up round the mandrel, the effect was much like a taut curtain. Obviously this lacked 'hoop' strength, and this was overcome by sticking this carbon strand to a fine fibre glass scrim, but by a clever method of cross-laying a proportion of the carbon fibre, a new generation of blanks emerged which did away with the scrim, making for slimmer and stronger blanks, necessarily more expensive and usually designated by the letters I.M. (intermediate modulus). I knew that I could have a really fine blank with this material, but, unhappily, the extra fine tips posed a problem for standard rolling tables. Hand rolling the tips was an option, but it proved expensive. Having been turned down by two leading manufacturers, I was relieved when the British firm of Bruce & Walker told me that they had the necessary know-how to undertake my design ideas.

Thus began nine months of trial and error testing, visiting the factory near to Huntingdon, and throwing the lines with the prototypes. The problem was not in the casting. The new material from the USA had the power to put a size 2 line well over twenty yards, and stream fishing would not require more than this. I had hit on the length of 9.6 ft. My first experiments with ten foot blanks showed that I should either have a tube which was too soft, or else needing extra carbon which would raise the line size by one unit, which I did not want at that time. Later I added the ten footer to the range for sea trout and mayfly, a tale to be told in due course. The problem lay in developing a rod action which would combine sufficient line speed for casting, but also having enough shock-absorber effect to allow for playing fish on very fine leader points without breakage.

Let me explain. The factor in setting a fly hook is the weight of the rod tip, and, necessarily, my design would have a very light tip. I thought it would not drive home a hook size larger than 12, and small hooks are matched to fine leader tippets. I envisaged a nylon diameter equivalent to a breaking strain of not more than 3 lb in regular nylon. There are many new leader materials on the market, but my personal preference is for the old-fashioned nylon monofilament. So, the marriage had to be a '*ménage à trois*', the three partners being the rod tip speed for casting, the tip-weight to set hooks of up to size 12 and the test curve to enable a good fish being unable to break the tippet on the strike and in subsequent playing.

After a long period of fishing with these ultra-light line rods my friends and I settled for a tippet breaking strain of 2½ lb.

As a side issue, when carbon rods first came into use I was involved with the French hook manufacturer, Viellard Migeon, in designing a range of fly hooks for them. I worked for two weeks in their factory at Morvillars, with their leading design technician, Monsieur Billet.

In earlier times, when hooks were hand-made, in spite of the sentiment towards hand-crafting, it was difficult to cut a barb accurately to a chosen depth of the metal wire – you need only glance at ordinary forged salmon irons of that era to discover that anything up to 30% would be cut. Modern

The 9½ ft ultra-light line rod points to Loch Toftingall (Caithness).

machines allow for greater accuracy to be standardised, and I recollect that 10% was normal. I wanted a micro-barb hook, for easier striking with the lighter tips and also for less damage to the lips of fish. This was achieved, but the average angler is less sophisticated and I doubt the product was a commercial success. It suits my rod design perfectly.

Someone once remarked unkindly of fishing ideas, 'we do not invent, we only rediscover'. There is a germ of truth in this, and it is sensible to use and build on the wisdom of the past. When I was pondering on how to marry these three requirements in a rod action it hit me forcibly that it had been done before, by Charles Ritz with his famous 'Parabolic' rod action. Ritz, too, had combined tip speed with a supple action which came in when a good fish was hooked. His purpose had been to 'detune' his rod to suit a very fast-line casting method which was characteristic to him. So I asked Ken Walker to achieve a parabolic action for my rod design.

To cut a long story short, by patient testing and travelling days, he accomplished it to perfection.

I was delighted when the very first nine-and-a-half footer came into my hand with the action I was seeking. It included some minor features I sought. It was unground because I did not wish to use a gloss varnish for display. Carbon, unlike the earlier glass fibre, does not absorb water, so it needs no damp-proofing. A raw carbon blank, straight from the oven, still retains tiny ridges from the cellophane wrapping used in its rolling procedure. If these were ground away in an ultra-light line blank I thought there would be a significant reduction in strength of the carbon wall. I also prefer the spigot joint. Every joint must be a dead spot, but spigots less so than the cheaper and easier to make overlapping joints.

Now I had to confront the two fears – prejudices if you like – against the use of light lines.

This is a British phenomenon, and if you are interested in angling history, you will discover that it goes back for over a century. The fiercest controversy was over the preference that the great Skues had for very light cane rods made for him in the States by the famous firm of Leonard, which, even in those days, weighed just a few ounces. The debate, fought out in the letter columns of the angling press, was indeed heated for it impinged on the reputations of renowned British manufacturers, and their sales performances. Skues was never reluctant to advance his opinions. He ruffled feathers. However, some of the fears no longer concern us. The balance of a rod and reel, important in those days, is no longer of concern, but the ability to strike and play fish and to manage line in wind was an objective criticism, and if it applied in those days to line sizes equal to today's five or six, what about my proposed two and three? These were puddings I knew I had to eat and prove. This I will describe in the subsequent chapter.

Just as a gun needs to be loaded, so does a fishing rod. The completion of the equipage was simplicity itself. Any good lightweight reel would serve, with the obvious consideration of sufficient backing. Obviously, too, the techniques for which the rod was designed required a floating line. The double taper profile was preferred because of the special casting methods to be adapted to the ultra-light line, specialised casts such as 'switch' and 'double switch' to cope with difficult winds and high banks.

Tactical choice of leader make-up will also be discussed subsequently, but I have always believed that to transmit power and good turnover along the line to the fly, for accuracy and precision, the diameter of the leader butt should not be less than one third of the diameter of the fly line tip. Of course, with such a fine fly line tip, this is simplicity itself.

At the moment when I was on cloud nine with my ideas being translated into a finished rod, disaster struck in the shape of what was fondly described by politicians as the 'recession' – I had another word for it. My colleagues and I (we were a truly co-operative firm) were compelled to close our city shop by a combination of a savage increase in business rates and a hike in the bank rate. Then, being in my early sixties, I lacked the motivation to start a rod making firm to sell my design ideas. I retired, but with the interest of making the rods on a small scale for a handful of connoisseurs of fishing with ultra-light lines, for wild fish in the main.

It was with some reluctance that I named the rod. It was to have no promotion, but reflecting how Stewart of old had opened up stream fishing in the trying conditions of summer, bright sunlight, low water levels and spooky trout, I baptised it the 'Brightwater'.

I now go on to describe the experiences my friends and I had in answering the challenge of playing larger fish and coping with adverse winds, but there was one final question to be answered.

It has been my experience that there is a temptation in manufacture to guard against guarantee claims, especially in mass marketing of a cheaper product, by adding a margin of material to the blank, to strengthen it. This was not possible, clearly, in my design, nor would I have accepted it were it open to me. What would be the breakage rate in such a light tool, given that my shop experience was of around 1–2% of rods sold over the range? I guess that to date over a hundred light line specialists have taken the 'Brightwater' and so far one has been broken, my own. I walked through a gate in Upper Teesdale, carrying my rod butt first in the recommended fashion, but without realising that the gate had a strong return spring. It snapped shut behind me, like the gates of Hell, decapitating my poor rod in the process.

I will not weary you, patient reader, with accounts of complimentary letters I received over the years, other than to say that a rewarding number arrived. This book goes on to discuss my own application of the rod to different sorts of fishing. The rod has, and is meant to have, defined limitations which are now clear to you. It was natural that I later received enquiries for a ten-footer, for other techniques, including sea trout fishing by my expert fishing friend, Colin North who had used the lighter tool for that species. I, myself, found I couldn't set a large mayfly hook at long range from the banks of a loch. The rod was not intended for this fishing. To start with, I experimented with a six inch extension butt, and I went on to ask Ken Walker to make me a ten foot version of the blank, but this necessitated a bit more carbon in the blank wall, bringing the line loading up one size, to AFTM 3 to 5. I was reluctant in a way, for in making this modest concession, I feared that there would also be a temptation to use the heavier weapon when the lighter one would have been indicated . . . back to the old fallacy of letting power replace technique.

Another experiment I trifled with was to interest myself in different rod actions for upstream and downstream wet fly fishing. A tradition of rod design in the past was that options were offered between fast dry fly actions (upstream) and soft wet fly rods (downstream). The parabolic action I preferred could best be described as 'medium fast' though it is more subtle than that. I did copy in one blank the age-old soft rod for downstream fishing. Historians please note, this was true to the ancient Greenheart tradition. It was fun to fish with, and I still have it, but it was not always practical to carry two rods to the river, to test the wind, to choose the rod, only to find after a mile or two that the direction of either river or wind changed. The original design serves both purposes well, the parabolic action is, indeed, multi-purpose as Ritz intended, and I'm happy to stick with it.

It was pleasant to rediscover Ritz, for he was a prophet before his time, and it wasn't until I was older and wiser that I came to appreciate the wisdom in his radical ideas.

There is an interesting side-issue to modern rod design which arises from the development of professional casting instruction. Many professional tutors say that distance casting depends on the 'speed' of the rod action, which is true. The fallacy is in the belief that distance is the only criterion in rod design. It is not, and, strangely this relates to hook design. Formerly, hook points were hollow ground as the trade grew out of the old needle-making industry. This meant that hooks penetrated by puncturing, there was no cutting edge. Modern automation gives the point a cutting edge which aids penetration, and this is important as obviously today's rod tips are lighter than in days gone by when bamboo and hard woods were used in fly rod production. The difference is easy to see if you can compare a modern machine-made hook with an old hand-ground one, it is as if you were comparing a sabre to a rapier. The problem is that under pressure from a stiff rod, the hook that cuts its way in can also cut its way out again, losing the fish. I have seen this on many occasions and this explains why the fish escape through being held too hard. The parabolic rod action gives that extra shock-absorber effect, which is particularly important if you are using stretch-free nylons or fly lines. The above description interestingly demonstrates why such point-designs for hooks as arrow or spear points have never proved popular, and on one occasion when I was asked to test such a design, under even fairly moderate rod pressure, the hooks cut themselves free whilst the fish were being played. I must confess that on occasion I used this deliberately to fish 'no kill' on chalk streams, knowing by experience how much pressure to apply to the fish to allow it to escape without handling or netting.

My time in the fishing hook design department was well spent, for another change from the old days is that machine manufacture has not yet copied the hand-making skill of tapering the hook eye. This entailed grinding down the wire so that the shank was tapered, and fined down to fold it over. A remarkably neat hook-eye resulted, closed up very tightly. Modern machines simply bend the wire to form the eye, often leaving a gap between the end of the wire and the hook shank where the leader knot can fray or escape. This is a reason why we cannot finish the flies we dress with the tiny heads so beloved by our forefathers. It is important to mask that gap with the tying thread. There is an advantage to the modern way, for the old tapered eyes were a source of hook breakage unless the tempering of the hook was critical, and I recall this happening to me occasionally when playing a trout downstream in very fast water. I mention this as there is a sentimental attachment by some anglers to the 'good old ways', but some of them were far from efficient.

My final thoughts on rod design were caught up in a furious debate at one of the workshops run by the Kent branch of the Salmon & Trout Association. I kept quiet, for it was between two recognised experts with conflicting opinions. The first gave it out that nine feet was the optimum length for a good casting rod, that snake guides were an abomination and that the scroll shaped cork handle was far superior to the cigar profile. I was convinced on the question of guides, I had to add a smidgen of extra carbon to my blank to accommodate ceramic-type lined guides for it's amazing how much the weight of guides influences rod action. The blank is so slim, though, that the cigar handle is by far the most comfortable. As to optimum length of nine feet, I have heard this before from casting experts, but they overlook the simple fact that rods do more than cast. At its extreme, a nine footer would be nonsense on a moorland beck, and in-efficient when it comes to working a bobfly when drifting a Scottish loch. So I still treasure the advice Stewart gave so long ago for the upstream wet fly method . . . short line, long rod . . . but relatively speaking . . .

This customising of my own rod design was great fun, but I was yet to encounter the two fears that those who have never used such a tool would raise . . . an ultra-light line in a strong wind? A big fish taking control . . . so, read on . . .

Wild brown trout from a highland loch. Taken on ultra-light line.

A New Approach to Fly Casting

I have a confession to make. I have been classed as a professional casting instructor, although this is only true in the sense that I practised this as a retirement hobby.

I have come to understand that like many sporting activities, it cannot be taught from the printed page, nor even by visual aids. The reason is simple. When demonstrated and taught physically the actions are explicable, but when discussed, on the printed page, as in this ensuing section, they appear to be confusing, and this cannot be avoided. The basic reason is that the differences between good casts and bad ones are subtle and often slight, such as small changes in timing for example. Should I avoid discussing the subject? By no means, for the intention is to encourage the reader to take a fresh look at the technique which is at the heart of our sport, and which, in my opinion, has deteriorated over recent decades due to changes in the sport itself.

When I came to the testing of the prototype rod a discouraging aspect became apparent, which simply put, is that when an angler casts with an ultra-light line for the first time he lacks the 'feel' that a heavier line conveys, of loading the rod as the line is extended. If, for example, one is casting a size 7 or 8 line with its appropriate rod, there is a definite sensation that the line is pulling against the rod tip during the backwards and forwards movements of the rod. It is this sensation which allows the caster to time his casting movements and the pause between the two. Because a size 3 line is so light in the air it is difficult at first to develop this feeling, and usually the caster then compensates by applying more physical force in the form of leverage. The spring-action of the rod is lost and performance is poor. The timing of the two casting movements is not felt.

There are two ways in which the caster can help himself to improve timing when first using a very light line. The 'feel' will develop with time and usage, but to start with, a simple catch phrase should be said to oneself during the casting action. My own recommendation is based on the slow swing of the pendulum of a grandfather clock, simply 'tic-toc'. The assistance comes from realising that there are three elements to using the rod as a spring. The first is the physical action of the caster. The second is the weight of the line in the air, pulling against the rod to make it flex, and the third, usually overlooked, is the stickiness of the line on the water's surface which resists the momentum of the rod to lift it off. It follows from this that the lower the rod tip at the beginning of the back-cast, the greater is the resistance simply because there is more line to lift. This, too, impels the rod to flex. This, in turn, helps to develop that essential 'feel' of the line pulling in the air.

The greater flexibility of modern carbon blanks, say when a choice of three line sizes is recommended, also helps the newcomer to ultra-light line casting, because he can choose the heaviest line, a size 4 for the nine-and-a-half footer and he can come down to a lighter line when he has grown accustomed to the rod.

It is well known and true that a fly rod operates as a spring. It is the purpose of a casting instructor to convey this to the novice. In so doing he has to overcome the muscle-memory which the novice has acquired over his previous lifetime by using all sorts of sporting equipment or tools. Such things as golf clubs, tennis rackets, cricket bats and hammers are used as levers, so it is automatic that the learner unconsciously tries to use the rod in the same way. This is what we call 'muscle-memory', a convenient term borrowed from golf professional instructors. The fly casting instructor has the task of teaching his pupil 'to make the rod do the work'.

It astonishes me to see the wide variations in the time it takes for the learning process. This has nothing to do with intelligence. A few newcomers to the sport overcome muscle memory literally within minutes whilst at the other extreme I need two or three sessions to start the novice on the right road. The average learner should leave me after a two-hour session ready to start casting a fly in anger against the fish.

The problem is that I know of no other implement we use in life which operates on the spring principle, other than a fly rod. In the old days, the coachman's whip would have served as an example. It is a paradox that fly casting is very simple, two short arm movements with a pause between to allow the line to extend in the air behind the caster. It is common sense that to make a spring store energy it must be firmly anchored at its base. Taking a watch spring as an example, if this were broken then it could be wound up for ever without producing a single movement of the second hand. The angler's wrist is the anchor, and the only significant fault in fly casting is to allow the wrist to hinge backwards at the summit of the fly cast as the line is going behind. There are many adjustments, described as faults, but this is the significant one, and many dodges have been adopted by instructors to prevent it, such as stuffing the rod butt up the sleeve or even strapping the rod butt to the wrist and using artificial restraints. These are the instructor's 'false friends'. This wrist rigidity is a bad way to teach because wrist movement has to be learned. This is the wrist controlling the rod to add line speed and zip to the cast but not allowing the rod to control the wrist, causing it to hinge. We call this latter fault 'wrist break' and it causes the energy of the spring to be dissipated, to leak away.

Happily we have some advantages over the golfer, the best of which is that most of us are not in a highly competitive situation. The way a man casts is more a matter of opinion than fact. I see many anglers who have casting faults when compared to an ideal, but they succeed in throwing a good line because they have adjusted to those faults. They are usually completely unaware that they have them as the line flies out nicely. Unlike the golfer's swing, which can be standardised, the fly cast is not so disciplined. This is comforting to know.

Ideally, the perfect cast is when the rod and line form the stem of the letter 'T', with the shoulders as the cross piece. Ideally, too, the shoulders should not swing during the cast, though it is tempting to do this to add power. Many casters swing their shoulders, yet they put out a reasonable line, and this depicts the fact that, providing the caster makes the rod flex, he can adjust to a certain factor of imprecision. Very few casters avoid an element of leverage in their technique. The truth is, though, that such 'errors' – if I may unfairly call them that – also involve an element of fatigue.

So what we have in the normal overhead cast with a single-handed rod are two arm movements with a pause between. The first arm movement sends the line behind the caster against the blocking action of the wrist, and shoulders. This winds up the spring. The pause is to allow the line to extend behind the caster, fairly high in the air. When the line is extended it signals this by a tug at the rod tip. Then the line is thrown forwards over the water, the stored energy of the spring is released, and this is felt down through the rod to the caster. If done successfully, the 'rod has done the work' and is seen and felt to be so doing.

This is elementary stuff, but it follows that if the line is comparatively heavy, then it is felt in the air to be pulling against the rod tip and also against the angler's left hand, should he be right handed. This loading-up of the rod spring with a heavier line helps casters of all levels of experience. An ultra-light line, on the correctly balanced rod still loads up and still stores energy on the back cast, but is much harder to feel. And so accustomed are British anglers to the feel of heavy lines moving in the air that when they first use a very light line they are disconcerted by its absence.

It is normal for the newcomer to light line fishing to compensate for the absence of 'feel'. A danger is in applying leverage by turning the shoulder in an attempt to add more line speed. From my very first trials with the prototype ultra-light line rod I began to realise that I had to rethink my fly casting ideas. Theoretically a thinner line should meet far less air resistance compared, say to a heavy one. Yet sceptics cited strong winds as a problem for light lines. They were partially right, but why? There are two reasons, one simple, and one not so simple. The first is that it is necessary to build up more line speed with a light line. This is plain common sense. The casting method had to accomplish that.

The second is the problem of the 'loop' of the line in the air. In a perfect cast the line unrolls over the water, and if you look carefully you see that there is a point when you can judge how wide the distance is between the two parts of the line as it turns over itself. This is what we call the 'loop'.

This distance is the same on both forwards and backwards casting actions, as if the one were a mirror of the other. When the distance is short it is called a 'narrow loop', and when it is large it is called a 'wide loop'. As a rule, the narrow loop is the efficient one which good casters seek. With a heavy line it is not vital for normal distance, but with a very fine and light line the loop is vital. In my dalliance with tournament casting my mentor was always calling to me to 'tighten up your loop'.

So I was confronted with two problems. How to increase line speed? How to develop a nice narrow loop?

The simpler the problem the simpler it is to solve. The line speed can be increased in the air by line haul, that is pulling down with the left hand during the casting action. A single line pull on the back cast, to be released as a line shoot on the forward cast is probably all that most anglers need. In fact most casters develop this automatically as their fishing life continues. The improvement comes rather through straightening the line in the air than by increasing its speed. The double-haul is a more sophisticated and efficient way of accomplishing the same thing except now there are two pulls on the line, one on the back cast, one on the forward cast with a feed-back of line behind, between the two hauls. Not only does this increase line speed, but it also straightens the line in the air which combines the two essentials for distance casting. It is better to throw a straight line than a wiggly one. You can throw a fast, straight line farther than a slow, wiggly one.

Now, many years ago when I was dabbling with competition fly casting I had to understand how to vary the width of that loop. It depends on two factors. The first is the degree to which the wrist is opened. As I explained, the wrist is used under control. Cocked forwards at the beginning of the cast it is said to be 'closed'. During a good cast the wrist is then opened sharply to a short degree to add line speed on the back cast, and closed smartly on the forward cast for the same purpose. I knew that if I opened my wrist early on the back cast, controlling that opening to move the rod butt just three inches or so from my forearm, then I would have a narrow loop on my back cast providing that I did not lay the rod back too far. If you think about this carefully it is easy to understand.

The problem is that one cannot see what is happening behind. I once saw Jim Hardy giving a demonstration of double haul casting at a game fair in Sweden, and he was able to bend backwards far enough to follow the path of his line visually to the rear, but most of us cannot manage this. It occurred to me that if I laid the rod on its side, in front of me to make side casts, then I could easily see the whole process. Moreover, I could control the whole operation. I could see the timing and extent of my wrist movement. I could see the line extending behind to judge its extension and I could pick two points opposite within which to keep the rod movements confined. These latter points are, of course, where muscular power is applied, and I call this the 'power arc'. I could also see that essential loop and tighten it up.

This is worthy of further explanation as it is a fine way for an angler to tighten up his technique. The rod is laid flat and the side cast is performed in front. Three things should now be checked. Firstly, the timing, for by turning the head the exact moment of line extension on the back cast is clearly seen. Next, the wrist should be watched to check that it opens early and not too widely. Last of all, two points on the opposite bank should be selected, and by disciplining the wrist action, the rod tip can be kept within those two targets, an arc of about 60 degrees.

To write these things down on paper is to invite confusion, though if they are thought about carefully they describe the actions which are crystal clear in demonstrations.

These were the considerations which flowed through my mind when I was pondering the need for developing a casting technique for the ultra-light line rod. Just then a wonderful coincidence happened. I picked up Charles Ritz's famous book and straightaway I realised that he had confronted the same problem many years before. Because of his association with Frank Sawyer who, in his time had advocated a light line (size 1 in those 'silk' days) for nymph fishing, then he, too, had the problem of increasing line speed with a narrow loop. Being one of the most dedicated and intelligent anglers of recent times, he took nothing for granted, and he reconstructed his own casting method to suit his needs on the clear streams of Normandy. The result he described as 'High Speed, High Line'.

Ritz had the misfortune to visit this country when fly casting was going in an entirely different direction. This was many years ago. A group of good casters had taken over the British Casting Association and their aim was to have tournament casting accepted as a recognised Olympic sport in its own right. Until that time, casting competitions included events with normal fishing gear, the 'Skish' events, but to purify the sport, these were cancelled, and with that departed a good part of the audience and amateur participation. I will not detail here the equipment requirements other than to say that this was confined to specialised gear with which no man could possibly fish. Unhappily these people ran the demonstrations at game fairs and other sporting events, and poor Ritz was ridiculed, for the method he had developed not only looked strange, but it was designed for a different purpose. The idea of detuning a rod action, to make it slower seemed absurd to those who were obsessed with speeding up rod tips to obtain maximum distance. The idea of using a short power arc seemed silly to those who insisted on a long and low lay back of rod and line, the exact opposite. So although the Ritz idea interested American and Continental anglers, here, in Britain it was thought to be too daft for words. In passing, a tournament technique requires a fair amount of leverage whereas the aim in instruction of normal casting is to develop the 'spring' action.

What were the essentials of the Ritz cast? Firstly, the rod was thrown upwards from the shoulder on the back cast, instead of backwards from the elbow which is our traditional style. The wrist was opened very early as the rod was lifted. The rod was stopped early, without lay back, and from this firmly locked position, the rod and line were punched forward smartly, with a strong wrist snap from a completely locked position. This gave a beautifully narrow loop, and the line fairly whistled out to turn over above the water with a high degree of accuracy.

Snags? Yes, one. Ritz locked his elbow so that his stiff arm was raised above his head like that of a soldier on parade. 'Tennis elbow,' whispered Bernard Venables in my ear when I was describing this method during an after dinner speech I made as a guest of the Wilton Flyfishers. Yes, this was true, Ritz disciples had their fair share of this painful complaint because the stiff arm was simply giving too much strain. Then an American angler told me that the famous Lefty Kreh cast in the Ritz style, but with his arm relaxed by bending the elbow slightly throughout the cast. As soon as I managed this – and it takes some practice – I had a new casting method to match perfectly my ultra-light line rod.

I gave demonstrations at various places in strong breezes to prove that the finer line can be driven through the wind as efficiently as its heavier counterpart. I proved this to members of the Craven Flydressers Guild one windy evening on the Wharfe and to Yorkshire Gamefishers on Fewston reservoir, also on a windy day. I was amused to learn of a historical parallel from fly fishing's history when the father of the dry fly, the great F. M. Halford himself, confessed to his friend Marryat that he couldn't put his fly line straight into a strong wind. Marryat then showed him how to cut down hard with his rod tip on the forward cast to drive the fly under the wind as it were. Ritz, too, rediscovered this for his book.

If you have the patience to adopt what I call the 'Neo-Ritz' method I feel sure you will have no trouble in acclimatising yourself to light line fishing. The two make a perfect marriage.

I have to coin these two expressions. The traditional way of fly casting in this country, with a single handed rod, is to throw the line backwards from the elbow. In fact, casting used to be taught with the pupil holding a book under his arm which he was not allowed to let fall during tuition. You see this style everywhere because it works and it feels natural. I call it the 'English style'. My improvement, which I call 'Neo-Ritz' throws the rod upwards from the shoulder instead of backwards, and as this feels unnatural at first, it is harder both to teach and to learn. It gives a great advantage when using the ultra-light line, and because it encourages a narrow loop, there is a higher degree of accuracy.

It is unfair to criticise 'British' fly casting. It works, and it suits the natural use of the elbow joint. There are a number of reasons why the Neo-Ritz style is rarely seen. Yes, it is harder to learn because as soon as you throw the rod upwards rather than backwards, the timing of the wrist movement changes. It has to be earlier and sharper. The forward cast also changes, for from the completely locked position, the rod is punched forward at the same moment that the wrist snaps smartly shut. In a word, the actions must be far more precise. I have a worry that our traditional 'elbow' casting is here to stay for a number of reasons. Our fishing is mostly easy, thanks to our stocking policies and the drift-fishing from boats on still water. Then we have formalised instruction, testing examiners, and this tends to standardise methods of instruction. The result is that unlike some other lands, we use much heavier fly lines to gain the line speed which the method does not easily confer. Yes, it works well enough: but is it the best?

Ah, that's opinion, and my choice is for a method which gives a far faster line, greater accuracy and allows me to use much finer lines with a friendlier rod action . . . but then that's what our sport should be about, choice and experiment. I would be unpopular if I argued for harder fishing, it goes against human nature, but if it were harder then technique would be improved because that would be a necessity, for the developments of a few decades ago, especially on still water, came from fisheries which had much lower stocking levels than would be acceptable today. I can make a personal choice, to hunt the wild brown trout in the wilderness, and that challenge gave me the ultra-light line and this new casting system. Please don't believe that I am claiming to have invented it, except insofar as that many of us adapt to a personal style. The credit for the rethinking of traditional ways must go to that very clever man, the late Charles Ritz.

Monteviot water, River Teviot at Jedburgh.

19

The Compulsion for Distance

In a sense this chapter is archaic. The interest in shooting head casting was at its height some twenty years ago when reservoir bank fishing was more popular. There are several reasons why casting habits changed. Firstly, a general increase in personal affluence made boat fishing affordable to more people. Secondly, heavier stocking programmes were introduced, the result of competition from the smaller, commercial fisheries. Then semi-shooting head fly line profiles were made commercially in a single unit, popularising the bug-tapered fly lines long used by bass fishermen in the Southern states of the USA. Finally, 'home-made experimentation' gave way to a wider range of the off-the-shelf-tackle items in the shops. Perhaps I should add that the once popular casting competitions also fell by the wayside. Nevertheless, there is still a minority of bank anglers looking for distance, and carefully crafted shooting heads still outperform other systems, and occasionally there is another minority tactic, putting a lure down into very deep water, say from a dam wall in search of the bigger cannibal trout, and the very fast sinking shooting head accomplishes this more efficiently than any other system. I also add some extra fly casting wrinkles to enliven this specialised section of my book.

The preceding chapters have introduced and developed my ultra-light line equipage and tactics. These are the bases of my fishing for wild brown trout.

There is a strange psychological aspect to bank fishing on still water fisheries, 'the grass is greener', but this translates into the belief that the further you can cast, the more fish you can catch. This is seen to be true, for as a general rule boat anglers take more fish, but I doubt this is related to the distance they are from the bank. On the contrary, they delight in moving in so close to shore lines that on occasions I have had to cease casting as I could drop my flies into the boat, and this happens even on remote lochs with only myself on the bank and one boat on the water. It is not the distance from the bank which gives the boat angler a better chance, it is the larger amount of water he covers on a drift. General rules cannot be made for all still waters, but it is true that reasonably shallow water provides more fly life than deep water, for sunlight and oxygen are vital to life. It is true that on popular reservoirs the constant invasion of the margins by bewadered armies of anglers drive fish from the shallows, and there are factors, too, such as light intensity which, when too strong, makes fish seek the more comfortable depths.

There are times and places when a longer line is necessary for the bank angler, with the proviso that wild brown trout come to the fly so quickly that it is more difficult to strike them at very long range, say in excess of thirty yards.

This was the problem encountered by those reservoir anglers following the last war when boats were in limited supply and relatively expensive. Tom Ivens, and his friends, such as the late Cyril Inwood, developed the method of using a long, butt actioned rod, a double taper line (silk in those days), and a double haul casting routine, which gave them a distance somewhat over thirty yards. This made sense, for reservoirs like Ravensthorpe, Eye Brook, and later, Grafham which had extensive marginal shallows. I remember the dejection I felt when first fishing Grafham from the bank, on a sunny day, to see the lake floor clearly at the fullest extent of my casting range.

I have explained also that in my turn I developed the light shooting head outfit as an option to the heavy split-cane reservoir rods of the day.[1]

This alternative method for those with modest physique was based on a lighter rod with a short shooting head. For those with an interest in angling history, I found the Hardy JJH 'Triumph' rod perfect for the work, as recommended to me by that champion caster of the time, the late Captain Tommy Edwards. Later, I was to develop my own fibre glass blank, the 'Two Lakes' which became one of the best sellers of that era. Surprisingly, it took many years before the tackle trade took an interest in this development, with ready made shooting heads, one of the reasons being that at first silk lines were the mainstay of fly fishing and heads were only used in tournament casting.

Much has happened since those days. The weight-forward lines brought an extra yard or two for the bank angler, though, strangely, they were developed at first to help those who had to cast short lines to fish at close range. Exaggerated versions of this line were evolved, long-bellies, bug-tapers for bass fishing in the USA and more recently, 'triangular tapers'.

These were all based on the common sense fact that by increasing the weight compressed into the forward part of the line, and at the same time reducing the thickness of the shooting line behind this head, the result was a projectile which, propelled at speed, would drag out far more of the shooting line. The two improvements were the speed of the head and the reduced diameter and line drag of the running line through the guides.

This development was one reason why the made-up shooting head fell in popularity, but it also coincided with a change in fishing habits. Still water fly fishing became very popular. The demand was met by an increasing number of stocked reservoirs with more boats, and smaller commercial fisheries. This latter did not require distance casting expertise.

In the first twenty years or so after the war there was a necessary trend

[1]*Fly Fishing Tactics on Still Water* (Muller, 1973).

towards home tackle making, the famous *bricolage* of the Gallic race, and this also motivated a greater fishing expertise, for you cannot develop the one without the other, you are made to think about your fishing.

The mass market of later years created the shelf-product. Being the owner of a tackle shop I noticed that the once popular market for rod kits to be made up at home dwindled and died. With that died the famous specialist suppliers of yesteryear, such as Eggerton at Merton to whom rod builders went for best quality greenheart and split cane. This brought about a subtle change in the psychology of the customer, the tackle buyer. For example, an experimental home rod builder would tailor his own product to his fishing needs, both in major functions such as weight, length and action, and in small ones, too, in colour, finish, choice and number of guides. Now it is the other way round, for no matter how wide the choice, he still has to fit his requirements into the mass-manufacturers' assessment of the popular market, decisions which may be made well to the East of Suez. Then, advertising is King, and many choices will be dictated by cosmetics. The home rod builders still exist, in very small numbers, and they are the most expert anglers.

Part of this off-the-shelf philosophy astonished me, for so many years after I had urged the tackle trade to interest itself in my shooting head idea, the ready-made shooting heads appeared on the shelves of tackle shops. And paradoxically, this was a discouragement to the fishermen who tried them, for in a word, they were too short, mostly cut at thirty feet. It is necessary to go into this thoroughly.

What is a shooting head outfit? Basically, it is an exaggerated form of the weight forward line. The head itself is joined to a finer running line behind.

What is the difference between a shooting head and a fly line? In use, the fly line increases its loading of the rod as it is extended in casting, therefore it has flexibility which the caster can feel. In short, he works out the comfortable length of line into the air until it flexes the rod comfortably. This explains the wide variation in line-weight recommendations for modern fly rods, such a rod might have a choice of 5, 6 and 7 AFTM weights. The shooting head, though, is of a fixed weight, therefore it has to be precise, so buying one off the shelf must be a hit-and-miss affair. I met many anglers who fell into this trap, only to find that their favourite rod was either over or under loaded. This is true for weight-forward lines, but the dealer overcomes this by recommending one size heavier than the equivalent recommendation for a double taper even though in AFTM terms the weight loading is the same.

It is obvious, then, that the correct shooting head for a given rod is a ratio between length and weight. The correct weight to work the rod must be within the length of line which the caster can comfortably manage in the air. At one extreme, the average caster would find forty five feet to be too long to airialise, and thirty feet too short to give him enough shoot to drop his fly up to forty yards away. This means that the caster has to make his own shooting heads to fulfil these precise criteria, cutting the head from a double taper line. For precision, there is no alternative.

To explain my own method to do this: if I wish to suit a rod which loads up nicely with a size 7 line, then I start by cutting a size 8 line in half. I then join the half line at its butt to my chosen shooting line, and start to do some experimental casting. This must be a temporary join which is easily detached. At first it will be overloaded, then by clipping back carefully and cautiously from the butt end, I arrive at the right length–weight ratio. This is my master-head, and as in my earlier days I had access to accurate balances when I needed an alternative head for the rod, I simply weighed out the new line against the master, it was that simple. This way I could make up shooting heads for different needs, sinkers, floaters and sink tips. As a very general rule, and it is only a rough guide, they were usually about thirty-six feet long.

Let me briefly describe the faults of getting it wrong. If the head is too short it will not drag out enough line on the shoot, and if it is extended too far during the casting routine there is a tendency for the shooting line to dip downwards between the head and the rod tip, technically known as 'overhang' and this destroys distance and turnover. If it is too long, then it is unmanageable in the air, the caster cannot airialise all of the head comfortably with a sensible length of shooting line behind. If it is too light, the caster cannot feed line back between the two movements of the double-haul (as we see later). If it is too heavy the head lashes back and forth so fiercely that turnover and good fly delivery is lost. You can see the need for precision in making up a shooting head; it requires patience and care.

In my early days I used a simple monofilament nylon for the shooting line. Care is needed to choose the best strength/diameter combination. Too thick and you lose distance. Too fine and tangling becomes a problem as well as discomfort in handling. There is a price to pay for the extra distance which shooting heads convey, you will rarely have a tangle-free day. In recent times some specialised shooting line material has been made available through the trade, and choice is a personal preference. There is a flattened nylon. There is also a memory free nylon. I have been comfortable with a hollow braided nylon which is pleasant to handle, somewhat prone to tangle and which gives a lesser shoot as against a shiny nylon monofilament. The neat use of modern sleeves and superglues makes more efficient joins than in my earlier days, and I find that a sleeve, which can be heat-shrunk over the join, is very good. A final point, I prefer to use a floating running line for all heads irrespective of floating or sinking type. This gives clearance on the retrieve over marginal obstacles such as rocks and weed. Also gentle 'takes' are hard to see at very long range and one develops the habit of watching little kinks in the shooting line rather than the distant position of the fly or lure.

The leader make-up for shooting head fishing also needs great care to arrive at a good turnover. It is sensible to fish a single fly at long range, but if a dropper is needed, it should be on a short link and high above the point fly, more than a yard, simply to reduce the risk of tangling. Tom Ivens hit on the plan of making up a double-taper leader by knotting in a thicker belly about one third of the way down from the leader butt. His leaders, though, were made from numerous nylon sections, and today four sections, stepping down to the desired tippet diameter, would be sufficient. The second section from the butt would be the thicker one to give the double-tapered belly.

Two general rules apply. It is harder to fish very fine tippets and small flies with a shooting head outfit. It's possible, but it is not easy. It requires exact timing in the casting process to avoid 'cracking off' and making wind knots. Secondly, achieving an elegant turnover of the leader is the problem when casting a shooting head. Failure is usually caused by the head travelling at too fast a speed, and sometimes the line 'bounces back'. I find that it helps to raise the rod tip as the line is shooting out on the forward cast, and then to allow the shooting line to brush over the forefinger of the left hand gently to slow it down as if the action were to allow the leader to overtake the shooting head. In passing, just in case you have seen that declining phenomenon, a tournament caster in action, you will notice that he turns his rod sideways on the back cast, to reduce drag through the guides. This is not advisable in our scaled down routine for practical fishing as it can cause the hook to foul the line. The reel should be kept vertical in relation to the ground throughout the whole casting action, that is with the rod not being allowed to twist outwards. This is also a good discipline for wrist control.

The shooting head outfit is suited to the double-haul casting method. This gives the best results in distance, but it is not strictly necessary. A normal single-haul cast will also deliver.

We are again indebted to Tom Ivens's classic early book to prove that the double-haul method can be scaled down from its out-and-out tournament application, which, amongst other things, would be exhausting to perform over long periods of fishing, as distinct from the short bursts of energy on the competitor's platform. We have to decide the distances we wish to reach, and this has to be sensible, for whereas by straining for short bursts, many achieve membership of the fifty five (yards) club, over water for long periods of time it doesn't make sense. Realistically, upwards of forty to forty five yards is a logical compromise, and in spite of our sport's tendency to be 'optimistic', this is a creditable performance beyond the reach of 'normal' technique and gear, bearing in mind the aim is to achieve a steady fatigue-free routine. After all, Tom Ivens, in his time, was happy with thirty yards which was exceptional for those days.

I explained before that a double-haul cast is simply one based on two pulls of line with the 'free hand' during the two movements of the fly cast. The first pull coincides with the back cast, the second with the forward cast, and there is a feed back of line between the two movements to make the second haul possible. In competition casting, with the head lashing back at tremendous speed, the rod had to be laid right back simply to give the caster time to fit in the three arm movements pull, feed back and pull again. As he was on a platform, high above the water and without fly, and no obstacle behind, this was no problem. The angler lacks these advantages. If he lays the rod back too far, the line falls low and is likely to foul bankside vegetation. This is the reason why both the tackle outfit and the casting method have to be scaled down for application to practical fishing.

I have explained that I first developed this light shooting head tactic to suit my physical limitations. I had a sore duodenal ulcer which disliked being pulled about. They did not have the fast-healing drugs in those days. My aim was to have an easy routine, based on timing and technique. After the line had been retrieved ready for the next cast, I aimed at two gentle double-haul 'false casts' to give me enough momentum to bang the fly out to the required distance. I could keep this up throughout a fishing day without feeling as if some washerwoman had put me through her wringer. I witnessed a similar approach when watching some golfers. A powerful man hit his ball with a tremendous swing, and as it sailed down the fairway, he grunted with satisfaction. A slip of a lady golfer then teed off with a perfectly timed, almost leisurely swing which took her ball well past that of her male companion. Timing and technique beat sheer brute strength and power. It is hard to convince a learner of this truth, especially if he is young and strong, for in his mind he relates distance casting to physical effort, but 'it ain't necessarily so'.

This is so important, that I emphasise it again. The natural temptation when switching to double-haul and shooting head is to go in for maximum effort, it's a psychological thing, and a huge mistake. The advantages come from developing a smooth, well timed and almost gentle technique. You will reach out farther than with any other system, but without the fatigue of someone employing a normal 'reservoir' outfit.

Another difference is the stance. The competitive caster stands sideways on if right handed, his left foot and shoulder is advanced. I knew a successful competitor who practised with his back pressed flat against a wall, which explains the position. It allows the head to be turned backwards to watch the back cast unroll to get perfect timing. I soon discarded this for fishing. It is uncomfortable, and when wading, the safe positions of the feet in the water must be the first consideration, good balance is required for safety. Nor did I wish to keep turning my head. The precise tackle make-up is important so that, in practical fishing, hour after hour, I had to develop my double-haul casting by *feel* alone. Both in making up the shooting head, then later in use, I began to realise that the two line hauls did not need to be fast and furious. The working distance came with reasonable gentle line hauls, flowing sweetly into each other. The rod then did not need to be laid right back, just slightly past the vertical position before being blocked. The difference is that there is a strong element of leverage in tournament casting which I had to discard, even if only because that, too, is tiring over long periods of fishing time.

A note of explanation is necessary here. The fly fisher has to keep his line relatively high on the back cast, therefore he has to 'stop' his rod earlier and higher than the tournament caster who is on a platform high above the water, and with no hook on his line. To the best of my recollection, there was no penalty if a competitor allowed his line to hit the ground or water behind, I often saw this happen. In fishing we cannot apply the exaggerated low lay-back of the competition caster.

In teaching the double-haul method over many years I realised that the problem for the beginner was that he found there was not enough time to fit in two hauls and a feed-back of line between the two rod movements. The single haul is an easy and natural action, pulling line on the back cast, releasing it on the forward chuck. I reasoned that if the caster could confine this to the forward cast alone whilst learning, after a while he would be able to fit the first pull into his back cast.

In its hey-day, shooting head operators used such devices as line rafts or line trays to mitigate tangles. They are useful, but I developed the habit of letting the retrieved line fall in wide loops onto the water.

At the time I write, although I have encouraged the Salmon & Trout Association to get our sport back into tournament casting, with as yet, the result unknown, because competitions lack the popularity of times gone by, readers may realise that I have been discussing a scaled-down tournament method. It is much like detuning a racing engine to be used for road work. Although there must be precision, especially in the tackle-make up, which is part of the fun, it lacks the out-and-out performance of competition work.

I was often asked what sort of rod suits a shooting head? The plain answer is any rod will do, even double-handed salmon rods have been loaded this way. It is certain, though, that ultimate line speed is not suited to practical fishing, and therefore a parabolic action is best for single-handed trout fishing. Bearing in mind that striking fast-taking brown trout at long range is not easy, I go for a ten footer to take a size 8 shooting head, probably around thirty-six feet, but precisely loaded as described earlier. Distance casting with normal fly lines predicates a fast-actioned rod simply because the fast line travels further, but this is unsuitable for the system I have described because it makes timing of the casting movements too critical, and above all, it is unnecessary.

This outfit has its place in my armoury. My rod is optimistically called the 'Whopper Stopper' for it is out of place against half-pounders. I prefer it to waddling across rough moorland with a float tube outfit strapped to my back.

Many years ago, when we had a Casting Club in the South, I was impressed with the theory of 'ovality' which said that as a rod flexed its round section flattened, thus losing power. I made up two rods for the platform, of hollow glass, and I had stuffed two buttresses into the top section to counter this effect. On my very first cast there was a resounding crack and the rod butt shattered. My reserve rod met the same fate and I had to complete my own performance with a normal rod someone had loaned me . . . like Lazarus of Old, as the saying is, I came fourth and lost my beer money!

I must add my personal reasons for this chapter. I am not intoxicated by distance casting. I have discovered, as I grow older and more experienced, that I could catch as many trout as I wanted without disturbing the far horizon. I do remember my early still water apprenticeship, and the satisfaction I felt through solving the problems of distance casting. A multitude of hours was spent in practising and experimentation, and a good few pounds were wasted, both sterling and avoirdupois. A frustration in those days was that with the exception of Tommy Edwards, none of the High Priests of professional casting were willing to give me help or advice. For the reasons I have stated, they wished to keep any tournament-type practices well removed from practical angling. In retrospect, I realise that this was a valuable lesson as it compelled me to go back to square one, to rethink everything for myself, and it also put me in contact with bass fishermen in the Southern States of the USA, and later other anglers in Scandinavia, who had adapted shooting head and double-haul to their own needs.

This is one reason why I have written this chapter, for although the search for extra distance often may be illusory, and it may unbalance tackle in relation to the size of the quarry, it is also great fun which increases the mastery of equipment and the improvement of technique. Secondly, there are times and places where it is tactically advantageous to throw a very long line on still water. There are fish tantalisingly beyond reach or depth with normal fly line, and you may lack the means or inclination to go afloat. The funny thing about double haul casting is that it does take time and practice to get into it, but once there it becomes automatic. I double-haul all the time now, irrespective of the rod and line I am using, and without even realising that I am doing it. It's second nature to me.

You have decided to yomp to a distant hill loch. It may take you two hours or more, so fell-walking boots are the best footwear. You must travel light, for tripping over heather is hard going. You cannot wade; even if you lugged waders with you because the edges of the lochs plunge straight down into deep holes from ancient diggings. This loch is like a pudding, the shallows are far out and the dark depths around the margins. The fish are rising around weed beds well out in the loch on the top of the pudding, say forty yards offshore. The insects they feed on are harboured in those weeds. You see the fish beating up the weed margins to scatter their prey into the clear water close to the fronds, and that is where you must put your flies. You can reach this place with a shooting head, not with a normal double taper line. Although in acidic peaty country, the loch is alkaline, a long worked-out marl pit, having the reputation for dour, but hefty trout. A three pounder is on the cards, so you are not under-gunned for the quarry. Yes, I know several lochs in Sutherland and Caithness which fit this description exactly.

I have described the need to put a very fast sinking line from a dam wall for fish which traditionally lie deep, and I imagine that those attacking schelly and char, especially from the bank, would use the system, especially as, say at Haweswater as one example, there is no boat fishing as I write.

A classic case for the very fast sinking shooting head was the Queen Mother reservoir. The vast, deep lake had been stocked with brown trout and as the years went by there was a population of huge cannibals which stayed very deep for most of the day, perhaps hunting small fish by night in the margins. The only way to attack these monsters was by getting a huge lure down to them with a Hi D shooting head, using lures, like my own Beasties, or another famous one designed specially for that water, the Blackbird. I recollect that such a fish seized my friend's lure when he was armpitting his rod to light a cigarette and it nearly took the rod with him from the dam wall! Alas, this fishery is no more, but ethically, this specimen hunting for the *ferox* type of trout is commendable and in no way similar to dragging pellet imitations around fish cages. I have enjoyed doing it; were I more patient I would do it still.

I reiterate that it's not my intention to instruct in casting in this chapter. This cannot be done by the printed page, there really is no short cut to taking professional instruction. I know, as a callow youth my first attempts at fly casting were from a book, and it was damned hard work.

I have some feelings of doubt, for this has been a sort of 'master class' on distance casting when, more and more, it is falling into disuse due to the popularity of float tubes, boat fishing and competitions. Twenty to thirty years ago you would have seen perhaps as many as one in three of the bank anglers on reservoirs using shooting heads with a good double-haul technique, and perhaps those days are past. There are still some applications for it. I have mentioned the extensive marginal shallows on some reservoirs and the opposite application is where you need to get a very heavy shooting head down very deep, either from a boat or a steep dam wall. Nearly all still waters which have large populations of stunted wild trout will also have a number of large cannibal fish, four years plus, which feed on them.

I now add some discussions of other specialised casting techniques.

I have described earlier how the salmon fisher's Spey casts with double-handed rods can be adapted to single-handed trout rods. These are the 'switch' casts and although they would have been used by experts in times gone by, you only need to do some reading of the dusty tomes, to realise that today they are rarely practised. Perhaps there has been a decline in skills, who knows?

It is simple to relate them to the salmon Spey casts to make them comprehensible. The Spey casts were invented to cope with the tree lined banks of that river, and they still serve where the long line of the overhead cast is impeded by obstacles behind the caster.

As time passed, anglers discovered that the Spey casts were more effi-cient at coping with windy conditions, and also the system was more leisurely. It was extremely pleasant to work down a pool, rolling out a line with a carefree action, entirely safe from making wind-knots.

In single-handed work it makes sense to confine it to places where the line cannot be thrown to the rear, places with high banks and cliffs, high trees and in rocky gorges. The cast is still governed by the wind. Just as there are two versions of the Spey, double and single, so there are the single and double switch.

Entire books and videos have been devoted to Spey type casting, but once its mechanism is understood, the mystery can be removed. The final part of these casts is simplicity itself, the roll cast, perhaps the easiest fly cast in all of our fishing, and the 'switch' element is simply to position the fly so that the roll cast can be made. Why? The normal salmon cast is down and across so that the fly winds up below the angler 'on the dangle'. And the line cannot be rolled across the river again without crossing itself and fouling leader and fly. So the fly has to be brought up close to the angler so that it can be roll cast again.

If there is an upstream wind, then it's not only easier to bring the fly to an upstream position, but a strong wind may even snatch the fly into the air and carry it above the caster. This is the position of the 'single switch', and as the fly is upstream of the caster, so must he use his upstream-arm to bring the fly into that position. Once the fly is there, the rod is lifted to form that classical letter 'D' of the easy roll cast.

If there's a strong downstream wind, then the fly is brought towards but below him, close enough again for the rod to be raised to roll out the line and fly. Again, common sense tells us that the caster then uses his 'down-stream' arm for the cast. You see how simple it is, the aim is to use the wind to help position the fly for the final roll, and not to fight against it. That is the common sense reason for the two optional casts.

The problem is that the caster needs to be ambidextrous! For if you think about it, there are four possible permutations, two choices of either cast on the left or right hand bank.

The secret is in timing, for the positioning of the fly must be a continu-ous gentle movement of the rod with just enough pressure to slide the line, leader and fly into the position for the roll cast which ideally follows without pause. The art lies in applying just the right amount of pressure to position the line and fly with the rod taken not too far back for the final throw. Happily, this comes with practice.

These positioning movements are semi-circular, much as if the rod were following the contour of an imaginary half-orange. In the single switch the rod just performs one such curve, sliding the fly upstream, but in the dou-ble switch it comes back again along the same contour, hence the term 'double'. At the end of each movement the rod is lifted upwards and the line bowled out. It all flows together.

In former times this last roll cast was a thorough bang down, literally bowling the line over the surface of the water, but modernists today give the rod a short, sharp, higher snap of the wrist sending the line over the water as in the forward cast of the normal overhead cast.

It is clear that the rod spring flexes as this is done, mostly by the drag of the line through the water, and this makes both casts efficient when either wading or close to the water, and it is not efficiently done from a high bank. There is a 'flip' version in the double switch which makes the cast work from a high bank. In this, instead of the rod following the second contour back again, on the second movement the rod is flipped over, the reel facing skywards, rod tip low to the water, and then the line is dragged in towards the bank just on the downstream side of the angler and the rod is lifted into the classical 'D'.

Now, I am aware that no one could possibly teach themselves this casting routine from this printed page. It is not possible. When I teach Spey or switch casts I give this information to the 'pupil' before I begin to instruct, and I warn him that at first it will seem to be a mind-boggling heap of indigestible information. But as the actual teaching begins, I slot it in as we proceed. Even the sequential photographs of days gone by, as in that classic book on casting by Edwards and Turner (*The Anglers' Cast*), were not much help. The reason is clear, that switch casting is a continuous process, smoothly flowing, but descriptions and visual aids break down into jerky sequences. My purpose here is to explain the actions at an intellectual level, but there is no substitute for personal instruction, and the rub is that hardly anyone today goes in for such technical casts because they think it unnecessary in our easier fishing climate.

There is a slightly comical side, because when I recite the above information to a pupil at the start of his lesson, an expression of absolute confusion comes across his face. Then as we progress, it all begins to slot in. Alas, on this printed page I can only give you the same information, my aim being to motivate you to take it all further. I would never write a 'how-to-cast' book as I firmly believe that person to person instruction is the only safe and sure way to learn, especially advanced techniques. You need someone by your side.

Is it necessary to learn these advanced skills?

There have been occasions where I have found these things to have been invaluable, times and places where other companions would not, could not fish. I have in mind the gorge running up to the High Force waterfall in Upper Teesdale. Only the south bank is accessible, but this is hard going, a sheer cliff behind with many gallant trees clinging to its steep sides. A fast, turbulent current boils down from the falls, tumbling over rocks. There are good fish here, but the place challenges every casting dodge in the book. I fish it upstream, right-handed switch, then back down again, left-handed double switch. It's the only way, and one afternoon, I took nine sizeable trout in two hours' drizzle. I hope this provides the incentive for a number of you to take your casting further, but to give yourself practical advantages in your fishing, and not a collection of party tricks.

I now describe how to mend a line in the air, it is easy enough to do, but in passing I point out that this also allows a fly literally to be cast around a corner, say to a fish lying upstream and in front of protruding vegetation. The cast is bold, it has to be aimed directly over the obstacle, then the line is flipped around it on the forward cast, making a curve on the water, looped around the problem. The fly comes back along the line of the curve without fouling. Besides mending line in the air to counter drag, this also gives a dry fly a longer drag-free ride. An upstream mend, perhaps easier than throwing a wiggly line, is the usual medicine to such an illness.

I summarise, too, that the so-called steeple cast is also the best way to push a line into a head-on wind. It is necessarily a clumsy cast, the line has to be snatched from the water with the arm locked, the rod is stopped early and snapped down again so that the tip virtually touches the water. It is possible to push a fly into a strong wind, albeit with a terminal splash which cannot be avoided.

Now, these are all dodges to deal with tricky or unusual situations. There are two keys to them. The first is to understand intellectually what has to be done. The second is a paradox, for although I stipulate instruction, there is also a certain measure of imprecision in fly casting, it is tolerant of a fair measure of adjustment. Two examples are from the Spey/Switch casts, for the classical positioning of the fly involves those satisfying, curving movements of the rod, but some modern casters simply snatch the line backwards in a parallel way; this works. And we have seen that there are two versions of the final roll delivery of the fly. There is one unalterable rule in all fly casting, that is to make the rod function like a spring. The flexing rod has to be blocked and wound up against the body, or it simply won't work. Within that golden rule there are many variations, opinions even.

I conclude, as I began, that the purpose in this chapter is not to teach: it is to convey an understanding of how basic technique can be developed to improving distance and coping with tricky conditions, of wind, of obstacles, of river conditions. Such an understanding of the 'how' and 'why' is an invaluable background to learning. It cannot be a substitute for instruction.

Part Two
Rivers and Streams

Ultra-light line fishing in low, bright water (River Ure).

The Upstream Wet Fly

This section deals with the specialised technique of upstream wet fly fishing with traditional North Country spider patterns. Although we have progressed in technique, historically we are indebted to W. C. Stewart, a border fisherman who, some century and a half ago, wrote his famous book in which he gave the reasoning for upstream fly fishing on the fast rain-fed rivers he fished. Before Stewart, for the most part, anglers fished 'down and across' and this left them fishless during the summer months when the water was low and clear, and the trout easily spooked.

In spite of my hero-worship of this great man, I must avoid the danger of becoming a mere historian. It is both essential and interesting to study the writing of that handful of iconoclasts who revolutionised the way in which we fish, but more than that, the intelligent angler builds his own technique on those foundations. I have explained earlier the advantages which Stewart gave for fishing the wet fly upstream.

The *Fishing Gazette* of the time explained the tremendous boon his book conferred on anglers of a century and a half ago, for with their horsehair lines, which were incapable of being pushed into a strong wind, when the water was low and bright in summer, they simply had to give up fishing. The limitations of their equipment were not relieved until the heavy silk line came into its own towards the end of the nineteenth century. We cannot appreciate the difficulties of playing a fish downstream, in a fierce current on a single horsehair leader the breaking strain of which would have been no more than three-quarters of a pound.

There was another advantage for the upstream technique which still applies today. Anglers fail to appreciate that fish can simply drown if water is forced under their gill covers, and this happens when the head of a trout is coaxed downstream for any length of time.

Although it is not a clear advantage, as will be seen, upstream wet fly fishing, involving as it does a shorter line with a longer rod, gives more precision in casting, and lies which are inaccessible to the downstream fisher are opened to attack. This is particularly true in upper reaches of rivers where, at summer level, boulders protrude above the surface.

I have described my basic tackle requirements, the longer rod to be loaded with an ultra-light double taper line, say AFTM 3 or 4. It is true that the weight-forward line is more efficient for most short-line casting, but the terrain of the rivers I fish, with rock-infested runs, high banks, often tree lined, means that I use the versions of the roll cast described elsewhere and the double taper line is more versatile for this work.

The better-class fly dressing books describe the structure of the up-stream spider flies. The traditional patterns suffice, simply the body colour, usually of thread alone, plus a sparse game-bird hackle, and such favourites as Partridge & Orange or Snipe & Purple have been killing fish since long before Stewart. Although I have found no disadvantage in using a man-made tying thread, the good, old Pearsall's 'Gossamer silk' becomes translucent when wet and it is available in the shades of colour required.

It is essential to finish the hackle with 'a kick', that is to force the hackle to stand out proud from the hook shank by bolstering it. This is easily accomplished by finishing the head and whip-knot immediately behind the hackle. Better still is the revival of the eighteenth century method of dubbing in a morsel of fur to bolster the hackle and to give the impression of the silhouette of the thorax of a sub-surface nymph. It makes sense to keep your upstream spiders separately from the other flies you carry. Winged wet flies are not suitable for this type of fishing, and I have a separate arsenal of spiders for downstream work, using longer hackles, dressed without a kick.

Two things need to be mentioned.

The idea of 'upstream' is not to be interpreted literally. The angler moves in an upstream direction. The flies are generally cast to fish that are upstream of him, but not always directly so. I have often thrown the flies at a fish rising behind me.

The second factor is that the difference between upstream and down-stream fishing is that the former is targeted at the particular lies of the fish, and at rising trout, whereas downstream work is aimed at sweeping the water by fishing down and across with a long line, sometimes to rising fish, sometimes just covering runs and lies.

This is a generalisation which, characteristically, has its exceptions, but the conclusion is that upstream fly fishing requires a high degree of accu-racy. It is this precision which deters some anglers. The problem with dogma is that it disguises plain common sense. And common sense is itself so simple that I am tempted not to write it down. I do so because it is so often overlooked. For example, the difference between 'fishing the rise' and 'fishing the water' is determined by whether or not the fish are seen taking the floating fly from the surface, or bulging to nymphs just below. These are easy targets to attack, but in their absence it is necessary to read the water and then cast to the likely holding places of fish.

The next common sense guide to the possible trout lies is that trout like to occupy quiet places where they do not expend energy to maintain a position against the force of the current, but, at the same time, they have to intercept food items brought down to them by this current – the obvious lies, close to rocks, in quiet bankside pockets of water. I remember with pain my first expeditions to fast rivers of the North when I passed by the torrential shallow runs between quieter pools in the belief that no sensible trout would be in the white water. I realised that I was wrong, for here and there are the tiny patches of dark sanctuary. I saw only the overall turbulence of the run without studying it carefully. Such lovers of clean gravel as the March Brown and Stone Fly nymphs live there. And then, one day, I saw a trout turning its flank in a golden gleam as it swooped on a nymph.

You may imagine how daunted I was to fish a fast run in the upstream style. I still commit the angler's sin of arriving at the stream and, without waiting, plunge in to fish, only to find that in my excitement I have missed a rod guide when tackling up. For the newcomer, say from the easy-going South, it is worthwhile to walk the river in the company of an experienced local angler. I remember how foolish I felt the first time I missed the rise-form of a trout in turbulent water, the breaking of the surface into a pattern which was different to the regular confusion of the current. My companion showed me how to read the bed of the stream which was faithfully copied by the map of the surface above.

Coming up from the South I had become accustomed to a gentle rhythm of fishing. The very first cast upstream shocked me out of my easy going ways, for as soon as the line fell onto the water the flies and leader hurtled back towards me, the line went between my legs and I had the most horrendous tangle of flies and leader. Fishing up a fast run is hard work! By persisting, I grew accustomed to it, and the 'short line' injunction was made very clear to me.

The aim is to control the line so that the flies come back with the current at the same speed as the water. As soon as your flies fall, the left hand[1] begins to retrieve at that rate, then a lifting of the rod tip completes the recovery, flipping back into the next cast. Then you edge a step or two forwards, if wading, to make the next cast. Even when there are no target fish showing, there is a need for accuracy if only to prevent the line fouling rocks. As these may be covered in algae or weed, flies will be lost to 'bad shooting' as the downstream current embeds them by its pressure.

The value of the long rod is that the fine, floating line can be flipped over or around rocks. Plain common sense also dictates whether to wade or fish from the bank. As an example, I wade a favourite river, Upper Teesdale, in the wider stretches above Middleton-in-Teesdale, because this gives me access to the far bank. The rougher stretch, from Widdebank Farm towards Caldron Snout I bank fish. The river here is so strewn with rocks, with deep holes between them, that wading is exhausting. The stream here being less wide, I can put my flies to the far side without leaving my own bank.

Leader make-up for upstream work is slightly different insofar as the dropper links must be short, say of four inches or so, and the flies knotted to the higher link of the water knot. Let me explain this. When you tie in

[1]Assumptions are made in the text that the angler is right handed, for simplicity.

the dropper link, you have two tails to choose from. By choosing the upper tail, when the leader comes back downstream, the dropper fly and its nylon link are forced to stand away from the main leader. Not only does this encourage the fly to gain a clean and swift entry through the surface film, swimming in a natural way, but I have a feeling that fish sometimes come short to a fly when they touch the leader nylon with their snouts as they turn onto the fly.

The importance of the sparse hackle with a parachute-like spread is now clear. The reason – and it is essential – is that the flies must go straight through the surface film and appear to be lively in the current. The fly for the top dropper can be slightly buzz, say dressed with a stiff cock's hackle so that, in effect, it becomes a dry fly to copy a hatched dun. I prefer a small hackled black spider for this. I sometimes treat this fly with a floatant, but if a bright, stiff hackle is used, there is no need to be so fussy. More important, the spiders on the point and middle dropper are dunked in a sinking compound at the start of the fishing.

I cannot stress too much the importance of making the flies work from the instant they hit the water because time and current are both flowing rapidly. Unlike dry fly fishing, the line should be turned over low to the water, on the forward cast, and Frank Sawyer's dodge of pulling in a few inches of line at the straightening of the line and leader is worthwhile. He described this as 'pitching' when he applied it to nymph fishing. Usually, after the first few casts, the flies are nicely soaked and the casting rhythm is 'grooved in' as the golfers say. This sounds finicky, I know, but I regard it as the vital aspect of upstream wet fly fishing.

Let me add a few words about this 'pitching' because it is so rarely done. Most of us know how to release a few inches of line at the last moment of line-turnover to parachute down gently a dry fly. This works well. If, when fishing wet flies or nymphs, a short tug is given to the line, the flies behave in the opposite way, they curve downwards to go through the surface film, usually before the leader and line fall to the surface. It is a useful tactic when frustratingly, flies fail to sink or stick in the surface film at the start of a fishing expedition. This is often the case when the outfit has been used previously for dry fly fishing and a modicum of grease or floatant has carelessly been left on line or leader, soon transferring itself to the new terminal gear.

I should mention here that the popular leader link, a short length of hollow-braided backing line is unhelpful in upstream work though it has its convenience elsewhere. It becomes waterlogged and it unbalances the slim-tipped line I use. It is more efficient to strip the plastic coating from the core of the line tip, then to whip the core back onto itself to form a neat loop.

The reason why so many fishermen rarely persevere with upstream work on the faster rivers is the time it takes to become acclimatised to the faster pace. There are two consolations which they miss: the first is that striking is much more certain providing that the line is retrieved at the speed equal to the current, and on occasion some judicious mending has to be done to keep in touch with the flies. The hook is usually pulled straight back into the fish, except when fishing across the current when a downstream belly has to be avoided as much as possible. Management of the floating line is the secret to success, and in mending line the trick is to do this without disturbing the 'normal' flow of the flies with the current. The answer is simple, say in making an upstream mend to counter drag. The rod is pushed forwards, away from the body, before the upstream flip is made. The mend can then be made without affecting the flies, providing that this is done early enough. Drag must be anticipated, the mend being performed before it occurs – again, plain common sense.

The second consolation is that a higher proportion of fish are caught upstream than when fishing downstream, clearly so. This is true when playing fish which are above you, for the first temptation to the fish is to run upstream against the pressure of the rod, and this tires it more quickly. As I prefer to return most of my trout (we need to maintain breeding stock in wild fish rivers) I avoid drowning the fish which would be caused by keeping its head downstream. The pre-war writer, Alexander Wanless used to catch enormous sea trout and salmon on very light spinning lines of just a pound or two breaking strain. He accomplished this by drowning the fish, turning its head gently downstream so that water was forced under the gill covers, as previously described. I mention this because on rare occasions when a large trout is hooked, it is useful to know that if pressure can be eased off the fish will not run and leap.

There is a difference in the way migratory fish fight, for whereas they tend to run against pressure, in upstream fishing, a wild brown trout will eventually turn and dash downstream after the initial shock of feeling the hook. What does this mean? A typical reaction of the trout hooked above you is for it to bolt against the pressure of the line, but as its head is turned downstream, feeling the discomfort of water behind its gills, much as ourselves going in over our heads, it then runs down the line, and usually you wind up with the fish below you, adding its weight and strength to the power of the current. Only experience can teach the playing of trout in fast water, but as a rule it is wise to keep the rod high to prevent the line from fouling rocks. The fish will sometimes wind up downstream of you, with the current to help it, and if the trout is a strong and large opponent, you may need to go down to it, hopefully on the bank if you can reach it safely.

One possible problem from the careless playing of a large fish in fast water is that of the 'drowned line'. This is more common in salmon fly fishing where the line is so thick that the water pressure on it is alarming, the fish runs upstream against the pressure of a line loop being forced downstream. We sometimes have to play fish which have gone to the far side of the fast water before bolting upstream, but happily the fine diameter of my own ultra-lightweight line reduces this danger to a minimum. Even so, the greatest danger of playing a large fish in a fast run is the 'drowned line', fish and line going in opposite directions! The shorter line of the upstream method mitigates this, and it also helps to avoid the temptation to rewind loose line onto the reel whilst in the early stages of playing a fresh opponent. Although experienced anglers rarely panic when a big chap is hooked, there is always the temptation to 'do everything at once'. More fish are lost like this than in any other way.

I recall a typical upstream experience of mine. The summer heat in Kent was oppressive. I longed for the cool clean air of the Upper Pennines, so I phoned the High Force Hotel, in Forest-in-Teesdale to reserve a room and permit on the Strathmore Estate water. I arrived at noon. The weather was exactly what I had been longing for, a gentle upstream wind with periods of very light drizzle. Knowing that I had the afternoon before me I decided to fish the river immediately in front of the hotel. This is a fast, rocky run leading up to the spectacular cataract of High Force, the highest waterfall in England. The river here runs through a steep gorge, and the south bank is rough going, rocky, with low overhanging branches from the trees which sprouted out from the cliff side. I clambered along, sometimes perching on the narrow bank, sometimes wading out a yard or two into the water, and, for the most part, being forced to make side casts upstream, happily with my stronger right arm. Because of the 'assault course' nature of the place I fished only two flies, widely spaced, a Partridge & Orange spider on the point and a Williams Favourite on the top dropper.

The water was swift, as one would expect, coming down from the cataract. The stretch was not a typical fast shallow run. The depth was too variable for that, and there were dark pools between and behind limestone boulders. Here was a mixture of glides, quiet pools and white, rushing torrents. A sparse hatch of an undetermined fly was progressing with an occasional rewarding rise.

The advantages of side casting are that the lower the line over the water the less it spooks fish, and the leader and flies fall in a 'shepherd's crook' which means that the flies come back over the fish without being preceded by the line. The first trout was right under my own bank, in one of those sheltered pockets of water made by an indentation into the bank.

If such areas are large enough, the current swirls round so that paradoxically, the fish is 'facing downstream' whilst still facing the current. In small pockets, though, the current is virtually still, the bubble left by the rising fish scarcely floats away, and flies trapped there can be taken in a leisurely way by the trout in residence. The cast has to be accurate, falling within an area of just a few square inches. This first fish came eagerly to the fly and was duly hooked and released.

The next rise was in a glide of ebony water, the sky being sombre. This fish was slightly to the side of the glide as it tumbled over a rocky ridge, a position which afforded it shelter from the strong flow, but the stream bent slightly here, taking the morsels of food to the lie. It was a difficult throw, being mid-stream, and the back cast was impeded by the cliff immediately behind, a sheer face of rock. I was able to push the fly to the place by a switch cast, and this fish also fell victim to the Partridge & Orange spider.

This was how I progressed, an athletic afternoon and a respite from the heavy, humid weather I had suffered at home. After two hours or so I had taken nine good trout, and being fatigued by the long drive and the assault course, I called it a day. I have to record that the next morning dawned with a clear sky into which sailed a bright sun. There was no wind. The weather had followed me.

The delight of fly fishing lies in the many bizarre contradictions and paradoxes.

Upstream fly fishing is a simple technique, and at the same time, it is, perhaps, the most skilful branch of fly fishing for trout. On its day it outscores the downstream method. There are two exceptions. The first is simply that if the wind is blowing downstream it is just plain stupid to fight it, tangle will follow tangle. I have to confess, too, that it is more dependent on times of hatching flies when trout are taking on, or close to the surface. When there's no surface activity, with the dour fish lying deep, then the downstream man enjoys the advantage of sweeping his flies above the bed of the river, taking the occasional fish. Stewart admitted this, claiming that when the river was swollen after rain, then his upstream revolution ground to a halt.

Fishing upstream over a length of a fast river is hot and hard work. A bad southern habit I quickly learned to discard was being a beast of burden. Strolling from a nearby car park to the gentle slope of a grassy reservoir bank conditions us to carrying the well-stuffed bag, with other impedimenta. A capacious net bangs around the thighs, a heavy waxed-cotton coat completes the outfit. Most of this can be dumped on the bank. To lug this along the bank of the highland stream would reduce you to a puffing billy goat, and, to mix the metaphor, your sweating face would be as scarlet as a turkey cock. Upstream often means uphill, yes, rivers do run downhill! I only take what I can put into my pockets. The wading staff is essential, but the net can be left at home. A spool of nylon, a small fly box and a Swiss Army knife of the angler's variety is all I need. This occupies one pocket, the other can contain a modest drink and bite to eat if the fishing time is to be long. If the walk between fishing stretches is long, then clip-down waders make sense.

If you must carry a net, then the racket type is best, for the belt-attached telescopic variety is a delusion and a snare for rocks in the river and bushes on the bank. Companions have come out of the water between fishing runs, only to find that their nets are lying in the undergrowth a mile or two downstream! Landing fish by wet-hand is easy enough. Perhaps the fish has to be played slightly longer, but as soon as it turns on its flank it can be drawn across the water in front of you, easily to be grabbed and unhooked. Yes, wetting your hand is essential if you are to return the fish without loss of its body mucus.

There is a curiosity of upstream fly fishing with sub-surface spiders which is based solely on my own experience. I illustrate this with a typical example of September fishing on a favourite stretch of the Teviot. The bailiff had assured us that evening rises were out of the question at that time of the year, the middle of the month when the sun dipped early below the pines and the air became cool. It wasn't quite true, there were fish taking tiny midges. A problem with normal fly fishing in this un-stocked part of the river is that very small trout and salmon parr plague you when fishing 'down and across'. A persistently strong downstream wind had persuaded me to fish traditionally for most of the week, but one evening a light air began to move towards the West, not enough to ripple the water which remained like a mirror. In a smooth run above the cauld I could see the fish rising, a good number of tiddlers, but here and there in the expected places, bigger fish were taking just below the surface. Teviot trout turn to a buttercup gold when they grow to over half-a-pound, and I spotted the flash as they turned onto the nymphs. Whilst cautiously wad-ing upstream, I cast to various rises, and, strangely, the greedy small fish ignored the upstream spiders while the takeable trout took boldly.

I cannot tell exactly why this happened other than to guess that the attraction to the tiddlers in the downstream way is the dash of the fly across the current, but that the upstream spider, drifting back with the current, is not so attractive to them. I was so mystified by this phenome-non that I deliberately cast to some of the small fish, and in each case was refused.

Yet, in the morning, when being compelled to fish downstream in a strong breeze, I had hooked tiddler after tiddler on the same patterns of spider.

I will explore later the disappearing art of beck fishing on upland moors, but I mention here the old Clyde style of artificial fly which serves as an alternative to the typical northern spider. In days past before infor-mation technology, principal trout streams evolved their individual styles of fly, the Clyde and Tummel for example. These have largely disap-peared as angling literature spread knowledge and the result was a stan-dardisation. It is unnecessary to revert to the exact regional patterns of yesteryear, except for fun, but as there were practical reasons for their invention, we can learn from them in a general way. What many of them had in common was a slim upright wing surrounded by a sparse hackle. This wing was not made from neatly matched slips of feather, but was merely a bunch of wing fibre, say from a starling primary. I have a suspicion that the original Greenwell was fashioned in this way.

The hackle could also be from a cockerel or bantam cock. I dress these, too, on up-eyed hooks, but the dressing must be lean enough to let the fly pierce the surface film immediately it is cast up to a fish, and, in my expe-rience it is a valuable addition to a fly team as a top dropper. It has the virtue of working well as either an upstream or downstream fly. Any spider can be adapted to this style, but a favourite of mine is a variation of that old Grey Hen and Rusty. The body is made from a ruddy herl of the cock pheasant tail, and the legs are just two turns of a light blue dun hackle. I tear out a strip of light starling feather, fold it over to make a slim bunch and tie this upright for the wing.

If something works well, why bother to understand it? Yet I have to confess that for me the simple spider takes preference if only because its 'entry' is faster and cleaner than any winged fly, and this is an essential requirement on very fast water.

Logically, a wet fly has its wings dressed low to copy the hump-back of a nymph, this is accepted wisdom, and this neo-Clyde style doesn't conform. Again it is necessary to remember the 'behaviour' recognition signals. The simple fact is that a nymph swims to the surface to hatch, and in some way this upright wing conveys that signal to the fish. But it works, do we need to know more? In passing, the angling writer, W. H. Lawrie, painstakingly analysed the minute differences between styles of fly used in the past on various rivers. It was a scholarly exercise, there are small differences between the regional fly structures, mainly in length of body, but the upright feather-bunch wing and sparsely wound hackle, encircling the body and wings, are common to all of them. It was also, I believe, a style which developed independently in Wales in the old days.

There, having discussed the physical aspects of upstream work, I must add that it demands a much higher level of concentration than downstream fly fishing. The 'take' of the trout will signal itself in more ways than the unmistakable tug of the trout below you. Sometimes, as in nymph fishing, the line will simply 'stop', and at the other extreme there will be the splashy boil. You learn to recognise that golden glint below the surface as the fish turns on the fly. Although it sounds like mere superstition, on occasion you will strike into a fish without knowing why, an instinctive feeling that there ought to be a fish just there. And, although you may not realise it, you learn far more about the river and its ways simply because you have to.

How to conclude this exposition?

I confess that it is one of those rare aspects of fly fishing which produces success after a patient period of persistence. It does not come easily and I have known some companions who tried it briefly, then gave up in exasperation. You may understand the reasons. The sheer hard work and the 'speed' of the fishing is discouraging. You tend to cover a short length of river by the hour in comparison to the downstream angler, though this means that you are fishing with greater precision. There's another mysterious psychological aspect. Although it is a fallacy, the downstream man feels the line to be alive, being tugged by the current, whereas the upstream technique has a lifeless feel to it because the flies are being washed back towards him. It takes practice to keep in touch with the flies, and persistence to gain expertise is the gift of a minority, especially in these days of 'instant success'. It is one of the highest skills in fly fishing; it always was.

Author fishing fast water in Upper Teesdale.

Flies

I have explained the importance of the structure of these upstream spider patterns. You may be surprised at the absence of a comprehensive list of imitative patterns. If you have the opportunity to refer to Stewart's classic book, *The Practical Angler* you will discover that he relied on only three spiders for upstream work, and this is the joy of the method, that presentation is everything. The fly behaves in such a natural way that a small range of patterns suffices. Stewart's patterns were not as efficient as those improved by northern masters who followed him, and only eccentrics would prefer them today.

There are some general rules which apply.

It is sensible to use dark flies in the early and late season, and they should relate in a general way to the natural fly. The (female) March Brown is traditionally copied by a Partridge & Orange Spider. The Large Dark Olives and Iron Blue Duns are suited respectively by the Waterhen Bloa and the Snipe & Purple. In summer when the lighter olives come onto the water the Partridge & Yellow and Greenwell spider come into their own. If you want a buzzy top dropper I find that a small Kate McClaren takes some beating. These flies work for me, but if you stick to the basic rule, there's a tremendous choice, and confidence will build on success. Can I add a personal favourite? The dear old Dark Watchett, twisting purple and orange thread together up the shank with a smidgen of mole's fur at the thorax and a very sparse jackdaw hackle tied with a kick. It's a great alternative to the Snipe & Purple.

This is more than a pedantic argument in the 'presentation versus imitation' debate. If you have a riverside chat to local anglers they will tell you how the great fly hatches of yesteryear are no more, thanks to chemical treatment of land and other micro-pollutions. Unhappily, the imitative aspect has been demoted, though still useful in a general way. Would Pritt have used a dark Snipe & Purple throughout the season? I doubt it, but today it works well right through the summer, spring and autumn alike.

A Snipe & Purple Spider, dressed with a 'kick' for upstream wet fly fishing.

Sparser fly life means that for the trout, insect food is catch as catch can. If this is sad, it does convey a practicality to our fly boxes. I separate my upstream and downstream flies into separate small wallets, and, alas, that word 'small' is a sign of the times. I am an optimist, the rivers will one day run full again, and bankside meadows will be clouded with insect swarms.

I realise that upstream work on these fast rain-fed rivers is only popular with a minority of fishers. Once in a while, though, you will meet a wind which is friendly for the method, try it, and please persist. I know the first impression will discourage you. It discouraged me. It is probably the most demanding of all of our fly fishing skills, and the rewards do not come early. Once mastered, though, the catch rate will go up, for it is very efficient, maybe too much so?

A fast run in Teesdale – white-water fishing.

Down and Across

Sounds so easy, doesn't it? And in a way it is, the current straightens the leader, it brings the flies across the current from the far side, covering the lies. This is why so many text books speak disparagingly about it. They use that old fashioned word, 'duffers'. This must be put into perspective. Yes, it is a good way to start beginners on river fly fishing, and yes, the river does correct a bad cast.

Downstream fishing can, and should be raised to a higher level of skill. To understand why you should consult your inner child and play a game of 'Pooh Sticks'. Do you remember your A. A. Milne? The thing is that two young 'uns drop their twigs simultaneously from the upstream side of a bridge and the winner is the owner of the twig which first reaches the downstream part of the river below the bridge. This is simplistic, but by floating any piece of natural debris, a twig, a leaf say, the idiosyncrasies of the current are revealed.

This is our old friend, 'reading the water'. For that floating item reveals the flow of food to the fish, where it bends towards the bank, curls around a rock, is trapped against a bank, is carried backwards, or upstream in an eddy or even remains unmoving in an area of scum. Of course, there's no need to enjoy childhood games, this is an illustration of how to read the water, to judge how that food will be brought to the fish, above and below the surface of the water. It is so simple, and it is so often ignored by the fisher who steps into the water and mechanically sweeps the river below him, blissfully hoping that the current will do the fishing for him.

However, there's still a difficulty for this writer. How can I teach each permutation of current on this printed page? I cannot. All I can do is to stress the importance of learning how to learn from the river, and how to manage the flies in the light of that knowledge so that they are brought to the fish in the way that the fish expects to see them. There is that plain, biological rule to start with, that trout position themselves where they can harvest food with the expenditure of the minimum number of calories. If you link these two common sense factors to observation you can determine the critical areas through which your flies must fish *properly*. Take one plain observation. Fish must face upstream to breathe, but what is upstream? It is not always where you believe it should be. It bends, twists, turns, runs back on itself, and so will your line.

Properly? That is a relationship between depth and speed. I must apologise here for ruling out two fallacies.

The first is the depth at which the trout feed. In early season, when the water is cold, it is a fallacy to suppose the trout are lying deep. On the contrary, when it has been almost too cold for me to hold my rod, with a bitter north-easter blowing, snow flakes whirling or sleet rattling on my Barbour coat, hatches of Large Dark Olives, Iron Blues and March Browns have brought fish to the surface. Trout are more likely to be lying deep on hot, sunny days, especially when the sun is shining down the pool to dazzle them.

This question of the direction and intensity of light stresses the main message of this book, that *how* a fish sees the fly is more important than *what* fly it sees. (A cheering thought, you do not need to carry those huge wooden armouries of flies down to the river!) Two examples serve, they are an interesting contradiction. If I must fish downstream on an afternoon of bright sun when it is shining straight down the pool and into the lidless eyes of the fish from a high angle, then I choose a fly which is silhouetted against the light. That would be a pattern of sombre colours with a lively action in wing and hackle. Later that same day, towards late afternoon, shading into evening, the light intensity declines, its angle is lower and then the luminosity may fall away as the haze or cloud above the horizon diminishes its power. It then makes sense to choose a fly with either a silver or gold body to reflect the light. For example, if sedges were coming onto the water, the Wickham would be an excellent choice, both in giving an imitative impression of the natural fly in shape and colour, but also in providing a provocative target. If that same evening were overcast with no direct light, then I would revert to a sombre fly. This sombre fly, too, would remain on the leader at dusk, on into the first true hour of darkness if I decided to fish on into the night.

As I only write about what I do, I translate the above paragraph into an experience on the Monteviot water last September when my friends and I decided not to fish until five in the afternoon as the day had been hot, bright and without any wind. I chose to fish down a long run known as the Whittleinch stream. The river above boiled over a cauld, for although there was a good level of water from rain a few days previously, it had become crystal clear. The sun was still high and right into the eyes of the fish, so I started with a winged Blue Dun on the point. For the first hour the fishing was hard because of the water clarity and in order not to disturb the pool for later I moved very slowly downstream. I had a very bold take, netting a two-pound grayling, followed by a half-pound brownie. Just after six o'clock the sun was lower and the first sedges – big, chocolate coloured ones – started to hatch and a rise began. I then switched to a Wickham on the point and had an exciting hour and a half with trout and grayling. By half-past seven the sun was obscured and a grey, slowly failing light came over the stream. The Wickham was no longer favoured, so I reverted to the Blue Dun again. Another trout or two followed, capped by two sea trout which I had seen pushing upstream from the pool below. A curiosity was that the 'early evening' fish hit the fly very hard, but as the rise developed, the 'takes' became quite gentle, and at its height I could cast to a choice of several rises without moving down in my 'chesties'.

Let me take this *how* question a stage further. A factor very few angling writers mention is the angle at which the fish sees the fly, but it is of paramount importance. At one extreme it is easy to demonstrate when using a winged wet fly, for it is seldom a fish can be tempted if it is thrown upstream to a rising fish. Straight across the current, yes, that does elicit a take on occasion, but the majority of fish can be induced to rise at an angle downstream, providing that the fly is not dragging across fast water on an unmended line. This is simply because the fish is being given a broadside view of the fly, but the wing and hackles are mobile. When the fly is on the dangle and the fish sees only its rudder, they take less, with two provisos. You can still tempt the fish to take if the fly is above their eyes, and also if you give the fly a provocative movement instead of simply lifting off immediately the lines ceases to move round with the current. This was an ancient salmon angler's trick, known as 'dodding' in the old days. It is done with either gentle movement of the rod tip, or small retrieves by hand.

We know from the work pre-war by Arthur Wood on his Cairnton water on the Dee, that salmon take the well sunk fly when the air temperature is lower than the water temperature, and vice versa, but this doesn't apply to trout fishing. On the contrary, trout may escape bright sunlight by lying deep or in shelter of undercut banks and weed.

It is a fallacy that line control to adjust the depth of the flies is the same for upstream and downstream fishing. It isn't. When fishing upstream, where a floating line is obligatory, the depth of the flies is controlled by the free hand pulling the line, especially with weighted nymph. Downstream fishing does give the choice of using sinking and sink tip lines, of various sinking speeds by choice, though I rarely fish other than with a floating line. We owe a debt to the late Hugh Falkus who pointed out the paradox, that by raising the rod tip when the flies are swinging round, the flies are made to sink deeper, and vice versa. It is exactly the opposite of what one might casually suppose, but it is easy to prove experimentally by dangling a team of flies on a leader in the flow, and raising and lowering the line. You will see that Falkus was right.

There is a cautionary note about the weighting of flies. True, for upstream work, when the flies are scarce in the water, weighting nymphs is useful, but in downstream work, it is the force of the current which causes flies to skate on the surface when the line is not managed correctly. If the height of the rod tip is one control, the mending of line is the other. Line mending is the throwing of an upstream loop when the fly line is extended on the water. Very rarely, a downstream loop will add life to flies in a static pool. The downstream mend, too, is necessary to add mobility to flies when casting across a normal current into a back eddy by the far bank, for failing to notice this means that these fruitful food traps are often neglected by fishermen.

Line mending is easy to do, the trick is to push the rod well away from the body before the line is flicked over. This prevents the flies jerking in an unnatural way. Experience soon indicates when to make the line-mend to anticipate the target area. When using a sinking line, which cannot be mended when sunk, the mend must be done whilst the line is turning over in the air on the forward cast, and this is far less tricky than it sounds. In a sense then, height of the rod tip and line management determine the depth and speed at which the flies come to the fish in any condition of water. Good, plain common sense.

In passing, there's this mystery of 'drag', when fishing down and across. The force of the current is exerting greater pressure on the line in mid-stream, and even with sensible line management, because the flies are tethered to the line, there must be some centrifugal force to make the flies and leader swing across. No dry fly would be accepted, fished this way, except, perhaps by freshly introduced rainbow trout. The explanation is straightforward, for as aquatic flies swim to the surface to hatch, they are simultaneously being carried downstream. As your wet flies swing round in the current, if drag-free, they also lift upwards, copying that behaviour pattern perfectly. This is why the speed and depth of the flies have to be nicely calculated. When an angler finds that the same fly is taken again and again from his team of two or three he tells himself this is because it is 'the right fly'. It is more likely to be because it is in the right place and fishing in the right way.

It seems absurdly simplistic to say that the depth at which the flies work is important. Of course it is. It can depend on two or three inches.

An example of this was on the Teviot in early April when the weather was cold even for that season. My two friends and I had been fishing for an hour or two before the expected hatches of March Brown and Large Dark Olives which usually started around midday. When the hatch of the latter fly came it was one of the most prolific I had ever witnessed, myriads of them streaming along the surface of the water by the far bank. We were fishing wet flies across the river, covering the fish easily, but although the trout reached a frenzy of feeding, we hooked none with the prescribed Blue Dun winged wet flies. The downstream wind was too fierce to switch to dry fly, cast upstream. We had an evening inquest, but could not solve the problem.

Next morning I decided to fish a lower run, and I reflected on the phenomenon as I walked along the bank. I recollected that the trout had taken most of the duns on the surface, and I also realised that as we had been fishing for some time before the rise, our leaders, line tips and flies were thoroughly soaked, and the answer seemed to be that the flies were fishing too deeply, even though just a foot or so below the surface.

Suiting thought to deed, I greased the leader and cast so that my team would be just below the surface, weather conditions being much the same.

To my pleasure, when the duns began to excite the trout I was able to bag-up a nice catch. Further proof arrived the following morning when the wind lessened and one of my colleagues, reverting to upstream spiders, took a splendid fish on Dark Watchett just below the surface.

Just to think this through, to discover why the fish were locked-on to the natural flies close to, or on the surface film, their behaviour was not perverse. On the contrary, the nymphs were ascending in the fast, shallow run above the pool, and they arrived at the surface to hatch out where the trout were lying in that pool below. The cold air held the flies on the surface at that place, and a simple cause and effect resulted. The trout knew just where to look for their food, and, more important, they also knew where not to look. The fallacy was for us to inspect our flies, to peer at the surface to see if the fish were 'taking something else' instead of calming down and thinking things through. These are the occasions when one 'goes through the box' in a fever of anxiety, often to no avail.

Whereas I have stated that it's not necessary to become an expert entomologist to be successful, it is helpful to master the basics of the life cycles and behaviour of aquatic and terrestrial insects upon which trout feed. There are many excellent text books for anglers, and whilst it's not necessary to identify precisely every upright winged fly, knowing the difference between a dun and a spinner, and between a stone fly and a sedge is helpful. Sensible observation by the river, for example, will tell you where you may expect a hatch of March Browns in spring, you want to be at the right place at the right time. And they are kind enough to favour the same places on successive days, more often than not. On one occasion I profited from noticing that in a mixed hatch of March Browns and Large Dark Olives the fish were taking the latter and ignoring the former, and it was my own Blue Dun which scored.

These flies are distinctive, we can all identify them, but when later, in summer, medium and pale olives come along, precise identification is difficult for the casual, inexpert angler, and, thankfully it's not necessary: a general pattern such as a Greenwell will cover a multitude of duns, just as a Pheasant Tail will cope with most of their spinners.

Being aware that I have neglected to discuss tackle in the chapter, I confess that there is some truth in the old adage that a rod for wet fly fishing downstream should have a fairly soft action. The reason is plain common sense, that when a fish takes 'below' it is often an opportunistic snap at a fly which is travelling fairly fast. Such a fish can more easily bounce off a stiff rod tip than a flexible one which absorbs the shock. Also, when fishing a fast stream, fish become unstuck when held against the pressure of the current and a rod which is too stiff to cushion the combined force of water and its struggle. I did experiment with a soft-actioned blank, pretty much like the limber greenheart rods of yesteryear, but the reduced water pressure against my ultra-light outfit, coupled with the parabolic action proved that this combination was sufficient. It also saved me the expense, and inconvenience of carrying two rods.

In all my fishing I rarely use anything other than a double taper floating fly line. I anticipate a future chapter on still water fishing, where, from the bank, the vast expanse in front conditions one into believing that distance casting is the most important factor. There are two ways to cast a long line. Most modern anglers prefer to use some form of weight forward line which will drag out a good 'line shoot' on the forward throw once sufficient momentum has been built up by 'false casting'. A minority get their distance because they have the ability to lift a very long line from the water, and to airialise it, and they usually prefer a double taper line. It is personal preference, they both work well enough, but the double taper line gives that extra versatility, in roll and switch casting which is clumsily performed with the other line profile. On the other hand, I have little excuse for rarely using or carrying a sinking line, I expect it would enhance my catches, I am advised to do it under those hot, bright and airless days, but I prefer instead to fish early or late, and on days of cloud and overcast.

Flies: my conversion to *how* rather than *what* has been a long and slow process, for in my younger day, as a professional fly tier, I was intoxicated with Halfordian ideas of exact imitation. Now I realise it is important to strike a balance between these two aspects. The result is that my fly box is far less crowded, for two reasons. I know the rivers I fish and what flies come with seasonal progression. I know that natural flies which resemble each other can be copied by a smaller range of patterns. Here are some examples. On northern rivers in early season, we expect to meet the March Brown, the Iron Blue and the Large Dark Olive. They must be copied in two styles, for downstream or upstream work. The winged Blue Dun serves the last two for downstream fishing, but strangely, it also serves well if, in an unseasonably warm April, the first medium olives appear. The March Brown, a distinct fly, is deserving of its own distinct copy. For upstream work the special spiders are needed, and they have been discussed previously.

A whole variety of medium and light olives in summer suit the dear old Greenwell, again, winged for downstream, spider-form for up. I insist that when you sit at your fly tying bench you should first ask yourself: 'what will this fly do?' – then you take light conditions into account, as I have described. I now wind up with a small vest-pocket wallet, tucked into my waistcoat pocket. I add one proviso. Most of us wind up with confidence-building favourites. I rarely go abroad without my Dark Watchett spider, and my save-a-day fly is the Silver Invicta. And we all have a jinx fly, usually a famed pattern which lets us down. Mine is the renowned Butcher!

There is one other 'must'. Every fly fisher should carry a simple black fly, I doubt the exact pattern matters, nor whether you fish stream or lake. I carry two versions, spider and winged. The former is the Williams' Favourite, a plain black body, fine silver rib and black cock's hackle, and if you simply add a pair of grey wings slips – I prefer jay primaries – you have Richard Clapham's 'Lee's Favourite' – both are plain black gnats, but roses by other names . . .?

There are many traps for angling writers to tumble into. When research-ing my anthology of the old *Fishing Gazettes*[1] I encountered much advice on striking and playing fish. I am tempted to follow suit, but I know that experience, and the river itself will teach those lessons; some will be hard lessons, but mistakes are useful tutors. There is one significant danger in downstream fishing when a hooked, large trout dashes upstream, usually by the far bank, when the strong current in mid-stream bellies the line downstream. The fish is going one way, the line the other, and this exerts a powerful force against the hook-hold. Happily – or otherwise – no one has solved this problem, it's like the infamous 'poisoned pawn' in chess. Advice was given by a master salmon angler long ago, to try to 'work closer to the fish', no easy job, thigh deep in a rock-infested torrent. Again, though, it spells out the efficiency of my own ultra-light line gear, with far less pressure on the finer line.

It's sensible to take a note of the salmon angler's technique, for Ameri-can anglers are amused that we use such long rods, and they fail to under-stand that they are more efficient for line management. My tackle system serves the same purpose in this downstream fast-river fishing, for the finer line can be switched, mended and managed in a wind more efficiently. I wince to see many friends going out with their sixes and sevens, which I call 'heavy artillery'. It is a 'Catch Twenty-two' trap, for the ultra-light line system impels a higher level of skill in casting and line and fly man-agement, from this comes better catches and more pleasure because it is more sporting. The contrary is sadly true, that the heavy line outfit institu-tionalises the less efficient 'elbow' cramped casting style with its wide loop and slow, heavy line. Most of British casting is stuck in this groove, alas.

Much of the fun of fly fishing comes in personal choice of equipment. Some items make sense, and I repeat as safety measures, the necessity of wading staff, and, naturally, couple this to good anti-slip waders. Some rivers require chesties – my favourite Teviot does – but in Upper Teesdale I would prefer thigh boots. The water is dark, I never venture where I can-not see the bottom. It always makes sense to wear eye shades or glasses. Flies and hooks sometimes go into strange places! The buoyancy waist-coats add an extra safety margin when wading. It makes sense, if you need a net, to carry it by a clip on a D ring, high on your back. Trailing nets can trip you in the fast current.

Leader materials are the subject of lovely controversies, but truth to tell, regular nylon serves well enough, though I sometimes use fluo-carbon as short dropper links in very clear water. These things are personal choices, but nothing is a substitute for failing to read the lessons the moving water is anxious to teach you. Expensive tackle does not cure bad fishermen.

The number of flies? Although a team of three is the norm, I am often happy with two, a winged point fly and a fairly buzzy top dropper well

[1] *The Bright Stream of Memory.*

53

up the leader, and although this latter is made with a full hackle collar, I prefer it to sink just below the surface, otherwise it causes the tail fly to drag. At dusk I nip off the dropper and fish a single fly. This is the time when you only need a single fly. As drag is the killer, I avoid the convenient hollow-nylon join for the leader, I simply strip the plastic coat from the line core and whip this latter back on itself to make a very small and neat loop which causes neither drag nor wake. A small point, I usually make up my rod first and let my leader and flies soak in the water whilst I prepare everything else, especially when fishing the evening rise. It's most exasperating to have a team which simply sticks to the surface with rising fish all around. These are idiosyncrasies which accumulate during one's fishing life, and you may well acquire you own. They work for me.

When I give talks I am most frequently asked about my main tackle system and its make up. Here is a short list for my downstream work on a normal Border river of medium width, average size trout and grayling:

Rod: 9.6 feet (parabolic action) with DT3F line
Leader: 12 feet, tapered in equal sections to a tippet of 3 lb b.s.
Flies: mostly two, point, and a dropper a yard from the point fly. I am not
   rigid about flies, sometimes I add a middle dropper. Reduced to a single
   point fly at dusk.
If sea trout are expected, I go up to my 10 ft rod with a size 4 line.

The lonely waterscapes of the Flow Country

The Nymph of the Stream

It is true that nymph fishing on chalk streams has been written up by those masters of the past, Skues, Sawyer and Kite. Sawyer gave us three practical patterns, the Pheasant Tail, the Grey Goose and the Grayling Bug. As a man of his river he knew the same lesson of this book, that 'how' is more important than 'what'. It is strange that none of these masters devoted time to rain-fed rivers in other parts of the country. They may have assumed that the rough-spider tradition served the purpose, especially for upstream fishing, but this is a fallacy. The spider fishing is suitable for trout which are rising, or close-lying to the surface in anticipation. Even the great Stewart would fish downstream with sunk wet flies when the river was full, for his upstream revolution was intended to open up the rivers to those who normally gave up when the rivers were low and the water was bright.

The nymph is a tactical choice on these rivers when there is neither surface nor sub-surface activity, but it is in the nature of searching the water rather than the chalk stream method of targeting visible fish. This was never investigated by the three chalk stream men as far as I can determine from their books. Let's get down to some mechanics.

The very first choice: the number of flies, for we are not confined to a single fly as on the restricted chalk stream. The use of a dry fly on a dropper above the nymph not only gives two shots at the target, but the dry fly also acts as a sight-bob. To an extent it can determine the depth at which the nymph will fish. An alternative, to give greater precision in fishing to a chosen depth is to knot in a leader extension, then to superglue a tiny ball of polystyrene over the knot. I found this to be so effective that I had doubts as to whether or not it was ethical, but as I fish mainly 'non-kill', unless rules forbid, I shall continue to use this leader make-up. Again, the plastic ball is a sight bob which veers or submerges when a fish takes the nymph. It also determines the depth at which the nymph works.

When I had my own fishing tackle shop I was able to search the whole world for specialised tackle items. A tapered leader is essential for stream nymph fishing, but more than that, the taper must be steep, the leader having a thick butt. There are three good reasons for this. Firstly, it gives a good turnover because the power of the fly line turnover is transmitted efficiently right down the leader, giving accurate and straight presentation. Secondly, the thick belly and butt of the leader, tapering to a fine point, allows the nymph to hang in the water, and from this comes the third advantage, that if you get a good sight of reflected light along the leader, it's easier both to see the take of the fish as well as to monitor the way in which the nymph is behaving in the current. Alas, fishing is filled with contradictions, and this is one occasion when a shining nylon is an advantage – you can't win every argument, can you?

The dressings of both the Hare's Ear and the Pheasant Tail are simple, but I like to arrive at a two-tone effect to emphasise the thorax. The Hare's Ear has an abdomen of snuff coloured fur from a hare's mask, ribbed with gold. The thorax is of a darker fur from the same pelt, and a strip of any brown feather goes over the thorax for the wing case. I prefer the sepia, speckled feather strip from either grouse wing or tail feather, but it's not important which you choose. Tail whisks and hackle have proved unnecessary in my fishing. I make the nymphs in three different weights to suit both different depths and speed of water.

This weighting is achieved by an underbody of wire, one layer of fine lead wire for the lightest, some more for the medium sinker and the 'Titanic' has two full layers.

To identify these easily in my box I wind in a narrow band of fluo thread at the head as a colour code, being respectively, yellow, red and green for the three different weights. The Pheasant Tail is made the same way, and it is worth the trouble to find a centre tail with a nice ruddy glow to it. The two-tone effect in my PT nymph is due to the thorax being formed from some herl taken from a brighter red macaw tail feather, but you may find any contrasting feather, or a suitable dubbing, the effect is the thing.

When I first started to use nymphs on rivers I believed that a hackle was important, to give 'life' to the fly, and accordingly I tied in a tuft of feather below the thorax. On experimenting further I was astonished to discover that catches were never reduced by omitting this hackle. I imagine that the reason is that, when fished on a line and leader, the action is that of a swimming nymph, the legs of the natural fly being tucked well away under the body. I would need some specialist knowledge to know if this is true, but practical fishing proves beyond doubt that there's no need to tie in a hackle unless this gives you confidence, it certainly does no harm to do so.

I have discarded Sawyer's Grey Goose nymph in favour of the Hare's Ear, but on occasion I use his grayling bug, which is simply made by forming a carrot-shaped body of a buff coloured wool over a weighted underbody. For all the world this looks like a maggot, but in a large size it is clearly a mayfly nymph. Sawyer stipulated a certain Chadwick wool, but long ago I found a wool called 'old parchment' which does the job admirably. It is a buff colour with just a hint of pink. Since these three patterns work well for me, I follow Sawyer's philosophy of keeping to this small range, though I make two sizes, on 12 and 14 hooks.

I rarely use specific mayfly nymphs simply because most of the rain-fed rivers I fish nowadays do not have the natural insect. When I fished chalk streams, although rules may have been relaxed since, the dry fly rule prevailed except for the months of July and August. I use mayfly nymphs occasionally on still water and the same pattern applies for streams.

I have experimented with copies of Olive Duns, Iron Blues and Large Dark Olives without great success, but Skues pointed out years ago that a combination of Gold Tinsel and Hare's Ear, when wet, gives off an olive aura. He was not adverse to adding a pinch of yellow seal to mix with his hare's fur to enhance this effect. I'm sure that Sawyer was right in his keen observation that certain nymphs are harder to simulate, not so much in colour, shape and size, but because it's hard to copy their sinuous movement in the water, although perfectionists may experiment with the wiggle-nymph, which has the body in two separate sections, the latter being detached and thus able to sway about in the water.

Let me briefly sum up the position about my artificial nymphs. I use almost exclusively two patterns, the Hare's Ear and the Pheasant Tail, some of which I dress on long shanked hooks for the big stone flies. I reiterate, experience proves that for practical fishing, it is unnecessary to fashion meticulous copies of the stone fly larvae. My nymphs are dressed in different weights to suit water or fishing conditions. I regard it as important to use contrasting colour tones between abdomen and thorax. Occasionally I use the Sawyer Grayling Bug, a simple long-shanked version of which would suit the mayfly nymph.

There's an exception to this strategy which is an effective half-way house between nymph fishing and the upstream wet fly fishing, especially useful for 'fishing the water' rather than targeting visible fish. It is very simple. It is to cast a long-hackled Black & Peacock spider upstream, into likely holding places, letting it drift back with the current. These long hackles give an attractive mobility to the fly, but they also control its position below the surface whereas a weighted nymph would tend to sink downwards on the slack leader.

I admit that I have been fishing upstream nymphs on streams for a very long time, since first I read Sawyer's book on nymph fishing. In the early days I fished the single nymph, and as it was a question of searching the water, bringing the nymph through likely lies, I had to develop a sort of a sixth sense as to when to strike. The trick was to move my head so that I could see light reflected from the leader, and striking was at the signal of any unusual behaviour of the nylon as it floated downstream, sometimes swerving, pulling down as if into a hole, or just checking in the flow. On occasion the water would 'hump up' or else a flash of gold or white underwater would signal a take. It is strange, but the instinct does come, and one afternoon, on a Wealden stream, I caught five fish without knowing exactly why I had struck. Once in a while I tightened when I thought the fish should have taken the nymph from a certain place, but without any sign at all, only to find the fish hooked. More of this, later, it is the key.

Let me explain some of the tell-tale signs. Of course the 'golden flash' is when a fish turns underwater to take the nymph to one side, losing its natural camouflage as the light is reflected from its flank. The flash of white is when the triangle of its lower jaw is revealed as it grabs the offering. The checks, swerves and pulling down of the leader are simple enough to understand. Yet leaders move for other reasons, idiosyncrasies of the river-flow, but it's encouraging to know that with experience, just fishing time, one soon learns to differentiate the 'natural' movement of the leader to that caused by a taking fish, for the latter has a 'suddenness' to it.

In previous chapters I have been able to develop traditional methods to a more advanced stage simply because they had become 'frozen' by time. Anglers had the attitude 'if it ain't bust, don't fix it', which was fair enough. Nymph fishing on streams, especially chalk streams is far more modern, and it has been subjected to scrutiny and development to a high degree. The reason was plain: demand. 'Dry fly only' became quite restrictive as fly hatches diminished and the habits of fishing changed from the leisurely 'time by the water' of Halford's time when members of the Houghton Club would spend several days at a time by the river. In fact the affluent masters of the past might even rent a cottage in the river valley and pass most of the season there. Lucky men!

Today, a Test or Itchen rod would be allocated a fixed day each week. The tempo of the fishing has increased, the stocking become intensive and the patient waiting for sparser hatches is unpopular. An element of the change in fishing habits was that inventive brains had to turn to alternative methods, and as the normal downstream wet fly was ruled out, the upstream nymph had to be the answer. Though they might never have admitted it, this need for 'instant success' was part of the motivation for the intensive studies of post-war innovators like Sawyer and Kite.

This is not intended to be theorising, for it brings me to the differences in technique between Stewart's upstream rough stream spiders and the 'induced take' of Kite. When Kite first described how he provoked a trout into taking a bare hook it was thought to be the wonder of the world, but Sawyer had already described how the nymph should be 'lifted' in front of a fish to give the impression of its rise to the surface to hatch. When Kite did the same trick with a bare hook he was simply demonstrating the main lesson of this book – behaviour! Even that salmon fishing maestro of long ago, Balfour-Kinnear, advised his readers to do the same thing with a salmon fly when it was refused by a 'stiff' fish. He called it 'pulling off'. He also advocated moving the fly backwards and forwards when it came onto the dangle, to provoke a following fish. This was done by moving the rod tip, and this he termed 'dodding'.

I mention this because in normal wet fly fishing the depth of the flies can be governed by the height of the rod tip, but to give a weighted nymph a sudden lift in the water it is necessary to pull in line with the free hand. This has to be done at the critical time, of course, just in front of the trout's nose. Sawyer also invented the 'pitching' way of getting a nymph to curve down smartly on the forward cast, as it unrolled the line over the water, and again, this is simply a sharp pull on the line. The nymph curves downwards to go smartly through the surface film. Naturally he was casting at fish he could see, and he first described in his book how the trout revealed a white triangle of its lower jaw as it accepted his offering. It is a loss to us that as far as I know, neither of these two experts, unlike Skues, applied their ideas to the faster rain-fed rivers of the North and West where this visible attack is not possible.

Since those days we have discovered that the nymph has a wider application. I have used it in the classical way on chalk streams, and, because years ago, there was little, if any written experience about rough stream use, I developed my own technique. The difference lies in this question of stalking and visibility, because it was only on occasion that I was able to target a particular rise. Usually I was casting to hopeful places where the broken surface, reflected light or coloured water forced me to develop my attention to the way the leader and line moved after the cast. I soon came to recognise another advantage which the past-masters were not allowed to seize. The nymph is one fly which can be fished successfully in any direction, it is equally attractive to fish thrown down and across the river like a winged wet-fly. It makes an effective anchor-man to a team of wet flies.

It is interesting, though that neither of these intelligent men applied the 'science' of exact imitation to their nymphs – Skues had attempted it – and Sawyer's keen sense of observation made him realise that the sinuous movements of the Blue-winged Olive nymph could not be imitated. He did not bother with an imitation of it, and he generally failed when the BWO was active, a conclusion I can confirm by my own experience. The classic wet fly overcomes this problem. The small Snipe & Purple will catch trout when Iron Blues are hatching, but a pure nymph imitation rarely succeeds.

I was surprised that there was no appreciation of the importance of the freshwater Shrimp in those earlier books.

In the golden days of the chalk stream dry-fly you find frustration expressed by anglers when trout were beating up the weed beds for shrimp. This activity is easily recognisable, the trout has its head down in a weed bed, signs of turmoil on the surface, often the tail fins are flapping about through the surface. A shrimp copy is often invaluable at such times, a weighted body of olive dubbing with a gold rib and a palmered olive hackle. A strip of olive feather or plastic is taken over the back for the shell, varnished to make it shine, and to give it that characteristic hump-back, it is made on the special grub-hook. This is an occasion when precise imitation is needed. This is effective on chalk streams, but I gave it up when I deserted them for the rougher streams of the North.

In passing, a lady was fishing the Bolton Abbey stretch of the Wharfe when the large brown stone flies were hatching. These beasts are up to an inch long, and the local anglers advised her to turn over stones to find the larval 'jacks', but she was squeamish of creepy-crawlies. Hunting through her fly box she found a still-water Stick Fly. Although told it would be useless, she took eleven good fish. The stone fly larva is one of the glories of the fly dressing master-classes, the expert weaving bodies, shaping wing cases and copying every tiny anatomical feature. Great fun, but completely impractical. Again, behaviour is the key, and a large Pheasant Tail nymph on a long shanked hook will win hands down. That's good to know.

The most difficult aspect is when the nymph is heavily weighted and has to be fished deep, for it is hanging on the body of the leader and against the buoyancy of the floating line. There is not much to see. Normally a fly line is rarely perfectly straight, especially when cast upstream, and there are little wrinkles in it. When so much of the leader is below the surface, the key is when these wrinkles straighten as the line is checked by a taking trout. The time to use this heavy nymph is when the water is full and the surface completely blank, and at the other extreme, in very bright sunlight when fish lie deep to avoid the glare. When the sun is shining down on a pool fish cannot see a fly approaching them from above, the glare is blinding them. But the nymph fished below them will be seen and accepted under these conditions.

So, the key is persistence. Many fishers of rough streams will just try upstream nymph for a short while, and, on failing to notice the 'takes', they will return to some older, tried method – probably wet fly – without realising the opportunities they missed. Yes, the secret of successful nymph fishing, particularly on the rain-fed rivers, is persistence until your mind tells you that the normal flow of the leader has been changed. Use that little polystyrene sight bob or a buzzy dry fly on a dropper if it doesn't give you an ethical twinge of guilt.

And one cautionary word. Avoid the temptation to change the fly frequently. I find in a normal season I have used but two nymphs in different weights and sizes. They are the plain Pheasant Tail and the Hare's Ear.

As a matter of interest, as I write this book there has been a controversy in the angling journals about the roles played by Oliver Kite and Frank Sawyer in the development of post-war nymph fishing technique. This is of little practical interest and I do find it distasteful to read posthumous feuds between the adherents of both men. It is known that they 'did not get along'. They both made important contributions to the evolution of our sport, though, alas, within a limited area of fishing. I knew Kite, I met him on occasion in my early years at Two Lakes, one of the first commercial 'put and take' still water fisheries. I simply do not know who thought of what first. At that time I was running one of the earliest fly dressing evening classes in London and my pupils, too, divided into two camps, happily without rancour. It seemed like a rerun of the Halford versus Skues battles of yesteryear, and the way human nature works in this sport is to 'personalise' differences of opinion. Although I knew and liked 'Ollie', Sawyer's book on nymph fishing came to hand before I took a rod at Two Lakes. Strangely, I never met Sawyer, and although I was influenced by his ideas and methods, as we shall see I owe much to Kite on dry fly technique which is why I believe these feuds, which run down the years, to be foolish.

Yes: the tackle. It's quite simple, the ultra-light line outfit described before suits admirably, and coincidentally, on rereading Sawyer, I noticed that even in those split-cane and silk-line days, he favoured a very light outfit. His Number One size silk line would probably equal my own AFTM 3. As in dry fly fishing, precision and accuracy is aided by tapered leaders with relatively steep tapers and thick butts. There is a trend today to use brightly coloured fluo fly lines which make no sense at all when finesse is required. I don't wish to join the fly line colour controversy, other than to say that a light colour, as flash-free as possible, is plain common sense.

Now, if you force me to give one overriding advantage for the nymph on a rain-fed river, apart from the ones discussed, I would cite the numerous fish I have taken, fish which were rising where drag reduced the floating fly to impotence. On many fast rivers I fish, Teviot, Whiteadder, Tees, Ure, a favourite taking-place for a trout is in the first smooth-surfaced water above caulds or broken runs. Drag hits the floating fly immediately no matter what wiggles or angle-changes you put into the line. This is the one place where a nymph will overcome drag and I cannot count the number of fish I have taken in this way; indeed, I now look for fish in such positions.

A final note on the structure of the artificial nymph, a modern nymph dressing includes silver, gold or copper beads at the head. They are successful when used on the dressing, though, personally I favour the weighting to be in the thorax, covered by material. The reason, though, is not to do with imitation, but our fly rod blanks have thinner and thinner walls. A number of rods are shattered each year when struck by these bead-headed flies, and even with experienced casters, this can happen. As you will know by now, my personal rod designs are loaded with ultra-fine lines, it's the way I fish, and their blank-walls are necessarily slim, of a special carbon material to suit the fine tips and slim profile. I do not take a risk with loose missiles!

The Vanishing Becks

I indulge myself in this chapter. In a sense the title is less than true. There are two types of becks, upland and lowland, and the latter are often cared for by fishing clubs if only because their richer food supply allows trout to grow to a reasonable size. Many of these lowland becks are paradoxically in hill country, a typical example of which is the charming stream which comes from Haweswater, flowing through the picturesque village of Brampton. This is the Lowther Water, probably taking its name from the famous employer of the Wordsworth family in times long gone. The Blackadder would also qualify in my mind, a fascinating border stream.

We now need a way of classifying such streams, and the system quoted from Macan & Worthington's excellent treatise on fresh water biology, in the Collins *New Naturalist* series of books will serve us very well, starting as it does where water first appears in the highest fell country. The infant stream, without rainfall, has not enough strength to move small pebbles, and only tiny fish live there. This is the 'minnow reach'. As it gathers pace and more water, the first small trout appear, but food is scarce. This is our typical upland beck. At first glance no modern angler would look at it. Then the stream goes on to a lowland stretch, perhaps meadow land, where pools deepen and fish can grow to a respectable table size. This is the lowland beck.

I, too, would have ignored the upland beck had not a slim volume come into my hands, written by an enthusiastic explorer of the high country, Richard Clapham.[1] Now, Clapham was fishing in times which were far different to our own, the pre-war years. These were stark years for many folk, especially in the North. Wages were low, unemployment was high, and adventurous men found many ways to 'put something on the table'. I can just remember myself, as a young lad, paddling a spinning barrel across a marsh to gather moorhens' eggs which were highly prized in our village. Few coarse fish were returned in those days, my Grandfather had a way with them which made him popular in the war when food became scarce, even for the middle class.

Clapham had a fairly colourful private life, beyond the scope of this book, but he loved the high country, and his book depicts his tall figure, striding the moors, traditional creel on his back, breeks and boots on his

---

[1] *Trout Fishing on Hill Streams*, 1947.

legs, rod in hand. Although he is not one of the literary giants of our sport, the account of his fishing is intriguing.

To make these upland becks viable as fisheries the essential thing to do was to improve the shelter and the food supply. The book gives the impression that Clapham himself organised parties of Yorkshire working men to go into the hills with pickaxes and crow bars. At least the raw material was to hand, heavy rocks. Firstly, pools had to be made, then these pools would be linked together into terraces, by making small caulds.

One day I traced such a stream into the Pennine hill country. 'No good fishing there,' the warden told me. 'No one bothers, only very small fish,' though the becks served as a welcome resource as spawning grounds for the wild brownies which ran up from the reservoirs into which they flowed. He was absolutely right. As I clambered up the water course, intermittent sunshine revealed tiny trout scooting for cover as I spooked them. Yet I could see that long ago the beck had been worked on, for here and there were the remnants of small weirs, long since broken down by neglect and disinterest. I could also visualise where the classical pool-terraces must have been. I conjured up an image of the gangs of working men tramping into the hills, tools in hand, dressed in the style of the time wearing cloth caps and rough woollen jackets.

The work the teams did paid off handsomely, and it was amazing that within a few months the odd half pounders lurked in the pools, where silt was trapped to harbour fly life, where terrestrial insects could not escape easily and small fish, minnows and bullheads, collected. There was another reason for the increase in the weight and condition of the fish. Put simply, the pools protected the trout from over-expenditure of energy, to hold station in the current, shelter from floods and in harvesting food. A revelation is on the front cover of Clapham's book, depicting a leash or two of handsome beck trout, posed on his ancient creel, each seemingly well over half a pound. Of course this was fishing for the pot, purism gave way to worm and minnow, especially when some moorland peat coloured the becks after rain.

The fly rod was simply a practical tool, and the advice Clapham gave his readers was to 'fish fine and as near as you can' with a long rod – not dissimilar from the Stewart ideal of old. The 'cross country' cast would have been useful, line laid across intervening ground so that the angler could be at some distance from the fish. Upstream fishing would have been the rule of the day for the same reason.

The target areas on these becks would have been small, making for accurate casting, and this type of problem gave rise to the earliest weight-forward lines which were made for casting short distances, and to deal more effectively with winds which bounced off the fell-sides and came from all directions. If memory serves me aright, the very first weight-forward lines marketed by Hardy were named 'Fillip' and advertised especially for short-line fishing with brook rods.

Alas, Clapham gave his fly dressings, but not their styles. He used but two patterns, and I have to guess that his version of the black gnat – called Lee's Favourite or, alternatively, the Black Spinner – was probably fashioned in a style from the Clyde, a style which, like most regional traditions, has died on us. It was, unusually, a winged wet fly which could be thrown upstream, as well as down. The wings would have been simply a slim tuft of feather, probably starling, set upright, and surrounded by a sparse hackle of the same colour. The body was plain black silk with a fine silver rib. His other favourite was the standard Bracken Clock, though he used the local name, 'Kennedy's beetle'. He said, 'to tie your flies in imitation of particular insects is a pure waste of time'.

He proved this by trout post mortems which confirmed what we would all suspect, that their stomachs were filled with 'a hundred sub-aquacious titbits'. Some other advice was 'I don't worry about the colour of my flies'. Also 'the tail is an unnecessary appendage'. Both to demonstrate the improvements made in these hill becks and the skill of his fishing with only two patterns, Clapham would expect a bag of thirty to forty fish in a hard day's fishing.

This is the fishing we have lost. The lusher, lowland becks are cared for, stocked, and are fished in methods described earlier in this book. We can still find upland streams much as Clapham would have fished, they are few, perhaps the Upper Whiteadder and its tributaries like the Dye Water,

A lowland beck, Lowtherwater, near Haweswater.

or the Hermitage stream, but others have simply vanished as fisheries, probably because today we like our fishing to be easy. Is it possible to shoulder a rod and bag and hike into the hills, footloose and free? And could we collect bands of hardy enthusiasts to break and heave the rocks to make those essential pools and terraces? No, it is a world which has gone.

There remains, though, the lessons which Clapham has taught us, that often we carry too many flies, that presentation is the key and that it is a mistake to become hypnotised with finicky imitations on fast-water fisheries where food for the trout is often 'catch as catch can'.

Yes, long ago, too long, perhaps, a friend and I were in the Lammermuir hills when we came across a typical upland beck, and we unpacked our rods to fish it, much as Clapham would have done in years long gone. I turned up a book I wrote long since.[2] There was the photo my friend took, a much younger me, crouched expectantly over the stream. Now, if by some chance a keen angler has managed to restore such a beck to its pre-war glory, he has only to invite me, and I will go there post haste. Clapham tells us that on July 18th, in 1913 he creeled 41 trout, and he would have used a horsehair leader, which he preferred to the new fangled gut.

Envoi

In concluding this account of sunk-fly tactics I use on running water, please bear in mind that it has been just that. I only write about what I do, and what I have done. The tactics for nymph and dry fly apply equally for chalk streams as well as rain-fed rivers (subject to the rules of the former!). The upstream and downstream wet fly tactics are unique to the streams of the North and West. There are no revolutionary, miracle flies, and if I am a traditionalist, there's solid reasoning for it. If certain fly patterns have killed fish for centuries, being virtually unchanged, as the March Brown and Blue Dun, for example, then they pass muster by the only critic which counts – the trout.

Whilst I admit that some of the casting techniques are advanced, meant to cope with difficult conditions of wind or water, no one should be deterred by elegant demonstrations at game fairs, on videos and the like. The secret is to discover how to get the job done. There's no audience to impress. At first sight casts like my versions of the Switch seem to be fussy, and there's a temptation for the angler to pass on to an easier place. As other anglers have followed the same escape route, good fish are unmolested. Those very few anglers who practice to become ambidextrous, for example, are afterwards astonished at how much extra fishing space is opened up to them.

I emphasise, too, the danger of becoming dogmatic. The simple choice

---

[2]*Fly Fishing Tactics on Rivers.*

of whether to fish up or down should be decided by the strength and direction of the wind. You can also invent your own experimental methods, too. I once adopted an old salmon-fishing method of 'backing up' a pool when a strong upstream wind held back the line. It was a wide stretch of the Tees where normal upstream work was impossible. The trick was to cast across the current from the bank, then to make a few steps upstream, and by changing the angle of the line, some extra impetus was given to it, enough to take the flies and leader downstream and against the strong breeze. It worked; I caught fish. Good thing I used to play Pooh Sticks!

You will have noticed, too, the relatively small number of flies I use, and the simplicity of their structure. I do not scorn the current trend of the 'beautiful imitation', fostered by fly dressing competitions and books written by expert fly dressers. This is great fun, but the danger is that anglers might become brainwashed into believing that success or failure depend on this. It rarely does. The way the fish sees the fly is the key, more often than not, and the first thing a fly dresser should ask himself at his bench is 'how will this fly behave in the water'? He should ask himself the same question when he casts this fly.

The final lesson, which I fear few will follow through no fault of their own, is to match lighter tackle systems to an improved casting technique, for generally, in this land we outgun the fish we seek to catch, thereby missing much sporting pleasure. It goes beyond this, for using a much lighter rod and line gives a more efficient management of the line, leader and flies. In practice, the twin fears of the effect of wind and the playing of powerful fish on ultra-light line gear are fallacious, but the contrary is true, as I have discussed. I admit the problem is that the tackle trade is matched to our traditional heavy-line, and if the great Skues couldn't change this, though he fought his corner for decades, then I am unlikely to do so. Happily, I can still get my own rod blanks made for me by the firm of Bruce & Walker.

I finish with a foolish question. What is the purpose of these tactics? In asking this, of you, of myself, I admit to a distaste of the prevailing mood of fish-greed. This greed, the desire for 'instant success', has been fostered by changes in society itself. The stress of life is a factor, and another is the competitive urge which has entered our sport, whilst a third is the increased stocking of fisheries to attract custom. My discourse is not intended to further that trend. In fact I mostly fish 'no kill'. Nor do I wish to beat my companions, for as an instructor over too many years, I enjoy helping them (and being helped!). My aim is very simple. It is to increase your fishing pleasure, for a good river should be like a golf course, with hazards and bunkers to overcome. And fly fishing is surely a sport based on self-imposed limitations to be overcome by the development of skill.

Now, we move on to dry fly fishing.

Dry Fly Tactics

Anyone who is interested in the history of fly fishing will have delved into the old controversy which dogged the sport from the days when the invention of the heavy, tapered silk line and the split cane rod ushered in the use of the floating fly, to be cast upstream. The controversy was over the twin themes of 'exact imitation' and 'purism'. These do not concern me here, other than to point out that the previous chapters have been mostly to do with those rivers which receive their water mainly from direct rainfall. There are brown trout in chalk streams, too, so I must now cast a wider loop. These chalk streams receive their water in the main from the percolation of rainwater through the limestone, which gives them both the alkaline quality and their pellucid nature. From the richness of the alkaline streams comes the wider range of aquatic flies and the prolific hatches. These hatches gave rise to exclusive feeding by the trout which, in turn brought about the extreme philosophy of 'exact imitation'.

In my very early years I was impressed by this philosophy and one of my earliest acquisitions was a book by that celebrated High Priest of imitation, F. M. Halford. This book actually had a series of colour plates, much like the one from which you choose a wall paint, and you had to match the indicated colour precisely for a given imitation.

Things change. The fly hatches declined, due to the draining of the water meadows, the intensity of weed cuts, the diminution of flow, the use of pesticides and the rapid turnover of stocked fish. 'Exact imitation' exists still as a nostalgic vestigial philosophy for a few pedants, no doubt it's fun, but as a practical approach to dry fly fishing, it has been brought down to a sensible level.

I was fortunate to fish at Two Lakes – that famous still water fishery in Hampshire – at the same time as the late Oliver Kite. In those days I was launching my own fly dressing business and I asked Ollie if I could dress and market his dry fly patterns. He gave his assent willingly and he presented me with samples to copy. As far as I know, some of these patterns have never before been described in print.

This is interesting, for two reasons. Like Sawyer, Kite's name is associated with the post-war generation of chalk stream nymph fishing; they both wrote books on this subject. Kite's dry fly patterns are less well known, perhaps only his Imperial lives on, but he had a practical range of dry flies all made on the simple principle of a plain body herl and hackle, sometimes exposing a coloured silk thread which he specified. The dressing style was the same, a body herl, sometimes dyed, and the herl would always be doubled at the thorax, making a carrot shaped body. As few people today are familiar with the patterns he invented, and as I have used them over the years, I hunted through old letters and fly collections to revive them.

Only the Imperial is well known still. The tying silk was purple, hence its name, and the body was of heron herl, the slaty grey shade, and truth to tell, as the heron is protected, I use a similar shade of herl from the secondary wing quills of the pigeon, which makes a marvellous body. Yes, the herl is redoubled over the thorax immediately behind the hackle.

There was no ribbing on the samples I was sent, but I have seen commercial samples with a genuine gold wire rib. The hackles were a dark blue dun for early and late season, a lighter one for the summer months. This was an innovation, and the practical application was to encompass all the olive duns in a single base, matching the dark flies of spring and autumn, Iron Blue, Large Dark Olive with the dark hackle, and the summer pattern copied the various medium olives. A fly for all seasons.

Ollie knew that he needed a spinner pattern and this introduced his Pheasant Tail Red Spinner fly which killed quantities of chalk stream trout for me. His sample had white cock tail whisks. The body was a bright red tying thread, widely ribbed at the bottom end by cock pheasant tail strands which were doubled up at the thorax. The hackle was a deep, foxy red. Again, the strategy was to cover virtually all natural spinners with a single pattern.

I add some tips for perfectionists. The two versions of the Imperials are distinctive, so make sure that the two shades of blue dun are really different, a true, undyed iron blue hackle (almost black) for the early and late season, and a light slaty pale blue dun for the summer. Also, it is possible to remain true to Kite, but using a slightly darker shade of blue-grey herl for the early-season body. I mention this as the two samples I received from him were far more distinctive than copies I have seen tied by some subsequent dressers. You can also leave a few turns of the purple thread exposed at the tail end. I use genetic, undyed hackles for Imperials.

For the PT Red Spinner, the Kite sample he sent me used a really bright, pillar box scarlet thread, not the deep crimson shade, and this is exposed over the bottom half of the body, but the pheasant tail is thickened up at the thorax to cover it. I include here for convenience two of his still water flies, the Sepia Dun and the Apricot Spinner because they both have the same simple structure. The Sepia Dun is a still water up-wing fly which appeared at Two Lakes in April, but I have rarely seen it elsewhere. The body was of a goose herl, dyed a very dark brown with hackle to match. For the Sepia Dun, if, like myself, you prefer undyed hackles, then use a really dark red game hackle instead. It goes without saying that you can also apply the Kite style to designs of your own, in olives, iron blues and so forth, the simple style was the Kite 'thing'.

Two more horses joined his stable, as Kite decided he needed a special pattern for pale wateries, and the style was the same, a plain white herl with matching tail whisks and hackle. On the rare occasions I met the pale evening duns this fly was a supreme killer. I was fishing once at dusk on the Eden near to Appleby when the little white flecks drifted down prodigiously against the far bank and the succulent ploppings soon excited my attention. The white fly did very well.

For some strange reason, perhaps encountered on his own fishing place, he also made a copy of the relatively rare ditch dun. The sample showed a body of dark olive herl and a blue dun hackle. I did not have success with this fly.

The lake and pond olives have distinctly different spinners. The red-bodied one is served by the PT Red Spinner, but the other one has an amber body, hence Oliver's Apricot Spinner, body herl of that colour being topped off with a bright honey cock hackle. I do not know why he spurned a spent-wing pattern except that his fly dressing philosophy was one of plain practicality.

There was no spent fly in the collection, that is dressed with the flat, hackle point wings, and as I have never favoured the parachute style, I sometimes adapted his spinner pattern by dividing the hackle on each side of the hook with figure-of-eight turns of thread to achieve a spent hackle style which flattens the fly on the surface film. I have always preferred this style to the parachute fly which also lays the artificial onto the surface film, but the choice is personal rather than rational, I'm sure both styles work equally well.

It was also strange that he did not send me a sedge fly, but I imagine that as many good patterns were around, there was no necessity. Nor did he favour the split winged fly. The same is true of mayflies, he sent me no specific pattern, but again, patterns are legion and I was fortunate in those days to meet the companion of a famous chalk stream angler called Taylor whose mayfly inventions were honoured, though never written down. I believe Kite favoured Grey Wulff, as did many other 'Test' fishermen. After his death only three of the seven Taylor inventions survived, gleaned from the memory of the poor man's widow. The other four are lost to us, alas.

In those days I fished the Test and the first fly we encountered in numbers in May was the hawthorn. Kite sent me no specific imitation, but it was simplicity to apply his basic style, black herl body and matching hackle. It worked well and doubled up for the black gnats.

I recollect that in my earliest forays at Two Lakes I had no copy of the Sepia Dun and the fish would look at no other. Oliver opened a well stocked box and handed me a couple. I said to him: 'I thought you only used one or two patterns?'

His eyes twinkled and he replied: 'Don't believe all you read!'

I recollect with affection the day the small box arrived in the post, with the samples inside, all beautifully made. Truth to tell, when first I put a fly out at Two Lakes I was obsessed with the fantastic copies of still water insects by C. F. Walker. The colour plates in his book on imitating still water flies showed copies that were so close to the natural counterparts that even the human eye could not separate one from t'other. I was doing some finicky stuff at my fly dressing bench. Kite changed that philosophy, though I still needed a mayfly and sedge for the nearby river.

Finally, some additional tips for dressing these flies. The samples Ollie sent me had no ribbing, and I see no need for one, though there's no logical reason other than simplicity. If I ribbed the herls I would use the very fine round tinsel beloved by salmon fly dressers for their 'butts'. It is lightweight and soft. Wire tends to bury into herl. I prefer natural herls where possible and for the black gnat version, instead of a dyed black I use the very dark herl found on grey goose or crow primaries. The wood pigeon secondary is a wonderful source of body herl, the texture is just right and the three bars of different shades of blue dun satisfy me for the Imperials. Hoping not to upset purists, the Pale Watery is also made by me with a very light grey herl, also found on the pigeon feather, and a very light honey hackle. This is not a real concession to imitation so much as an attempt to give some contrasts to the brightness of the sky.

Kite did not over-hackle his flies, a four to five winding of a good quality feather is just right. With the exception of the PT Red Spinner, the tail whisks of the other patterns are taken from the same hackle as at the throat.

Another curiosity, Kite never favoured the traditional up-eyed dry fly hooks. The patterns he sent were dressed on his favourite hook pattern, the Allcock's Model Perfect, which were down-eyed. Later, when I was invited to the Viellard-Migeon hook factory in France to design a range of fly hooks I discovered the sound engineering principle which guided his choice. In those days dry fly hooks were not forged. Forging a hook means that the bend-section is squared off to add strength. The old Model Perfect hook was a good example of this. In his fishing, as in his fly designs, Kite demonstrated that paradox, skill is born of perfecting the basic simplicities, observation and application, for which there is no substitute. There plainly are no complex answers to spooked fish to be learned at the fly tying bench when the answer lies in correcting presentation.

It is not my purpose to criticise unduly the stocking policy of chalk streams, and the rainbow trout is beyond the scope of this book. I recognise that intensive stocking has been forced on fishery managements by simple economics, the high costs of estate management. The post-war trend in fly fishing has been to make it easier than at any time in the past. The chalk streams had to compete with highly stocked still waters, especially the smaller, commercial put-and-take fisheries. Rather than give you boring statistics, I will instead relate two personal experiences from the River Test, which I fished over many years. On one estate water, the keeper would record catches beat by beat on a weekly basis, and replace the fish which had been taken. This kept the number of fish constant. The

River Teise in the Kentish Weald.

two effects were that there was always a fish in a recognised 'lie', and that this fish had little time to learn how to feed on the natural fly because it had insufficient time to shake off the conditioning effect of receiving artificial food on a timetable in the fish farm. On another stretch where I had a rod, I could be fishing at one end of a beat when fresh fish were being put in at the other. Cynics thus dubbed the Test as 'the longest stock pond in Europe'.

This may seem to be a harsh judgment, but it is realistic and I allow myself a smile when I read the sentimental accounts which equate today's fisheries with those of long ago. It is not fair to criticise the changes, they are an inevitable result of economic necessity and fishing habits.

That age-old club, the Wilton Flyfishers remained true to the ancient traditions of maintaining wild stocks and there are other pockets of resistance here and there.

The streams with which I was familiar over many years were the Test, and its tributary, the Anton, the Itchen, Upper Avon, Wylie, and the Kennet. Even if it were possible to return to the spirit of the past, the democratic majority wouldn't allow it, as I know from having proposed on a Test syndicate fishery where I was a member, that rainbow trout and nymph fishing should be outlawed, only to find myself as a minority of one! The cost of the fishing was high, the members expected a good return on the subscription.

Let me discuss the Test in more detail. Although it is classed as a chalk stream, having its source springs in limestone, it is not a true one insofar as it runs through peatlands along part of its length, and this always impeded natural reproduction and a good growth rate. This is why the river has had to be stocked for a very long period of time. The early chronicles of the Houghton Club describe the transport of brown trout and grayling in Macintosh bags by horse-drawn carts long before the motor car was thought of.

I sometimes wonder if Kite didn't bother to send me a sedge fly because of the decline in hatches of the early season Grannom. These were a wonder of days gone by, when clouds of ginger sedges swarmed over the water, and the females, bearing green egg sacs, zoomed upstream in great balls. This fly depends on the ranunculus weed which old-time keepers never cut until it had flowered, but weed cutting is more ruthless today.

After the April hatches, May comes with the hawthorn fly, a terrestrial fly which comes onto the water from the may-trees. This insect is instantly recognised, too, for it is big, black and buzzy, with two trailing legs visible in flight. This is a happy fly for the fisher because one thing is certain, humans and fish see the colour black in the same way, and a suitable black-hackled fly with a herl body of the same colour will easily fool the trout. The Kite-type simple imitation was good medicine for this fly.

Here some confusion must enter, for the two flies of a chalk stream in spring are the inky Iron Blue and the Large Dark Olive, but these flies also appear on rain-fed streams at the same time of year. Happily, the dark

Imperial will serve both rivers. The Kite range of dry flies served me well on both types of river, for I shared with him the practical approach to what otherwise would have been a confusing mess of fly patterns. I need but add a competent all-round sedge fly, one or two mayflies and I am happy for any time of year on any river, not only in Britain, but in other European countries where I have fished.

The progress of the season produces a wider range of insects than the fast rivers of the North and West. The Test and Anton were rich in mayfly. The mayflies disappeared from the Itchen mysteriously many decades ago, though I have seen a scattering in recent times. The first appearance of the duns varies considerably from river to river. It always came later to the Wylie, but it persisted there far longer, even odd ones appearing in August.

It is necessary to put to bed an ancient tradition which is repeated par-rot-fashion in text books, that the trout refuse the duns when they first appear. I cannot imagine where this story came from, it is completely untrue, except on some lochs, the very first duns are snaffled as soon as they arrive. Sometimes a single mayfly dun loses its sense of time and hatches by itself quite out of its proper season, but it rarely survives more than a few yards before being intercepted by an aware fish. It seems point-less attacking trout with mayfly nymphs, they are so easy to catch on arti-ficial dry flies as well as this being most exciting sport. It is a tactic of some fishery managements to introduce their largest fish for the mayfly bon-anza. On the Test you may expect brown trout of several pounds in weight. My best fish on a dry mayfly was a fraction under six pounds.

Exceptions make fishing an interestingly unpredictable sport, and although I have never fished nymph at mayfly time on the Test, on occa-sion the trout did refuse floating duns as they were hitting the flies on the point of hatching. It is natural that on a day of cold wind the adult dun will take some time to emerge from the nymphal shuck in the surface film. It uses this shuck as a launching pad after its wings have hardened in the air. Being so vulnerable for a longer time the fish take that food item. The answer is quite simple, to clip the hackles very short below the hook so that the fly settles down into the surface film.

Past masters agreed that the fourth and eleventh day of the mayfly time were the best. On the fourth day of the hatch the duns are at their height, fish want little else. From the eleventh day, the female spinners are return-ing to the water to lay their eggs, and the fish usually switch to them. There is a time when you can see the change, it is a remarkable sight which fascinated me on the Test. I had been catching fish on floating duns in the morning. The fish took in the classic way, aligning itself to the float-ing fly and chopping it off smartly by interception. The rise to a mayfly dun is unmistakable, a nice, bold ring, leaving a bubble or two to sail away downstream. The male spinners were rising and falling in the air over the bankside meadow, the famous dance, and when a female wandered amongst them, the coupling took place and the first egg-bearing flies returned to the water. It was one of those magical evenings, the wind had fallen and the surface of the river was spotted with both newly hatching duns and returning spinners.

From a vantage position on a bridge I noticed that the way in which the fish were rising had changed. The violent swirls had given way to gentle rings. Then a 'spent gnat', the dead or dying female after egg-laying, was washing down towards me, side by side with a brown trout which leisurely turned onto it and sucked it down with very little commotion. The spent fly, being very low in the water, only required the effortless sucking in of water, to vanish into the mouth of the trout. This was a perfect example of the preoccupied feeding which, in turn, preoccupied this angler and the way he put his fly to the fish. Failure in these aspects is more likely due to the structure than the slightly different colour of material in the artificial fly. Trout instinctively know that duns are vigorously trying to escape from the water, but that spent gnats have nowhere to go. When fishing the spent gnat it is important to leave space for the fly to drift well past the target fish as the trout will sometimes follow the fly downstream before turning on it.

The other legacy of 'lost' flies came to me from a caller when I was a professional fly dresser. This is what he told me. A certain Mr Taylor was a prodigious catcher of fish on mayflies of his own invention, of which he claimed seven marvels, which his friends envied. He had suddenly died and his widow could only trace three of these patterns. Would I dress them for him? Would I not. The first two were dun imitations.

The first of these, dubbed 'Taylor's Green Champion', had tail fibres of black and white bars, culled I believe from Lady Amherst's pheasant. The body was of apple green floss ribbed with black button thread. There was a short badger cock hackle down the body and a larger one at the throat. The wings were two dyed green partridge hackles tied forward over the eye, but with a narrow splay. His 'Yellow Champion' simply substituted yellow materials for the green.

The copy of the spent gnat I called 'Taylor's Black Drake'. The whisks were the same as the duns, but the body was of white fluo floss crossribbed with black and scarlet fluo fine floss. Two pairs of black spent hackle point wings were tied on, flat, and a short badger cock hackle brought the fly close to the surface of the water. Normally I dressed these flies on the large mayfly hooks, but there's a curiosity, that trout are poor at estimating size, and I later scored well by reducing the size of the flies by dressing them on normal dry fly hooks, suitably matched to attenuated materials. This is useful as there's a tendency for fan-winged flies to spin in the air and to kink the leader.

Many years ago I acquired a book by Alexander Wanless. He had invented a range of dry flies for the once-famous firm of Milward. The range of Milward-Wanless flies employed detached bodies attached to minute doubles. They never became established in fly fishing history, but the idea of using detached bodies on small hooks is a good one now that the tips of our rods are so much lighter in striking. Plastic mayfly bodies can be obtained. I prefer to use them for Daddy Longlegs, for there is a curiosity about mayflies, that trout really do not refuse smaller imitations, dressed on normal dry fly hooks. I cannot account for this quirk in their vision, I simply know it to be true from experience. I suppose I dress my own artificials at normal mayfly size because these flies are so attractive. That's a good reason. I am as certain as one can be about the behaviour of fish, that generally, size is not a very important factor in dry fly fishing, they do not relate to it very well. That may start another controversy!

To complete a very practical armoury of dry flies for all occasions, a simple sedge fly is necessary, one which serves for the whole of that enormous range of flat-winged flies. There is a wide choice, Skues's Little Red Sedge, the standard Cinnamon Sedge, the Lunn's Caperer and Terry's Terror. They all serve well, I doubt it matters which you choose. I eventually adapted an idea of the late Richard Walker, to make a simple pattern with a brown body, palmered hackle ribbed with gold, and a bunch of red-game hackle fibres, tied flat for the wing. A further red-game throat hackle finishes off the job.

And I must add an old favourite, called either the Leckford Professor, if you are polite, or the Cow's Arse if you are not. There's a need for a safety fly which you can twitch off the bank to tempt a fish lying against it. The fly is reversed, two hackles, a natural red and a white are wound in at the tail end, the body in front is a silver ribbed dubbing of brown rabbit fur. Were I confined to but a single dry fly for ever, this one would be my choice. I have used it to copy almost everything I met on the Test and it would often bring up a trout nailed to the bottom. It is also a fine rough-water floater for those knotty whorls on weir runs.

There you are; given the wider spread of chalk stream fly life, I have had to fill your box, and make some concessions to the imitative theory, but I owe a considerable debt to Oliver Kite for convincing me of the need to rationalise my dry fly philosophy into a practical choice, so I built it around his utilitarian structure.

Now, when I first turned my fly rod towards the faster rivers of the North it was brought home to me that in dry fly fishing, more than anywhere else, the imitative aspect was overruling that of behaviour. With one notable exception, the fast-water March Brown, anglers were content to use without modification, the patterns which had been born on the southern chalk streams. There were rises to floating flies, indeed some very good ones, on the faster currents of the northern rivers, but no one seemed to have thought through the relationship between fly structure and the conditions of the water, which were generally more turbulent and vigorous than in the South.

The exception was the late Captain Terry Thomas who, many years since had described in a fishing magazine a March Brown he used on the River Usk. Designed to give increased buoyancy as well as visibility in broken water and light, he employed a soft brown partridge hackle in front of one or two stiff white cock's hackles. This was intelligent engineering.

Although I was content to apply Kite's patterns to any river, I also began to think of ways to improve buoyancy and visibility. I had seen trout rising in even the fiercest of white-water runs, the indication is a breaking of the surface pattern of the water, sometimes hard to discern. Often the give-away is a ripple breaking sideways across the spume. Such a fish is, of course, sheltering behind a rock or in a declivity in the river bed. It comes to the fly with panache and is great fun to hook in the savage flow. Sometimes, though, it misses the fly altogether.

At this time a new style of hook came along, with a wide gape and a bent shank, designed for the hump-backs of shrimps and grubs. I used this for a new style of dry fly, and to begin, I lashed a hefty bunch of hackle fibres on the bend of the hook, pointing down to make contact with the water. These not only gave extra buoyancy, but they acted as a rudder to align the fly with the fast current. The body was of any material to choice, but for the March Brown I used the corky underbark of the birch tree, an idea gleaned from a fishing magazine of the last century. This I ribbed with brown thread. In reality, though, I could select any quill, herl or fur according to the pattern. The secret was in the hackles, for believing in two-tone effect, I selected two of different colour. Usually one would be a smoky Blue Dun to create the misty impression of wing-shadow. The trick was to wind on one hackle in the normal way, then to wind through this the second hackle, though this one would be back-to-front. The result was a most inelegant-looking fly with its hackle points splayed like a porcupine. It did give remarkable floating power to the fly, especially when using quality genetic hackles.

This is an example where practicality is more important than display, for truth to tell, the resulting fly does seem to be rather ugly, except to the fish.

Almost any favourite traditional fly can be customised in this way. For example, an old-time killer for trout on light olives is the Ginger Quill, but I found it superb to copy the needle stone flies on rock-infested rivers. The tail whisks were ginger, the body a striped peacock herl quill, and then a light blue dun hackle was reversed and wound through a ginger one. I leave you to make up your own combinations, but instead of using wing slips, the light blue dun hackle gives the impression of them, and this makes for a much tougher fly for tougher conditions, doesn't it?

It's hard to know whether to classify the 'emerger' as a nymph or a dry fly. This style of fly copies the nymph as it is bogged down into the surface film, with the adult dun attempting to escape from the nymphal shuck. A true emerger copy has been around for a very long time, simply a Gold-ribbed Hare's Ear with the longer guard hairs picked out at the throat instead of a hackle feather. This pattern cannot be bettered to this day. A fly dressing friend, the late Jack Curd, went one better in that he laid a strip of the guard hair between the strands of tying thread which he had opened up with two needles. He wound this on as a hackle, then clipped short the hair to a bristle-collar. Anointed with a floatant, this fly scored for me under a hot sun on the Whiteadder when nothing else worked. It is a superb emerger.

There is a simple way to make an emerger at the waterside by clipping back the hackle of any dry fly to make a very short collar.

Although the downstream wet fly method was always termed the classic way of introducing novices to the noble art of fly fishing, I would plump for the dry fly, not only for its exciting visibility, but because it is not difficult for the beginner who has just mastered his first casting lessons.

Apart from developing accuracy, and the ability to drop the fly above the fish, the next step is to bring the fly to the fish without drag. It's a nice judgment to measure the distance above the fish where the fly must fall without alarming it, yet without the downstream force on the line imparting drag. The release of a short length of line as the turnover finishes on the forward cast shoots the fly upwards so that it then parachutes down gently. I understand, too, that American dry fly men side-cast to bring the fly over the fish in a shepherd's crook, without being preceded by line or leader. These things sound tricky, but the fact that everything is visible – cause and effect – makes it the easiest school for the novice.

On occasion it is necessary to bend the line and leader around a higher obstacle or a bend in the river bank, but the side cast, with its shepherd's crook finish can accomplish this – you may have to strike by sound! With practice, it is not too difficult to throw a curve around an obstacle protruding from the bank. If this were, say, a clump of rushes, the fly and line is aimed straight at the fish, over the rush bed, then, on the forward cast, the rod is given a sharp flip outwards and a nice curve around the obstacle is performed. An advantage of ambidexterity is that curves can be thrown in either direction, and happily the fly floats back to you along the path of the line's curve, not into the vegetation. As described before, both upstream mends or a wiggling of the rod tip will put slack into the line on the forward cast whilst the line is still in the air, and this is to neutralise drag.

False casting has traditionally been used to dry a 'used' fly in the air, but it is also a way of measuring distance in the air to the target area, feeding in some line until the correct length is judged to be airialised beyond the rod tip. In passing I must put to bed the nostalgic maxim that amadou is a wonder material for drying the fly. It is no better than a paper tissue, and a darn sight more expensive. Another tradition from the past was that a dry fly rod needed a stiff tip action. It doesn't, the medium fast parabolic action is quite suitable.

When I first came to the River Test, being allocated a beat, I was struck by the patches of bare ground or trampled grass here and there, until I related them to a right-handed cast to certain trout the survival of which was due to drag. Everyone stood in the same place to cast to the same fish.

This was one motivation for me to become ambidextrous, so that I could either change the angle of attack, or even change the bank from which I attacked that particular fish.

The large dry flies, mayflies and the occasional daddy, were so easily drowned when switching distance and direction, that I learnt how to take the fly upwards from the surface of the water with a snake roll cast.

Although on the hallowed beats background vegetation is usually cut back, occasionally a high obstacle intrudes. The oft-recommended 'steeple' cast has the disadvantage of banging the fly down heavily. We can thank modern salmon anglers for developing this higher flick for their roll-casts, as described earlier, and with some practice, the floating fly can be wafted down as gently as with a normal overhead chuck. The fly must be well anointed though, for you needs must pull it across the water before the final snap-roll is performed.

You will gather from what I have written, and the way I fish, that with the exceptions of mayflies, I do not relish the traditional split winged dry flies. This is true, though I love to make them. I must admit that once I was completely baffled by the refusal of an olive-snaffling trout, which I covered well without drag, to take my hackled fly. In desperation I tied on the same pattern, though with split wings, and it was immediately accepted. There seems to be no logic for this! It is things like this which defeat dogma.

In the old days I took the trouble to degrease the final few inches of the leader, to coax it to go just below the surface film, and this could make all the difference. In those days we had to stretch and grease the silk lines and this grease had the annoying habit of getting onto the leader. Yes, I am mildly sceptical of the wonder leader materials, but in dry fly fishing it makes sense to use one of the new 'invisible' materials for the last link of the leader, copolymer or fluo-carbon. In dry fly fishing, above all, nylon glitter is an enemy.

I admit this chapter has been heretical, for the great tradition of our literature, in its golden days, raised the dry fly to the pinnacle of our art. In fact it is probably the easiest of all of our tactics even though on occasion it may not be the most successful. The nymph practitioner will take more fish though this technique is slightly more difficult. Why? It is because he has two shots for every one of the dry fly man's, one for the rising fish, another for the fish which is not taking from the surface.

Trout are 'contrary critters', and whilst we like to make rules for them to obey, they sometimes fail to comply, so with some trepidation I give some general behaviour patterns. On chalk streams I was often told it was a waste of time to fish early as the hatches of duns never started till later in the morning. There's some truth in this, but this overlooked a fall of spinner, females which had been mating the night before and which came onto the water before sun-up to lay their eggs. On northern rivers, though, a summer fall of spinner would often happen after sundown. That PT Red Spinner was a sensible fly choice in both places.

One of the weather maxims I found to be true, when the ghostly white mist comes onto the water in late evening it does put fish down, presumably because the 'surface vision' is eliminated. Yes, fish do rise in rain, you can see them do so. But a strong sun slanting down a stream also diminishes a rise because it shines into the eyes of the fish (though grayling are less affected because of their shooting rise from the bottom). The 'red sky', detested by our forebears has never worried me or the fish.

A strong ripple from wind action is always a nuisance to the dry fly man because it cools the surface water, and possibly hinders the trout's vision. The worst wind is the gusty one which makes feathery arrows across the water; I hate that one. But the weather I detest the most on a chalk stream is a very hot windless day when the valley becomes a heat trap. Such days always have early mornings and evenings, don't they?

Every writer on dry fly fishing has used a few choice words on the 'angler's curse', a fly so tiny as to be almost beyond simulation, but on which the fish love to become preoccupied. One such curse is the caenis, a tiny whitish fly with broad wings, recognisable by its three long tail whisks, but thankfully its hatch, from the first duns to the spent spinners, is of short duration. Traditional advice was to use a very small hackled Coachman fly, but it never worked for me. I had occasional success with a minute Grey Duster. The real curse though is a persistent tiny, glistening black fly. This causes an invisible rise, until one sees the ebony pinheads floating downstream. The problem with this 'hatch' is that it can persist for a long time, and it excites the fish. On one occasion, when this happened in a fast run in Upper Teesdale, my friend and I took turns in chucking everything in the box at rising fish, but they were so locked-on to the little beasts that they would look at nothing else, neither nymph, wet spider nor floating fly. A curiosity of this rise, which gulled us completely, was that the rise forms were quite large, making splendid whorls in the surface as the fish gulped down sizable mouthfuls of water to grab the insects.

I try to add to the knowledge and experience of the past. Of course, I can repeat the classic truisms on striking, to leave that slight pause after the 'take'. And there are many cautionary tales on playing fish. I say no more; it has all been well written in past texts, and I leave you in the hands of the real teachers on these things, the river and the fish. One learns from mistakes in fishing, as in life.

Part Three
Still Waters

Calder loch.

A General Survey

It may appear astounding to make the statement that today we actually know very little about still water trout fisheries for brown trout. It is true if only because the natural trend has been towards the popularity of stocked fisheries, which means the rainbow trout. Taking growth and disease as two important factors in wild fish stocks, attention and research declined because there was little if any demand, apart from the academic. In short, interest would need to be supported by finance, but the commercial bias was in the stocked reservoirs and the smaller, commercial put-and-take fisheries. Here the problems were different. True, I have found tape worm in rainbow trout at Chew reservoir, and eye fluke in some of the Anglian reservoirs, but generally, the rod pressure and stocking policy ensures that the stocked fish are in residence for only a short time before capture, and this hardly allows for the disease and parasite problems to arise, except marginally. We have seen that the scientific study of Bewl Water declared that the average life span of a stocked rainbow in that fishery was sixteen days, a period which may have been shortened by the policy of intensive stocking prior to big competitions when normal bag-limits are suspended.

Does this matter? In the interests of true science, of course it does, but there is a spin-off from, say, a research project into the health of wild brown trout in still water, for apart from the general interest in disease or parasitism, the team of scientists would uncover valuable information of growth rates and general health and condition of the fish and fauna in the fisheries, which must interest local clubs and visiting anglers.

At this time there is one area of relative wilderness which attracts fly fishers in search of wild brown trout and this is the far North, Caithness and Sutherland. Having fished there over several years with friends, we were concerned to find high levels of parasitic intestinal worms in the fish in some lochs, and we persuaded the Charitable Trust of the Salmon & Trout Association to undertake a research project. An angler's interpretation of this project gives an insight into the situation of the brown trout in British still waters.

The money having been allocated, the team went from the Department of Biological Sciences of the Herriot-Watt University of Edinburgh[1], and it

[1]*Parasites of Brown Trout in Northern Scottish Lochs*, July 1997.

has to be said at the outset that it did an extremely thorough job. I think it must also have been an enjoyable task, for I noted in the paper they published that besides taking fish samples by seine nets, some were also caught by fly rods. From a fishery point of view this is important because it means sampling from the same stocks which you and I would also catch.

There was a problem insofar as research is often based on testing results against a standard, the standard being previous examinations of the territory, but not only had there been none previously, but because the commercial interest lies now in stocked waters, precious little work had been done anywhere else. As a casually interested person my only previous reference would have been the excellent book on the wild trout by Frost & Brown in the Collins *New Naturalist* series of books. Nevertheless this was a happy project for two reasons. Although salmon fishing provides the main attraction there, with rivers like the Thurso, Naver, Halladale and Helmsdale, there is a significant number of regular trout fishing visitors to the area, not only for the famed limestone lochs in the West, but also for loch complexes like Badenloch which are fished from local hotels like the Garvault establishment. This latter, rightly advertised as the 'most remote hotel in Britain' is a true angler's refuge, having access to boats on the three Badenloch waters, but also to several other lochs on the moorlands.

The second reason is that there have been changes in an area which has been stable for generations. Notably the decline in sea fish stocks due to intensive fishing which has driven bird predators inland and these birds are significant hosts for fish parasites. In passing, although not scientific, the angler notices such things as the number of parasites he discovers, say, in a Caithness trout caught not far from the sea, compared with the number found in one taken far inland, in such locations as wild brown trout fisheries in the High Pennines. One of my few quibbles with the report is when it gives the impression of normal, or expected levels of infestation for we simply do not know what these 'normal' levels should be. However, this book is not concerned with parasitism except insofar as it presents a problem or deterrent to anglers.

To summarise the findings, then to put them on one side, clearly the worms are the parasites which upset anglers because they are visible when fish are cleaned, both in the gut, and in the muscle tissue if the fish are not cleaned quickly enough after capture. There are many 'invisible' parasites which do not worry us unduly, we do not see them, and they are liver, heart and eye flukes. The report was pessimistic in the sense that it declares that nothing can be done to remedy parasite infection without knocking out a bird host, which, in an area beloved by the RSPB, is unacceptable. If wild brown trout were as important in the economy as salmon I would expect more attention, with investigation into the addition of a vermicide to trout food in smaller fisheries and trout farms, and the culling of stocks in lochs with a numerous stunted population, for it seems logical that growth rates of fish and parasite levels are linked, but the report failed to discuss this, alas. One promising aspect, the St John's Club which has the loch fishery at Dunnet, has constructed an indoor fish-raising operation which gets their brown trout off to a good start in a safe environment.

So, allow me to pass on to the angling questions of the report, for the two counties have an enormous number of fisheries which can be fished for a relatively modest sum. I use these as a yardstick, for there are also other relatively unspoiled areas, in Wales and the High Pennines for example, where similar fishing can be enjoyed by the connoisseur. How many lochs are there in that area of the far North? I haven't counted them, but in a month's stay I managed to fish in twenty two, all different. There is a range of choice between the specimen hunter's delight, say the Cross Lochs where he might have but one single take a day from a three pounder, or perhaps Yarrows loch in the east where half pounders would come to the fly eagerly all day. Between those two extremes are 'middling' fisheries where a day's hard work would produce hopefully half a dozen fish around the pound-plus mark, the sort of catch I would expect from Watten. Now, this is not a guide book; such books abound. Get one! The local lady-expert, Lesley Crawford has produced an excellent example.

A regular, good fly fisher becomes, unknowingly, a rough scientist for his findings coincide with research, for, as you would expect, he wouldn't need to know the pH of a fishery to realise that if it produced bigger fish then its food life would be richer and its water more alkaline. It doesn't always follow, other factors creep in, such as the spawning facilities for the fish, but it's a rough and ready guide. The research project, undertaken on ten lochs of different characteristics, bears this out, for the 'best' pH of the ten is Watten and this is justifiably a popular loch with its strain of Leven trout, distinct from other local populations. Toftingall, nearby, matched it. This is one of my favourites, being by preference a bank angler (Watten is best boat fished). Toftingall is cradled by pine forests, it has a prolific mayfly hatch and is scenically attractive.

The variables creep in when you visit nearby Calder, a vast reservoir with a good pH, but because of its great depth it produces a large population of small fish. Unusually, the study showed that Calder fish put on a growth spurt after their fourth year which I attribute to cannibalism of the older fish on the younger stocks. This is why the fishery gives up the occasional three-pound-plus fish, often of splendid shape and condition. This phenomenon is repeated at Cow Green, a reservoir high in the Pennines, unstocked, with a population of wild brown trout of no great size. Breeding there is favoured by the numerous sikes which enter the lake from the fells, but occasionally one catches a fish well over two pounds. These larger fish must predate on small trout and bull heads. It is this differential, the two strata of trout, which caused that idea of a special strain or species of predatory monsters known as *ferox*. Classically, they are fish with ugly, huge heads filled with needle-like teeth, but it 'ain't necessarily so' for at both the waters I mention those occasional larger fish can be of splendid condition as my cover painting shows. Nor is their diet entirely of fish. My Cow Green specimen came to a small black dry fly.

Although I do not know the water well, I would imagine that the spectacular Lake Vyrnwy produces a similar variation in its wild brown trout stock.

Were they of salmon-scale commercial interest these wild fisheries would benefit from culling, for in older times the rod pressure was probably much higher and performed this function, but today we simply do not value our wild fisheries enough because of the rainbow stocked waters. Natural stock pruning takes place, from the cannibal fish, parasites and from fish-eating birds. The latter bring the parasites, of course, but Darwin teaches us that by natural selection most species overproduce in order to ensure survival, and given access to spawning grounds, brown trout are too successful from a fishery point of view, though not from nature's. With very few exceptions, we do not manage wild brown trout waters, simply because the money isn't there. What you see is what you get.

I mention in passing that pH is only an approximate guide. A lake can be quite alkaline, but if it consists of mainly deep water, then obviously the food producing areas will be diminished. Probably the perfect fisheries of the far North are the old marl workings which are relatively shallow and highly alkaline, but some of them can be the dourest fisheries because of the rich choice of food. It is not merely that the trout become rapidly satiated, but because they see so much of their living food they become efficiently imprinted by its behaviour. In short, like a gourmet in an indifferent restaurant, a critical eye is cast on all offerings, and yours may well be sent back to the chef. I have not mentioned the excellent limestone lochs of Durness and Cape Wrath simply because I have not fished them, my fishing being in the central and eastern lochs of the far North.

I have mentioned that I am by preference a bank angler and as such I know that still water is a misnomer. It is moved by wind and temperature, but it has given rise to an uncomfortable belief that we should adopt the Spartan habit of fishing on the windward side of a lake. It should be enough for me to declare that over many years I have found this to be an absolute fallacy, and serendipity proved to me that the most comfortable bank on the lee shore was usually the most productive, especially if I could fish over a marginal area of quiet water into the edges of a ripple. There are probably natural explanations for my experience: trout, unlike carp, not relishing warmer water on the windward side resulting from thermal stratification of deeper lakes in summer, appreciate the attraction of terrestrial insects blown onto the water, or even the fact that hatching insects from the lee-shore water take longer to dry their wings when emerging from their pupal shucks and can easily be harvested.

Be that as it may, I have long disregarded those masochists who hurl flies into the dirty water on the windward side, into the teeth of a strong wind.

It is true that casting across a wind lane or scum line is productive, another sensible ploy. The attraction of wind lanes is a mystery I shall discuss later; it is as if the water in the lane is more sticky. Often it has an oily look to it, or perhaps the foam traps insects. Also productive – and again a mystery – is the water, say a yard or two on either side of the lane itself. The mystery deepens, for unlike the rainbow trout, still water brownies are not great rovers. You see a local angler, say at Cow Green, fishing along the bank. He covers an area thoroughly, then, taking up his rod and bag, he walks past a few yards of water where long experience tells him fish will not come to the fly. Often this may be a deeper declivity where fish may lie too deep to take the surface-fished fly. It is common sense that *relatively* shallow water is the more productive of trout food simply because sunlight warms and illuminates the lake floor. Now, although the brown trout are not habitual rovers, of course they move, they migrate upwind to intercept and compete for a drift of mayfly coming down with the wind . . . first come, first served as it were. These are an angler's practical observations; we haven't monitored trout movements sufficiently to understand them well, but, happily, those swirls on the surface reveal much to the intelligent watcher.

I should mention here that there is a unity between still water brown trout fisheries. Habits and conditions do not vary much between these lochs in Caithness and Sutherland, those in the more distant isles of Orkney and Shetland, the moorland lochs in Wales, say at Bugeilyn, and the lakes in the High Pennines. I find, for example, that in summer, a black hackled fly will kill on all of these waters, as will my favourite Grouse & Claret.

Traditions die hard. The sixty-four thousand dollar question is why? There is no reason why the southern rainbow angler shouldn't try with some success the tactics he uses on his local rainbow lake. I have seen such an angler being successful with Pheasant Tail nymphs on a Caithness lake during its dour period. I take a longer look at this. A visiting man must fish. If fate decides that he will have no wind, a water surface like glass under a bright sun which shines for longer than it does at home, then, when some of us would wait for the evening, which comes later in those climes, it makes sense for him, perhaps to fish slowly and patiently with a weighted nymph or a sinking line. He would suit his tactic intelligently to the conditions, whereas, although this used to be my way in my enthusiastic green years, today I choose my time when I know the traditional wet-fly team will do its deadly work under a sombre sky with a friendly ripple below it. This is the reason why there is the successful tradition, for it grew at a time when people did not travel much, when time was not money. There was no need to think about coping with hard conditions, one merely waited until those conditions changed. I met many anglers who, visiting that deservedly popular loch at Watten, were advised not to bother with the bright day, but by persevering with a 'reservoir' technique and fly, they scored, perhaps being the only anglers on the loch.

This is why in the far North I prefer to rent a cottage where I can make my own fishing timetable. I confess that I am mostly the 'wait for it' school of angler, leaving the hot, sunny days to the midges, but, yes, the patient fishing of the nymph does produce if you can stick it. Why? It's very simple. Trout cannot shut their eyes to glare. They seek the comfort of deep water unless there is a good ripple. That is where you need to seek them out. On occasion, when I have felt I needed to do it, fishing from the margins, I threw a weighted nymph far out on a long leader, then, putting the rod down, I left it until I knew it was on the bottom before starting a slow retrieve. I used a floating line, for sometimes the take would be a straightening of the little curls on the surface. Where mayflies abound, the matching nymph is a good choice, as is the ubiquitous Pheasant Tail. It is true that a propitious time is the actual moment of the very first line retrieve when the nymph 'lifts off' from the bottom. It is seen by an interceptor. Unlike rainbows, which sometimes follow before grabbing, the wild brown trout is an instant seizer, an opportunist.

So, having decided on which bank to fish, a further choice is between boat and bank. Of course, I do fish from a boat on occasion. Some of the lochs I discuss here require it. Both Watten and St John's fish better afloat, and on lake Vyrnwy it is obligatory unless the water tower is revealed as dry when the Liverpudlians get thirsty. Given a choice, though, I prefer the comfort of bank fishing (midges apart!). Over a season I would admit the boat outscores the bank in the numbers game, economically less so, if that is a factor. As a Senior Citizen it is, for me, but only a minor one. I have a definite philosophical preference for the bank, it suits my leisurely approach to the sport, the time to sit and stare, to investigate wild life, flora and fauna, local terrain. The fish catching is only part of my fishing life. Also, on some lochs there is an anxiety to get you afloat, to convince you that the grass is always greener (in an aquatic sense). Thus on the Baddenloch system, three vast waterscapes, I was told that everyone fished from the boats, the banks being unproductive, but it simply wasn't true. An exception is certainly dapping, hard, though not impossible from the shore. And dapping does produce the occasional monster trout from, say, Rimsdale loch.

Moving is important, for unlike rainbow fishing, you cannot wait for brownies to find you. It's the other way round, you need to cover water. This is probably the greatest error the rainbow man makes when first fishing a wild loch. He roots himself to his deep wading position, throwing a long line into the same water. It rarely works well.

The very first choice would be which sort of fishing do you want? Many small fish, a modest catch of medium sized trout (probably the favourite) or really hard fishing for a possible monster? It's easy to decide, for you give your preference to the local hotel, say Garvault or Forsinard amongst many, or you go to the tackle shops in Wick or Thurso. You express your wish, they will make the facility available to you. You can rent a boat and engine if you prefer and usually the permit-seller will put you onto a loch where the number of anglers may be controlled, two or four, say.

You should also ask about weather, for the strength and direction of wind will be important. A shallow, silty loch – and there are some – will be too cloudy to fish in a strong wind and may take a day or two to settle after the blow. Some very exposed, open lochs may even be too uncomfortable to fish from a boat.

For bank fishing, some lochs with steep banks do not require waders – I fish the Baddenloch system with wellies. Others, like Toftingall, are best fished with thigh or chest waders, as there are marginal shallows in the best spots. Some lochs require a good tramp, not comfortable going in waders.

Time of day? With reasonable wind, weather and cloud, any time will do, but late into the dusk on hot, bright and windless days. Early morning? That's the same thing, isn't it?

Perhaps not discussed by your friendly ticket purveyor is the dreaded midge, prolific on some banks on calmer, warm days, but this is an important consideration! The terrain is important, both in the far islands, the far North and the high Pennines, all moorlands in fact, to recognise the dangers of peat bogs beneath friendly-looking sphagnum moss. High lochs, exposed to winds and few anglers, have undercut banks on the windward side of the prevailing winds and even sheep paths can collapse beneath your feet. It has happened to me on two occasions.

Beware sheep paths! I once strayed from the route along such a path which led me straight to the edge of a precipice at dusk, high above Strath Halladale. Take a map and a compass, learn to read both. Wild fish are in wild places and some lochs will be along rough forest tracks with access by keys to locked gates. Bear this in mind!

Those of us who fish in such places take these things for granted, but having seen anglers from the quiet South, accustomed to the stroll across the meadow from car park to lake side, and remembering my first day on Balderhead when the rain was coming down sideways, I state here the obvious. Two years before I wrote this I was told of an angler who anchored up along a dangerous shore at Calder loch, stepped out of his boat onto the marginal 'land' and disappeared, never to return alive. . . .

What are the conclusions?

Yes, wild fish are mostly in the wildernesses of this land, the still waters having much in common whether they be in the high hills of England, the moorlands of Wales or Scotland or the distant islands. Yes, you can fish boat or bank, the latter being a good bet as it is relatively quieter than stocked waters. If you are unfamiliar with these waters, take care, no one minds a sensible enquiry.

I have mentioned before another mystery of still water which perplexes anglers. This is the thermal stratification of lakes. In summer time two distinct layers of water are formed, the warmer one floating on top of the colder one, and between them is a layer of rapidly changing temperature called the thermocline. When the wind blows constantly this latter situation tilts towards the windward shore where the warm water is deeper. On the lee shore, on a summer's day you can feel the icy water around your waders. It was thought that fish would not lie below the thermocline where oxygenation is poor and light is weak, but skin divers have photographed perch there, and the strange deep-loving fish like char live there, and are preyed on by the cannibal *ferox* trout. If we are honest, we must admit that our knowledge of trout movement in relation to these layers is incomplete.

We know that the autumn gales and the loss of temperature by radiation in the longer nights cause these deeper lakes to lose this stratification; the water assumes a more universal temperature and there are subtle changes in the behaviour of creatures which live on the lake floor. A sort of hibernation takes place, which may explain why we find so many 'empty' fish in early season. I shall investigate this further when I discuss the behaviour and capture of those cannibal monsters, the *ferox* trout, and to a certain extent, those strange snail- and plankton-eating specialists, the so-called *sonaghan* and *dollaghan* trout of Irish lakes, though they can become surface feeders when a good menu is presented, say in mayfly time when I have caught them. Of course these are all normal brown trout which have adapted to specialised feeding conditions, perhaps for reasons of age, perhaps because of competition for food supply, and perhaps it demonstrates the very first stage of mutation about which Darwin wrote so long ago. My guess is that it is not a hereditary factor; one does not catch baby *ferox*, *dollaghan* or *sonaghan* trout.

There has been many a debate in the angling press about stocking, the effect the introduced fish have on the natural wild population of a lake, and what is a true 'wild fish'. This matters far less than the purists claim. I doubt it does any harm at all to add stocked brown trout to a fishery. I have known many occasions when adding new blood has improved fisheries, especially when an earlier pollution took place, as in the Upper Tees. There are few truly wild fish in one sense, but in a practical sense, once fish have become natural feeders and reverted to an instinctive wariness of predators, to all intents and purposes they are wild. Does interbreeding do any harm? Providing the 'new' fish are free from parasite and disease, I doubt it very much.

My preferences

These are personal. I have developed two rods. Usually, my first choice is my ultra-light 9.6 footer loaded with an AFTM 3 or 4 double taper floating line. This sets hook up to size 12. I use a more powerful rod only for the mayfly time as a larger hook needs to be set. This is a ten footer with a size 4 or 5 double taper line. I choose thigh waders or wellies according to the bank conditions. I travel light, no net and a fly box, reel of regular tippet nylon, 2.6 to 3 lb b.s., some provisions for the day, usual tools. A wax cotton coat, map and compass if a good moorland yomp is required. Some anti-midge gunge is essential. I regard hat and glasses as essential. For the rest, flies and so on, the tactical choices decide that. Some writers give precise recommendations for keeping hunger and thirst at bay, and, yes, take something, but I leave that to you. Although I gave it up long since, when I was addicted to specimen hunting I used a powerful trolling rod with a very fast-sinking shooting head. For occasional dapping a long rod is required, from 12 to 15 feet and specialists are content to use telescopic coarse fishing rods, beloved by holiday anglers. The blow-line is easily made from nylon carpet yard, joined to a running line of regular monofilament nylon, wound onto a large-drum coarse fishing centre pin reel. Tie a granny knot into every yard of the blow-line to stop it fraying.

And read the section later in this book for the tackle make-up.

A final note on the edibility of wild brown trout from someone who doesn't care much for them!

You will find intestinal worms in many wild fish. No turbot is without its friendly neighbourhood nematode. Only one rare species can invade the human gut of a person who is in poor health, but proper cooking destroys them all. To keep the worms in the gut where they can be evacuated, either clean the fish quickly on capture, or freeze them immediately you return with the catch. It is foolish to leave the offal either close to or in the water, it simply speeds the infestation. Remember, parasites are a normal part of nature, they are in most sea fish but supermarket buyers rarely see them. It is a cosmetic problem, really.

Finally, and for the record, although the worm appearance caused my friends and me to ask for the research project, as we fish mostly no-kill, we did not notice an appreciable falling off in trout condition and appearance in Caithness and Sutherland, except in lochs mentioned in the report. The area is still a trout fisher's paradise. The other restriction is that the RSPB now own large reserves at Forsinard and they restrict fishing on certain lochs when the divers are nesting – enquiry should be made.

This has been a general survey of the still water conditions for brown trout over the United Kingdom. Now it's time to get down to catching them!

Boat Control

I am a bank angler by preference, simply because, as the years go by, I find it more comfortable to stroll along the bank of lakes and lochs, but also for two oblique reasons. I am nosy about wildlife and often dart off into trees or meadows to investigate, say a strange-looking fungus. The other reason is that bank fishing has this casual opportunity of being able to sit down, stretch my legs, open the flask and relax. Being cramped on a boat seat for hours reminds me more of the politician who sat on the fence so long that the iron entered his soul.

You will gather from this that I was an habitual boat-fisher who changed his fishing habits with advancing years, and, though still enthusiastic, it became a more relaxed affair.

Quite some years ago, when the large reservoirs like Grafham opened, vast drifts were available to the angler, and intelligent boat fishers like Bob Church experimented with ways of changing the steady drift before the wind. They borrowed from the East Coast herring drifters the technique of using a lee board. As its name implies, it is simply a board clamped to the side of the boat, about a third along amid-ships, and the wind and water pressure changes the angle of the drift from being before the wind and wave to running across them. Whilst this undoubtedly improved fishing with, say a sinking line and lure, I never found it improved catches for the traditional short line with a worked team of flies, the so-called Scottish loch style.

This was eventually forbidden by Authority, for as the lee board was just a wooden plank clamped to the gunwales by a G bracket some considerable strain was being put on the boat's structure, and sometimes the boat canted over alarmingly in a strong wind. Not only that, when the reservoir was shared between boat anglers and yachtsmen, the latter naturally laid off a course to miss a boat they assumed to be on a normal wind drift, suddenly to discover that it was cutting under their bows. When lee boards were outlawed then some anglers discovered they could achieve a similar result with a large rudder, but in those days it was mildly surprising to see an angler preparing his boat. He staggered down to the jetty with boards, clamps, boat seats and drogues. The boat became a miniature merchant vessel.

I deal now with the modern boat seat which is laid across the thwarts, raising the angler quite high above the boat, giving it 'top hamper' which can be uncomfortable in a strong wind. This is probably safe from fish-spooking in fisheries devoted to the freshly introduced rainbow trout, and I imagine its benefit is thought to be an advantage when working the top dropper on the surface. In my experience, when used on waters which hold mainly or solely brown trout, fish are spooked. I recounted an example of this when sea trout fishing on Loch Maree when, as soon as my companion raised himself in this way the fish ceased to come to the fly.

So, in my personal fishing the only controlling mechanism which suits me is the drogue, both to slow the boat and to adjust its drift. Long since I became disenchanted with the drogues made available to the angler through the retail trade and eventually I made my own.

The very first fault I discovered with 'off-the-shelf' drogues was that they were simply not man enough for the job. The control-lines were fine and flimsy. I had one snap on a drift in Orkney, in a strong wind just as I had hooked a good brownie, and the sudden increase in the speed of the drift lost me that fish. The very first thing I decided to do was to use much stronger rope.

I could never understand the reasoning for the hole in the centre of the canopy, and, on enquiry, I was given two reasons. The first was that it steadied the drogue which would otherwise twist and oscillate in the water. The second was that it made it easier to recover the drogue after use. Most of these drogues were just not big enough to slow the boat in a good wind, and again the maker's answer was that a bigger drogue would be cumbersome to carry and to deploy. I began to think how to improve the efficiency of the boat angler's drogue within a reasonable size format, though it would have to be a one-off for myself, for, being in the fishing tackle trade at that time, my opinion was that the real reasoning behind the existing designs was production cost.

I had in the past several years of sea fishing-boat experience where the sea anchor is a vital part of equipment. Firstly, that hole had to go, it served no purpose other than to reduce the efficiency of the drogue. The argument about recovery of the drogue was fallacious, for if the canopy ropes are long enough, one simply grabs one to use as a tripping line, as in normal anchor recovery, and one could even attach a tripping line itself to the canopy, but in practice this proved unnecessary. It is also sensible to be able to trip a drogue if it catches on an obstacle in the water, say a skerry, for then the canopy can be slid over it. Strangely, I do see on rare occasions a boat angler heaving at his drogue line without realising he should collapse it in the water before shipping it aboard. Drogues and anchors should always be tripped, that is pulled away in a reverse direction from their resistance, if only for safety's sake. The length of the four lead ropes to the canopy must be long enough for one of them to be used for tripping the drogue without undue stretching over the gunwale, and this was accomplished in practice.

How to overcome the oscillation argument and improve the efficiency of the canopy without increasing its size to an unmanageable amount? I

93

hit on the idea of making a flap along the leading edge of a square canopy which was folded in when carried, but opened up like a parachute by water pressure when deployed, to give extra resistance and to steady the drogue. This worked like a dream, the drogue was rock-steady in the water and had increased resistance. I give in the photograph the dimensions I settled on, for again, safety is a factor that must be balanced with efficiency.

Either for simplicity or out of laziness I abandoned the interchangeable canopy and adjustable collar design features, described below, as I did less boat fishing. I had a metal eye made in each corner of the canopy and the four spreading ropes were attached with dog clips. The idea was that I would be able to switch canopies of different sizes. I'm certain this was a great idea, but it complicated life too much, being too much to carry. The next idea was to have a sliding collar over the four ropes, one being doubled through it, so that the depth of the canopy could be adjusted. This worked in practice, but its effect was insufficient to make it a permanent feature. The drogue was also stored in its own carrying bag with drainage holes in each corner.

In the end, good design is a marriage of simplicity and efficiency, so the final result was the large canopy with no hole, very strong ropes and the folding flap. I have been using this same one for some thirty years, proof enough, and I had my design made up as a one-off for me by someone used to working with that material. It naturally follows that the canopy must be made of a really tough man-made material which cannot easily tear on unseen rocks. Imagine, for instance, the skerries in Loch Harray, Orkney. The main purpose of a drogue is to slow a boat on a wind drift, simplicity itself. It also serves to position the boat. Anglers know that a boat never drifts uniformly before the wind. With an engine at the stern and more hamper at the prow, the latter usually swings forward and frequent adjustments have to be made. With two leisurely companions this is of no great matter, given common sense, but I was amused when once I accidentally drifted through a flotilla of competition anglers to hear one bawl to his boat partner who was in the prow: 'you're nicking my water!'

It's obvious that careful positioning of the drogue can mitigate the effect of top hamper when the drogue is deployed from roughly midships. One colleague of mine has a running line from stern to prow along which the drogue line can be slid. This works well, but I dislike any obstacle like this upon which one can stumble. By experiment, as boats differ, the wind-effect against the higher prow can be largely overcome by deciding from which thole pin the drogue is attached. It will rarely be perfect, drifts usually need to be adjusted by a stroke or two on the oar, but it will serve well enough.

By now you should have gauged my boat fishing philosophy. Although I am in favour of simplicity, disliking lee boards, rudder controls and those high-up boat seats, I did pay great attention to drogue design, and not being over impressed with those available 'off the shelf' I had my own

The author's drogue. The canopy is one yard square. The folded-in flap, which opens under water pressure measures 3½".

made with what I consider to be improved and stronger features. There is another safety feature in this, for with every extra piece of gear you put into a boat there is an added pitfall for the clumsy foot which may unbalance the craft. In short, the less you need in the boat the better.

Of course, drogues can also be swum out from the stern or prow of a boat. This gives a change of angle to attack the fish, but it probably makes more sense for a single angler. Later I shall discuss the rather boring way of going after the deep-lying *ferox*, painstaking work with a fast-sinking line and semi-trolled lure, and the boat can be managed in this way.

My attitude to wind lanes, when brownie fishing, is different to drifting along them for rainbows. The latter love to cruise up wind lanes. Many years ago, when Hanningfield reservoir was on season ticket, and far less heavily fished than today, when that broad wind lane we called the 'M1' ran diagonally across the lake, I could start a drift along it. The light used to gleam on the oily water in the lane, and coming towards you would be shoals of humping rainbows, always moving upwind. It was possible to identify an individual fish and to intercept it. What is the magic of the wind lane? Everyone has a theory. Mine is that I believe the surface film in a wind lane to be stickier than outside it, and hatching flies, such as buzzers as one instance, are trapped there. The physics of this stronger molecular wall of the surface film in wind lanes are complicated, probably controversial, so I say no more.

Brown trout are not generally cruising feeders, and if you position your-self to watch a wind lane, say on a Scottish loch, when there is a hatch of fly, the chances are that you will see the same fish rising in the same place because it is waiting for the wind drift to bring the food to it; it does not go to meet it. Like all 'fishing rules' you also see this one broken, but it is a reasonable assumption on which to base tactics. Now, decades of experi-ence prove the importance of wind and scum lanes. A curiosity of brown trout is that many will also feed just to one side of these lanes, the reasons for which I not sure, but my own experience satisfies me that this is so. The fact is, as every experienced boat angler knows, that the positioning of a boat drift in relation to a wind lane is of vital importance.

I add in passing that I carry a small pair of pocket binoculars when boat fishing. I can usually spot areas where fish are rising, or, equally valuable, birds swooping close to the water are another indication. In this respect, do not discount the humble sea gulls, they are greedy snappers-up of hatching flies.

Plainly, it is effective to arrange a drift along the wind lane, if it is wide enough, or with two anglers because frequently two lanes are formed side by side with rougher water between them so that each angler can cover his own lane. When by myself, I try to attach the drogue at one end of the boat so that I can cast across the wind lane, as this gives the fish a sideways look at the flies, though upwind mending of the line is necessary to avoid drag. In either drifting fashion, it helps to put some angle into the fly-retrieve.

Apart from wind lanes, the drift along the shore line is the most produc-tive and popular, though care must be taken not to poach on the territory of bank anglers. In stocked reservoirs which are regularly fished, the nor-mal feeding zones of trout are hard to predict because of disturbance by waders and outboards. I recollect it was a writer named Bridgett who wrote one of the earliest specialised books on still water fishing who rightly told us that trout preferred to feed on the litterol zone of a lake. Translated, this means there is a perfect depth where the fish feel safe, but where sufficient light and warmth reach the lake floor to allow the fauna there to thrive. It is this zone which gives the bank angler his much loved 'edge of the ripple' from the lee shore. It is not scientific, but I simply look down into the water to try to judge the right line for the drift. It's a matter of careful control to manage a drift perfectly along such a line. More often than not we keep drifting diagonally onto the shore. This is when the less skilful boat man has to keep making his sudden, short engine bursts and he comes down onto the shore so quickly that he has to drop his rod to prevent himself from running ashore.

Common sense dictates that planning drifts along the edges of weed beds which are obviously food larders for the trout, should also prove use-ful. Not so easily managed are drifts around the sub-surface layers of rocks such as the famous skerries in Orcadian lochs like Harray. In fact success depends on fishing skerries properly, but the problem is simply that the visiting angler doesn't know their location, depth below the surface or their extent. He fears running his boat onto them or smashing the shear pin of his outboard. There's no real substitute for local knowledge other than to take time to survey a chosen area of water, to fix in the mind the position of the skerries there and to plan a drift accordingly. The temptation is always to rush into the fishing, but patient devotion to reconnaissance will pay off. That survey should include approaches from various angles because the wind may change from day to day. It does so on Northern isles.

When planning a drift along shore lines, weed beds and skerries, if two unselfish anglers are in the boat it makes sense for them to take it in turns to fish and manage the boat gently on the oars. A really skilful angler can ply the rod in one hand whilst managing a single oar in the other, but it takes some experience. Generally speaking, the deepest parts of lakes are less productive, but so many rules are broken by fish.

Although I have made some general observations and assumptions about the way in which trout find their food, actually, little is known about the movement of brown trout in still water. Wind lanes have caught me out. I have been undecided over whether the best rise will come upwind in the lane or come onto the windward shore.

I think it strange that so many boat hirers fail to provide a small anchor. I guess the reason is that they know that the majority of anglers are not great boat handlers. Many of them do not realise that you need to veer out two thirds more rope to the anchor than the depth directly down from keel to the lake floor. This is a golden rule on the sea to cope with the rise and fall of the tide, but it makes sense also on inland waters simply for boat comfort and steadiness. Accidents have been made by the ferocious pulling of a locked anchor, held fast in debris. Impounded water covers tree roots, hedges and old buildings. I usually take my own small anchor. The wide-pronged sort should always have a tripping line to allow for a reverse pull if the anchor is fast in the bottom, and some designs of anchor have folding flukes which turn inwards when that reverse pull is applied. These are the best type to use, with the proviso that an anchor should have an attachment point for the tripping line. The sledge type of anchor isn't best suited to inland water though it is first class in the marine environment, biting into the sea floor under tidal pressure. Even so, a *short* length of chain to the anchor is a sensible addition. One of my friends underwent an uncomfortable hernia operation after trying to retrieve an anchor from within a huge mass of weeds because he had no tripping line to it.

The use of an anchor is my tactic when I discover the concentration of rises at one end of a wind lane. At first sight this seems folly, given that there will always be an extension of the rise, say in a hatch of mayflies, sailing along the wind lane, but by extending the rope, the boat can also be taken downwind, too. Here, the flat anchor is useful, providing that the water is not too deep, say that used by Norfolk pike men, the so called mud anchor which lies flat. I mention this with some reservations because they can be awkward to retrieve for the unaccustomed angler and they are not recommended to be used on very rough lake floors. Although they do not 'trip', resistance can be reduced for recovery, given that you have made your own anchor, by attaching a line to a large staple in the side of the slab.

The way the Norfolk Broadsmen use the mud anchor is to have a long rope and they progressively veer out more line to allow the boat to drift gently down wind, so more water is carefully covered. When the rope is fully extended, the boat is pulled back towards the mud anchor, which is lifted aboard, and then the next piece of water is fished in the same way. This was taught to me for pike spinning, by my fishing companion on Hickling Broad, the late Edwin, son of the legendary Jim Vincent. I use this for smaller lakes, for trout, but a little thought reveals that it is suitable for relatively shallow waters.

I repeat, over and over again, that many of us overlook the basic simplicities of fly fishing, the common sense of it, if you prefer. Taking a wind lane, for example, in June when mayflies are hatching, we know that these fantastic flies hatch from nymphs which prefer a silty lake floor, and silt prefers to build up on the lee side of a water, that is on the protected side of the prevailing winds from the South-west, especially if shelter is also given by tree plantations. Given also that trout follow the advice of Macbeth to Macduff, to get in first, the top of a wind lane from that direction may well be the best place to fish. Trout 'know' that adult mayflies are anxious to get off the water, so the earlier they intercept them the better. With terrestrial flies, say spent daddies trapped in a wind lane, the rise may be spread further as these flies have nowhere to go. Yes, we have to make these sort of assumptions because we need a logical basis for tactical choice, but, again, this doesn't excuse observation, for fish often break the rules we lay down for them. It is where I believe fish to be rising within a certain area, often the start or finish of a wind lane, that I find an anchor useful to hold position. I feel sure that many a reader will recall times when he could throw a fly to a choice of several rising fish without moving himself, but then to his frustration, the boat drifted from there into a barren area. This is when you constantly see and hear outboard engines being used over and over again in short bursts to get the anglers back into the same short drift.

The above is heretical to the assumption that brown trout lochs should always be drift-fished, another reason why anchors are so seldom available. Unfortunately this rules out a slice of tactical choice.

It should have become clear from the words so far written that the drift of the boat is a relationship between the speed of that drift and the speed and fashion in which flies are worked. The novice may deploy his drogue only to slow the boat in a strong wind which, he believes, is moving the boat too quickly. That is one purpose, perhaps its main one, but a drogue is also used in lightish winds simply because you want to fish your flies slowly, perhaps to fish a dry fly without drag, or to modify the direction of the drift.

It is also plain common sense that if you fish a drift slowly you are covering more water because with 'fast fishing' there are spaces of water between casts which are not covered by the flies. I often use a drogue in reasonably light winds, for, paradoxically, that is when flies should be fished more slowly to counter drag and even the glitter and disturbance from the leader and its dropper-links. After a few boat sessions an angler soon recognises that the evening rise may be confined to a limited area of water in which the boat should be held as long as possible. The condition many of us hate on a big lake is the flat calm where we chase the few areas of ripple in which we want to hold the boat. It seems daft at first to put out a drogue in such light airs, but water is not only moved by wind. A counter-current, running back from a windward shore will continue to move for some time after the daytime wind falls away, and in some lakes other water movement from springs, inlets and from convection will carry a boat even when the surface indication is to the contrary.

If habitual boat anglers are frank, they will mention the irritation they have when they tangle with their companion's line. The cause is that, according to which way the boat is drifting, with two right handed casters, one is casting 'inside' the boat. It is a common sense reason to master ambidextrous casting, as discussed earlier. Then both anglers are casting 'on the outside' of the boat, with latitude in changing direction to cover rising fish. On a plain, straight drift, tangling is usually avoided, especially if both anglers are short-line fishing, and the more so if a word or two is exchanged when casting, but this all falls apart when one man sees a fish rise to one side, the back cast is then angled into the other man's line. Good fun, especially, I imagine, in competitions!

Of course, I have views on boats. I guess most old timers prefer the wooden ones which sit comfortably in the water and are wind-driven at a lower speed, so my preference is for the clinker construction. It follows that glass-fibre boats are less comfortable, and thankfully, the cursed alloy boat is seen less these days. Having first started boat fishing on Weirwood reservoir, I think in 1958, I was used to rowing, but 'instant fishing' has come in, and even small waters are blessed with the buzzing outboard. The stocked rainbow trout may not mind rising in water just ploughed up by a boat returning to the top of its drift, and even the common sense rule of not fishing this disturbed water is forgotten. You would expect, too, a bank fisher by preference, such as myself, to curse those boat men who, though having hundreds of acres to fish, churn up the water within my casting distance. It's astonishing how often this happens. We then exchange pleasantries.

Here I must philosophise. In my younger years I did prefer to go afloat, but this was in the days when, on most still waters, there was neither option nor reason for the dreaded outboard motor. This is a prejudice, I liked rowing. In those days, taking Hanningfield reservoir as an example, it would take me forty minutes to reach one of my favourite hot spots. It is a contradiction, too, that in many places where I fish, the boat anglers instinctively know that the best feeding grounds for the trout are close to the bank and they use a boat and outboard as a substitute for walking, which is why the poor bank angler has his own water invaded. A friend and I, fishing in Caithness, had to stop casting and wait while a boat which had invaded our area, was carried away from our bank. Literally, our flies would have sailed around the ears of the two boat anglers who kindly advised us what flies to use. This was a loch of several hundred acres on which we two, and these boat anglers were the only fishermen out that day.

I suppose it is our island heritage, which has deserted us now that we have become a nation of landlubbers who neither build nor crew ships, which assumes that every Britisher is automatically at home in a small boat. Unlike other vehicles, people go afloat with neither experience nor instruction (even on the sea), and some of them figure in the few hundred anglers who have drowned in recent years. You would think that intelligent coroners would make some observations about this. In my early years of season ticket on a famous (unnamed) reservoir, the cautious fishery manager would read the wind speed from his instrument, and put up a red flag when it reached a certain level, Force 6 I think. No boats would be allowed out that day. Commercial pressures came, the number of boats increased, outboard motors were added, the stocking ratio increased dramatically as the lake switched to day-ticket fishing. I was astonished to be allowed to take a boat out in wind strengths which, I believe would not have been permitted before. The one good thing was that after I left that water sailing boats were allowed, and hopefully they had a rescue boat to hand.

Having had refitted to my own designs two commercial sea fishing boats, I suppose I have ideas on boat design, but this is a field where more experience is needed. Even in small craft I have thought that an apparently 'safe' boat was inherently unstable, and, contrariwise, another of more delicate build was more 'sea kindly'. One develops one's likes and dislikes, and my own *bête noir* is a craft with a high prow which catches the wind. Happily, there's a good side to this, for fisheries earn a reputation for their boats, and a reliable folklore builds up in the boat fishing fraternity. We know where the good, stable and safe boats are, and the contrary is true. Fishery managers who pay attention to this, who care for the boats they have, are worth their weight in gold. And the plainest good sense of all, wear a buoyancy aid when you go afloat, remembering that old adage: there are old sailors and there are brave sailors, but there are no old, brave sailors.

I can only summarise some personal conclusions from long experience. I detest 'top hamper', that is any unnecessary obstruction sticking up into the air to catch the wind and spook the fish. I include in this those popular boat seats which are balanced across the thwarts. I will never again fish with anyone who uses one. I recollect that, long ago, when taking my navigation and boat handling instruction around the Solent, we used two boats one of which, of American design, had one of those very high 'flying bridges' in which the big game anglers delight. It was a pig to manage in a strong wind. The other, a sweet little cruiser, low in the water, was a delight, so nimble was it in any wind. I have to confess that the ungainly additions have been popularised for competition fishing for rainbow trout, but on a windswept Highland loch, to me they would be abominations. The secret is to take into the boat only that which you need, for extra clutter can be uncomfortable, perhaps dangerous when stumbling about on 'landlegs'.

A secret, too, is to stow gear away centrally, for on one of my favourite waters two anglers capsized their boat – *there's no boat that cannot be capsized*. The accident happened when the two anglers were enjoying their lunch break with both rods fishing over the side of the boat, propped against the gunwales. One rod jerked down savagely to a 'take', both men dived for it, over went the boat. One survived by clinging to the upturned craft, the other drowned. In a strong wind, if someone suddenly lurches for something he needs against the side of the boat, perhaps stumbling, then that's dangerous. The obvious thing is a net, it's vital to have a long shafted boat net, for leaning over the side, stretching to scoop a fish into a short one is about the daftest thing you could do.

So, common sense, before you take the boat out, stow things centrally; important things should be within reach, but only take what you need. Danger comes from unexpected quarters. The angler who landed on the far bank of Calder loch in Caithness, jumped out onto the bank, or so he thought, but went straight down twenty feet and he, too, drowned. Yes, boats can take you to distant banks, but if you do not know the terrain, take extra care. The undercut bank, ground eroded away from wave action on the windward side, can collapse beneath the feet of both the careless bank angler as well as someone landing from a boat, and these traps for the unwary are characteristic of lakes and lochs on exposed heath and moorland. Believe it or not, our sport probably claims more fatalities than any other.

A warning which I obey myself. There are some places where local anglers will tell you that the stronger the wind and waves, the better it is to go afloat. I am told this often by boatmen on the great loughs in Ireland. And I do see tiny boats tossing about in incredible 'seas'. Not only is there little point in being scared and uncomfortable, there must be an element of danger in it. If in doubt, don't go. If you are susceptible to *mal de mer*, fresh water does it as easily as sea water. My old acquaintance, the late Richard Walker was a martyr to it on Grafham. Follow that unfailing cure for it: grass. No, you don't eat it, you find a nice patch and lie on it!

We cannot always avoid strong winds. Weather rarely remains constant all day, but the sensible thing is to shelter under a lee shore and to avoid being pinned against a windward shore. This latter danger happened to me when fishing with Mrs Lesley Crawford on Watten when a sudden gale sprang up, and there were some hairy moments in bringing the boat back up wind. The same dangers exist as at sea when caught in a big wave, the main one being of 'pooping', that is waves breaking over the boat to flood it. Careful attention to motor speed when heading into the wave line is important, and avoidance of being caught side on by heavy wind and water. I try to make for the nearest lee shore, then creep back to base along it. If I am really alarmed, I come ashore, pull the boat well up, fix it firmly and either wait for calmer conditions, as in a squall, or walk back to base. I have done this twice on open waters which provide practically no lee.

You will have noticed the simplicity of my boat fishing management. The location of fishing ground has been made on the bases of hope, observation and common sense. I read occasionally of fish-finding electronic devices and so on which I certainly employed at sea. I would be tempted to use one when patiently trolling for *ferox* trout in wide expanses of water, but in normal brown trout fishing, for reasons of safety and comfort, I prefer an uncluttered boat. My own rule is to keep things as simple as possible.

It is the sudden, fierce squall which worries, and happily it is usually of short duration. The weather sign of an approaching squall is the signal of a rush of cold air before the storm hits. This is the 'nose of the squall', caused by cold air being pushed forward by the heavy rain, and birds will be seen to circle upwards, going high. It is said by some observers that there is also an uprush of air in front of an approaching squall which takes the birds high. If I stress these things it's because it's more sensible to be a safe coward than a drowned hero.

There has been much emphasis on safety and weather in this chapter. I confess I am alarmed at the cavalier attitude of many boat anglers to safety, and the phrases I dislike the most when it blows up are 'don't worry, I'm used to it' or 'it fishes best in a good blow'. This was probably my own careless attitude, years ago when I believed that nothing much could go wrong on inland fisheries. A long experience of owning two sea fishing boats changed this, frequently taking the boat out forty miles or so to fish distant banks like the Galloper – check it on your charts. Without careful attention to meteorological reports and ensuring that all equipment was on the top line, trouble could ensue. Although it never happened, there was always the thought if, due to some foolish oversight, one had the humiliation of calling out the rescue services. Almost better to drown than face that.

All sensible boat anglers going to sea build up a team of reliable crew and checking everything becomes a routine habit. It frightens me to see the careless attitude of some boat anglers going out onto what is almost an inland sea, and although it will never happen in our carefree sport, I would like to have an element of instruction on small boat management as a condition of hiring, and afterwards the production of a certificate that it was done. As I have described with the earlier lee boards, large drift-rudders and now those high boat seats, the fishing tactics should not reduce safety. And perhaps the wearing of buoyancy aids should be compulsory. Nor should fishery management on vast, open waters be frightened to call off fishing, and even fishing competitions, if the weather is bad, or call boats in if it worsens. Perhaps insurers could look at this? I would regard Force 6 as a danger level.

Why this? I expect many fishermen of my age have lost friends and acquaintances, or we know of someone who has. I trust, dear reader, you will ask yourself, is this true of you? We then learn a hard lesson. I lost a good friend who was preparing his sea boat for a fishing trip. He was an experienced man but he thought it safe to take his battery to his boat by small dinghy, though the creek was troubled by a high wind. The dinghy capsized. He drowned a few feet from the shore and in only seven feet of water. *I end by repeating that warning.* No matter what we are told of unsinkable boats with foolproof buoyancy chambers and the like, there is no boat made which cannot capsize. So make safety your very first item of control.

Afloat on Talyllyn Lake.

Organised Bank Fishing

The very first, simplest things are to know where you are and to know where you are going. An advantage – depending on your energy and point of view – is that you can yomp to distant lakes and lochs. In remote places this may mean bogtrotting over untracked moorland. It makes good sense to master some basic map-reading skills, for like the open sea, there may be few, or no landmarks. This is important, for in lonely places, especially if you are close to the sea as in Shetland where they boast that no place is further than three miles from the coast, there is the danger of that cotton-wool sea fog, known affectionately as the 'haar' in northern climes, and by the Sussex County Cricket Club as a gentle 'sea fret'. A point to remember is that a compass is used not only to pin-point your destination, but also to remember the reciprocal direction reading to know your way back.

It is not my purpose here to give a map-reading course, but there is one tip I have found useful on occasion, which is use a wrist watch as a rough-and-ready compass, when the sun is shining. If you can find north and south, then you can know the other cardinal points. You simply point your hour hand at the sun. South will be half-way between the sun and twelve noon *in winter*, and axiomatically north will be precisely opposite. This is for Greenwich Mean Time, of course, and it follows that in summer, south will be between the sun and 1.00 pm. Naturally, this applies to the northern hemisphere only. You would need to reverse these positions for the southern hemisphere.

As much of my fishing has been in remote areas, I cannot resist the temptation to explore lochs which involve moorland tramping. I emphasis the importance of neither taking chances on vague directions given by friends nor even guide books. For my own comfort I usually take a staff, for on heather moorlands especially, the drainage ditches and potholes are usually covered by heather. The other danger I have mentioned is the moss-covered peat hag, a tempting trap for the unwary. One other thing is worth mentioning, a pitfall my son and I fell into in Shetland where this is not uncommon. Many moorland lochs lie in valleys, and one strolls down long slopes without realising the distance. We had parked our Mini on top of the high lane, then eagerly marched down to the loch shining in the sun, below us. After an hour or two of fishing, I glanced back and was horrified to see that our car had become a tiny black spot on the high horizon. It would have been of little enjoyment to plunge uphill through the tangling heather in the dark, so the evening rise was curtailed.

There are some other common-sense preparations to make for yomping to distant lochs. The first is to ascertain the type of footwear needed, bearing in mind that lightly fished water may not need wading, for hill walking in waders is a severe penance. Mostly I go in fell-walking boots, occasionally wellies. Then I plan on how little to carry, for weight screams after an hour or two. The experienced walker's rucksack is the best way to carry supplies, it distributes the weight evenly on one's back. Your choice of provender I leave to you, but it is wise to take some. I never take a net, fishing catch and release doesn't require it. The choice of flies can be kept to a few well-known patterns, black always being a very useful colour and the pattern of little importance. A spool or two of nylon, a fisherman's knife and my light-line rod, reel with d.t. floating line, complete the gear set-up. A small point on flies, if you include some palmered patterns, say a Soldier Palmer or Kate McClaren, then a smidgen of a floatant will convert them into effective dry flies should the need arise.

I do not bother with a sinking line, preferring to carry a few weighted flies, some tied on 'wee doubles', but for those who prefer to use one, it is easy enough to switch spools on the reel, and pointless to encumber oneself with the stockie-basher's delight, the extra rod.

Yes, this is plain common sense. The reason I mention this is because there is a trend towards overloading on southern reservoirs. One sees the multi-layered fly boxes containing myriads of patterns. This is not necessary. Certainly, I take such a box on my travels, but I select some favourites to put into a vest-pocket wallet. If you stick to locally recommended traditional patterns which have killed trout for centuries, they will rarely let you down.

Now I will add a strange precaution for yompers. Learn how to take a hook out of flesh, it's a long way to the nearest hospital. Of course, you will always wear eye protective shield or glasses, won't you? The trick to pulling out a hook is to push the eye downwards to the level of the skin so that the point aligns with the hole it made going into you, then to give it a smart tweak along that line. Some people loop a piece of nylon around the bend of the hook and use that as a puller, grabbing both tails of the nylon. Also, do it immediately after the hook goes in, for flesh hardens up around unwanted intruders. Done smartly, the sensation is a slight sting as the hook comes free. It goes without saying, for catch and release fishers, that barbless hooks give little trouble, but you can use micro-barbs, or flatten the barbs with your forceps. The occasions when I have hooked myself have been when changing a fly when a gust of wind flicks the rod over. Of course, the addition of a small first-aid kit makes sense. A foible of mine is to carry some analgesics because a characteristic of remote lochs is often a bright ripple and staring for hours at tiny flies in that broken light sometimes produces a headache. My preference, both for guarding against water-glare as well as to protect my eyes is to wear one of those large polarising eye shields rather than the normal spectacles. And on one occasion I blessed my staff. I put my knee out on the far side of Cow Green and I was faced with a long hobble back through the heather.

A problem which we rarely solve to perfection is clothing. The heavy-duty waxed-cotton coat we start with becomes a sweat-producing hot-house, especially when pumping up a fell-side. Everyone has his own solution. Mine is to wear a lightweight waterproof coat over a pullover, this latter being taken off and stowed in the rucksack when the going gets warm. A lightweight pair of waterproof trousers also takes up little storage place in the rucksack. For rain, I also store one of those towelling scarves.

Of course, I cannot avoid the dreaded midge; I've mentioned the obvious precaution of taking a deterrent, the unguent being far more efficacious than the spray. I could not shroud myself in one of those nets. These irritating pests swarm on windless days, the bank angler is a martyr to them, but I mitigate the nuisance by planning my visits to the midge-places in early summer and autumn when they are not quite so pestiferous. Happily, the former coincides with the mayfly time. Folklore has it that a sprig or two of bog myrtle, stuck into one's hat, keeps them away, take that for what it's worth, or rub the crushed leaves into your exposed skin.

If we turn to the written wisdom of the post-war experts on bank fishing on English reservoirs we cannot help but notice the emphasis placed on distance casting – the grass is always greener. But many of these reservoirs, like Grafham, have extensive marginal shallows. Again, when fishing very deeply with a fast-sinking line, a longer line means a greater depth. This is less of a problem on the wild-trout lakes which are less heavily fished. When I have fished from first light at Blagdon and Bewl Water I have been struck by the way in which fish would be rising almost under the rod tip until the regular anglers plunged into the water to their wader-tops and the first boats began to churn up the margins.

It is sometimes useful to throw a long line on wild fisheries, again, if the marginal shallows are extensive, but on other waters you can actually overcast the trout if there is a shelf which falls suddenly into deep water. I experienced this when bank-fishing in Calder loch, in Caithness. I was double-hauling to a distance of about thirty yards, but always rising the fish when I had retrieved between five and ten yards of line. I mention this, because the choice of line profile depends on the way in which you achieve distance. Most anglers build up line speed by false casting and shoot line for distance. A minority prefer to lift a long line from the water, and airialise it without much of a shoot. The former type of casters will probably prefer to use a weight-forward line, and the latter will use a double-taper to avoid the nuisance of 'overhang', that is a dip in the line between the rod tip and the line-belly when it is in the air. I prefer to use a double-taper line because it has more versatility, an example of which is the snake-roll to take a dry fly upwards from the surface when a swift change of direction is needed to cover a rise.

Another reservoir practice is to use a very long leader, some anglers making up lengths of over twenty feet. There is sense in this when fishing for rainbow trout which may follow a fly for a few yards, sometimes hitting the fly over and over again. This is not the habit of the wild brown trout, they come but once from where they are. Nor are they unusually 'gut-shy' in waters which are usually under far less rod pressure. I do not find it necessary to use leaders of more than twelve feet, the more so as I never favour the use of the brightly coloured fluorescent lines which attract some anglers.

The question to answer, probably before setting out to a still-water fishery, is 'which bank'? I make it a habit to get a weather forecast to discover direction and strength of the wind. Taking into account the size of the chosen water, some, like the majority in Shetland, can be fished around in a day. I recollect the first time I fished the far bank of Rimsdale, believing that when I reached a distant headland I would be at the far end of the loch, only to see the shore line receding to the horizon. Here, choosing the friendliest bank in relation to the wind would be sensible. Before deciding I also glance at a map to discover the extent of bays and woodlands to give shelter under the lee. As in river fishing, it is unwise to punch into near-gales.

Another problem to solve, before deciding where to fish, is the depth of the water and the nature of the bank, and the only reliable guide is local information or, failing that, a prior visit, if you are a newcomer. Some fisheries, and Rimsdale is a good example, have shelf-like banks and wading is neither necessary nor sensible. However, the ground is often soggy, there are ditches and streams to negotiate, but as there is a considerable amount of walking to do, to reach the main water from the lane, knee boots are a fair compromise.

The depth of the inshore water is also important, shallows and sudden deeps near to the bank being unproductive extremes. On occasion these features cannot be avoided. Scarhouse reservoir, for example, has deep water very close to the bank, but, happily, here and there one discovers some shallower bays. Referring again to the furthest bank of Rimsdale, when this loch is at normal height, the spits of land protruding into the body of the water are often the most productive places, and again, a glance at the map in relation to the wind will show where wind and scum lanes will develop from such features. A land spit is a vital feature for bank fishers because it changes the nature of the water around it, and this, in turn affects the whole food chain. It is common sense that silt builds up in its lee, fauna finds protection and fish find the fauna. In short, the spit forms a food trap.

A shoreline bulge, the miniature delta, is also a favourite fishing place of mine. Two I call to mind at Cow Green reservoir, on opposite banks, are amongst the most productive fishing places in that lake. These deltas also act as food collection places and the shelving floors in front of them, usually progressive slopes, shelter much food material for fish. A feature of Scarhouse reservoir along the open shoreline is the shelf cut away by wave action with deep water beyond – a danger to unwary waders. These are less productive because insect and other fauna are not protected from the strong wave action against the shore which gets a constant battering. It's interesting to watch local anglers who, perhaps without realising the physical causes, walk smartly past such places to the next bay, spit or delta simply because long experience tells them they are less likely to catch fish there. Without knowing why, such anglers are building up a mental picture of the features of a lake and the way they determine the food chains.

We do not need to know all of the physical characteristics of lakes, but we do need to realise that the term 'still water' is a misnomer. A lake is a living, active entity simply because water is moved, by currents, by the wind and by temperature. It has been estimated, for example, that water entering Windermere at one end, takes nine months to flow out of the other end. I have discussed the thermal stratification of a deep lake in summer. You may imagine that like the sea, there is a continual fall of vegetable and animal debris to the lake floor, and if light and oxygen there is very low, then decay can scarcely take place where it is very deep. The movement of fish in the deep, colder layer in summer is a mystery, especially as one supposes that the debris on the lake floor would rapidly deplete oxygen stocks there, and is this a factor in the migration of char and the big cannibal trout into the shallower waters in May?

Such worries might discourage a novice angler, bemusing him as to where to choose his bank-fishing place, and with what fly? It need not, for experience builds up into a store of local folklore about which it is foolish to scoff. Also, one can use common sense to determine the likely food traps. Referring back to my dislike of fishing into a strong wind, at first sight this might seem merely a matter of comfort – and that is a useful bonus – but the windward shore of a lake is usually one facing the prevailing winds which batter it, dispersing silt in which many insects thrive, and exposing mainly the large rocks. Again, it might be thought that silt would build up against the windward shore, being driven by wind and wave, but deeper thinking shows that the particles are too light to settle, they are driven sideways to pile up in banks, along deltas, spits and the edges of bays. Where rush and reed beds exist, they also collect silt and vegetable matter to shelter insects, especially where they rot down and die at the end of these beds. This is equally true of weed beds, and again, common sense tells us that fishing around them is productive.

This ability to survey what to some would appear to be a featureless expanse of water reduces the odds against you. It boils down to this, that silt traps are also food traps, be they underwater ledges, buildings which were covered by water when a reservoir was made (such features are easily seen in the clear water of Haweswater), underwater lanes, ditches and hedges in such lakes, and even tree stumps. Such features exist for decades after the dams are constructed. On the banks, reed and rush beds, weedy areas, deltas and land spits serve the same purpose.

Some anglers will avoid a strong wind blowing into their casting side, although various methods of line control can mitigate the danger of hooking oneself. As a matter of interest, bearing in mind that weather is a fickle mistress, over recent years when fishing in the far North, I have found that wind direction from the North and East has prevailed in May and June, and switches to the South and West as the summer develops. There are many old anglers' maxims and rhymes about fishing winds, but cold winds which chill the surface naturally retard fly hatches, and the worst, in my own experience, are the winds which flurry in gusts, sending arrows of ripple scudding across the water.

The danger I mentioned in the boat fishing section, that a strong wind will make shallow lochs with silty beds quite cloudy, is an even greater curse for the bank angler, so yet another aspect to check is the nature of the lake floor, during and after gales. Suspended silt impedes the trout's vision, but it probably de-oxygenates water, as does algae.

I mention algae because on occasion I have been compelled to fish during a flare-up of phytoplankton which makes the fish dour and unresponsive. However, I did succeed once or twice when the grass-green algae was in abundance, looking much like a hundred gardeners had dumped their lawn cuttings into the water. This type of algae tends to float in a layer in the top few feet of the lake, and having travelled a long way to fish, I guessed that there must be clear water below. Fishing the flies well sunk, I did manage to winkle out the odd fish. Algae tends to flare up in nutrient rich water when rain is followed by sun, the rain brings nitrates and phosphates from the land to fertilise the water, and it is not until these nutrients have been used up that the water clears again.

Choosing which lake to fish is the most basic form of preparation, and I have discussed how, in a wilderness area like, for instance, Sutherland, from a simple viewpoint there are options for many smaller fish, a reasonable bag of medium sized trout or a dour loch with legendary monsters. Taking into account the factors of weather, the choice is easier to make. So let me put this into a day's perspective for myself, based on a rented cottage near Wick, on the eastern side. It is mid-June, so I would prefer to go where there is likely to be a good hatch of mayfly and I can fish from the bank. I prefer to hope for a reasonable bag of trout around the pound to two-pound mark. I take out the large-scale map and note that the wind direction would give me nice shelter from the far bank of Toftingall loch which produces good mayfly and free-rising trout of medium size. I note that the map shows a nice stand of trees along that far bank to give some shelter from the wind which is given as fairly strong. The map shows some spits and bays, there are two streams to cross, so I know I shall need waders, but the walking distance is not excessive. A phone call to Hugo Ross's shop in Wick reserves me a bank fishing ticket, so I drive in to pick up the keys to the forestry gates. The previous days have been calm, it's not a gale today, so I know the water will be relatively clear. Had there been gales on the preceding days I should have chosen another loch, perhaps Stemster, which has a hard rock floor and where the water remains clear in the strongest of blows.

The last thing to examine during the planning of a trip is the strength and direction of light, though this is mainly for comfort, it is unpleasant to face a glaring sun. Of course, it makes sense to fish early and late in such conditions, though I am reluctant to advise holiday anglers, with limited time, not to go out. The saving grace is that in many wild-brown trout wildernesses the weather is changeable, especially in the islands where even in high pressure areas, little white clouds will bubble up to give broken light. If I had to choose my favourite fishing conditions, they would probably be sunny days with a light breeze and cloud shadows chasing across the water. To sum up the preparation, instead of dashing off to a recommended loch or lake, study a map and weather conditions, relating the latter to the former, and although this is plain common sense, I have neglected to do it on occasion, and paid the price. And I know from the company I keep that the majority of fishermen pay this no heed.

So far I have discussed planning to fish waters which are occupied by brown trout, 'wild' in a liberal sense. There is an increasing number of anglers who seek out the brownies in mixed fisheries which also contain rainbow trout. Enquiry sometimes shows that the brown trout take up refuge in corners of such fisheries, for the aggressive rainbows literally bully them. This was typical of a small club lake of some five acres where I was a member. Here the minority species tended to take up residence in deeper water, or they were localised in certain bays. This sounds like folklore, but I am convinced by experience, that there is truth in it, as if the two species had reached an understanding as to territory. There are many lakes where a rainbow stock has been added to an existing wild brown trout population, examples being Hury and Grassholme reservoirs in the Upper Pennines. I know anglers who deliberately and successfully target the wild fish in those two lakes. So, although it does sound like unreliable folklore, bear in mind the territorial behaviour of brown trout, and quite often the experience of regular anglers will prove to be a useful guide.

This is quite the opposite of the rainbow trout, for what is termed 'practice' by competition angling teams before their matches is a way of discovering the areas to which these roving fish have migrated, often due to mysteriously active feeding grounds. Although I have no statistical evidence to rely on, my feeling is that the turnover of stocked brown trout is slower than rainbows, if only because the latter is a much hungrier fish. What I call 'wildness' is all in the mind. I am happy to catch brown trout stocked into a lake like Talyllyn because I regard them as a stable population, feeding naturally. I am less happy when a silly rainbow latches onto my fly at Vyrnwy when I am after the wild brown trout there. This is why all brown trout are grist to this book's mill.

110

This has been about the *general* planning for still water fishing. The particular tactics, choice of flies and tackle make-up follow. You will have noticed that I am a traditionalist, especially in the choice of flies, which will be discussed later in the tactical considerations. I mention now that within the traditional framework common sense can still be applied, and I give just one instance. If I fish that well-known killer, the Wickham, as a point fly below the surface, then a sparse palmered body hackle is sensible, but if I wish to use the same pattern as a top dropper, to be greased and fished in the surface to imitate a hatching insect, then I also dress a few samples of the Wickham with an extra collar, four or five turns of hackle at the head of the fly, in front of the wing. This is another argument in favour of *the behaviour of the fly* being its most important element. Many patterns of fly can be given such treatment.

If I have had a fault in my bank fishing it is probably in trying to cast too far, and such is the nature of the wild places I prefer, that wiry heather or cotton grass has only to touch the leader on the back cast to produce the most horrendous tangles. My leader set-up for bank fishing is usually of two flies only, very widely spaced. The point fly is commonly a winged pattern, to sink below the surface, and the bob-fly is a well-collared palmer as described. Occasionally I take off the top dropper, if the water is very calm with the gentlest of ripples far out. The less commotion in the surface film, the better. This is a theme to be developed later.

I end this section with some personal comments about various categories of still water, for we have been brought up on that casual classification of 'rich' and 'poor' waters, the former mostly being described as alkaline, the latter as acid with special reference to peat. The scientists have given us some ten-dollar words to go with this scene. The rich lake, receiving nutrients is called 'eutrophic'. The poor lake is said to be 'oligotrophic', being very poor in nutrients, whilst between the two come the 'dystrophic' lakes, those lovely beery ones we find in airy uplands. There are so many exceptions as to make this a problem for the angler. Cow Green, for example is surrounded by peatlands, yet bars of different types of limestone give the water a reasonable pH level. Old marl workings, too, are often in peaty areas, but they may give us eutrophic lakes, I would cite Watten as an example. The Cross Lochs, surrounded by heather moors, have one of the richest insect populations I have seen, its trout, though dour, are of a healthy and hefty condition. I mention this because when I first suggested to one or two chosen friends that they accompany me to some wilderness areas their immediate reaction was that, in comparison to the famous limestone lochs of the far north west, rightly famed, fishing on peaty moors would be just for stunted tiddlers. Delving into the geology reveals a more complicated picture.

It's funny that so much of fishing is plain common sense. If you plan a trip to a far-off place there's an easy way to solve this problem. Ask! When last in Orkney, I had paid a few quid to join the local association, and on contacting one of its officers, I was immediately told which lakes were 'on' and which were 'off', and this is characteristic of those lochs. In Shetland, the same modest fee gave me a most accurate guide to the loch system there. In the far North, both tackle shops and hotels, many of which sell permits to non-residents, were equally helpful. You need not be a boffin to make your choice. Things are not always what they seem, the great swathes of terrain seen by the geologist as barren may hide a farmer who has treated his land with fertiliser which leaches into the lake. 'Ah', says the boffin. 'The water must be barren, it comes from those Ice Age volcanoes'. But he doesn't see the farmer's hopper raining phosphates onto his meagre grassland.

I asked a farmer at Hundland loch – he had kindly given me permission to fish his lake – 'What's the fly here?'

'Oh, it's that dratted Warble Fly. Gives me a mort of trouble.'

I haven't yet found an imitation of the Warble Fly.

Bank fishing on the Reay lochs, Caithness.

The Mysterious Ferox

When I was young, those large cannibal trout which inhabit both rivers and lakes were thought to be an entirely different species, hence the name *ferox*. Modern thinking has reduced them to being normal brown trout which have become largely cannibal due to their age. Earlier, I related this to the life history of the brown trout by Frost & Brown in Collins' *New Naturalist* series of books. They implied that the feeding behaviour of trout changed after the fourth year of growth, but it's not as simple as that if only because trout feed on smaller fish from a very early age. What really happens is that the balance of the diet of these *ferox* moves towards other fish as they grow older, larger and more powerful. I have mentioned also that perhaps eye parasites play a part in this, diminishing visual acuity.

Recently fish farmers have used the term 'special strain' in relation to huge rainbow trout. I am doubtful if this is valid in relation to *ferox*, and for the sake of convenience I will continue to use this term. Having worked with bacteria during the first part of my adult life, I was happy to accept that there was a strain of these flora if they passed on an acquired characteristic, say resistance to antibiotics. But as the fresh water Biological Association showed at Cow Green, the enormous cannibals would enter the sikes to breed with lesser trout, therefore, there was no distinct progeny of *ferox*, nor would I expect there to be. The development of a specialised feeding habit does not constitute a distinct strain, nor even a sub-species such as our forefathers believed. It is curious, though, that some, not all, develop certain physical characteristics to suit their feeding behaviour, notably the long, needle-like teeth which I have seen on occasion. Also, there can be a marked deterioration in body condition, many of these fish are dark and lank. Whether this is a result of ageing, or of diet you may determine, though if impaired vision is a factor, then that may explain it.

Some other factors intrude. There are eutrophic lakes where the average weight of the trout is high because the food supply is rich in relation to the fish stock. These are **not** my *ferox*, they reach good size within a shorter life period, and their diet is what a fly fisher would term as normal. My *ferox* live in lakes and rivers where there is a distinct size difference between the vast majority of trout which seem to reach no great average size, and these bigger cannibals which prey on them almost exclusively, and on other small fish. These lakes would be oligotrophic in the main, and the rivers would similarly have stocks of small brown trout, though possibly with runs of migratory fish.

The mystery of these cannibals is why, for a large part of their time, they dwell in very deep water. This has been proved over and over again by the majority of catches coming from deep trolling. Perhaps the classic example is that of the immense Queen Mother reservoir to the west of London, which was formerly a stocked fishery open to fly fishing, though this is no longer the case as I write. Early stockings were of brown trout of normal stockfish size. The fishery changed hands, became more commercial and the managers switched to rainbow trout. Catches of the brown trout were scarce. This is not an unusual feature of mixed stocking, when the rainbows are introduced the brown trout seem to disappear for a year or two.

The water, being so wide and deep, was trolled with sinking lines, and really big brown trout were taken on occasion, so that those anglers with a liking for specimen hunting, developed huge trolling lures, some of several inches long, and with extra-fast sinking shooting heads, some memorable fish were taken by day in very deep water. This was duly recorded in the angling press. A friend and I spent a rather tedious day trying to catch such a monster, only to miss one when the rod was taken downwards with a tremendous wrench. This is an opportunity to follow the previous chapters about the nature of different still waters, because a characteristic of a *ferox* water is that it has great clarity.

The trolling successes prove that such fish chase and catch their prey, though I am curious to learn if, like older pike, they also scavenge from the bottom. It is hard to explain this habit of the very deep dwelling places, for both light and oxygen are poor there, especially as these lakes stratify in summer, as previously described. Yet, undoubtedly, this is what they do, but how and why they do so I leave to researchers to discover.

There now follow logically two distinct feeding patterns. In some of these lakes there are other species of smaller fish which also inhabit the deeps, notably char in lakes like Windermere, and Crummock water, and whitefish. The cannibals follow the char when they come into shallower water in May and early June and on occasion they are caught on normal fly, they have not lost that side of their nature. I also believe that throughout the year, they come into the margins by night to predate on smaller fish which live in the shallower water. This past year I saw a tremendous commotion at dusk as a great trout was hunting through the surface at Cow Green, and two of us who fish regularly there believe that these fish-eaters normally lie along the valley where the Tees flows through the body of the lake.

Perhaps controversially, I believe that water clarity is an important factor for *ferox* lakes, and scientific data shows that two such lakes I know, Windermere and Crummock water have mean clarity levels down to eight metres from the surface.

114

Personally, I went through a phase of specimen hunting. My early book *Big Pike*, published by the *Angling Times* many years ago, was probably the first to be devoted to specimen-sized fish of a single species. I switched to other fish, until I had satisfied myself with those rated as specimens, carp, roach, eels and so on. It is a respectable and worthy fishing philosophy. A noted specimen hunter was Fred Wagstaff who applied himself to *ferox* with notable success. And a hero of my youth, and of my angling club at Canterbury, Warren Hastings[1], devoted himself to that vanishing race, Kings of the weirs, the great Thames Trout which were undoubtedly *ferox*.

I do have one *ferox* to my name, not a monster, and in fact it was never weighed. It was taken at Cow Green some years ago, and its size differential and its characteristics in relation to the run-of-the-mill trout I catch there persuades me that it belongs to that race. My friend, Colin North took another from Loch Maree.

With a fly rod, the trolling method is clearly the best, but it is slow, patient work. I would prefer to do this by slowly rowing a boat with the appropriate line or shooting head deeply sunk behind it. I do have expectation that a favourite rainbow lure of mine would be excellent medicine. It is that brilliant streamer: the Grey Ghost, invented by the famous American fly-dresser, Helen Shaw, which, when worked, looks for all the world like a small fish. My two changes are to swap the four grey cock wings feathers for those of dark olive or green to match our own baitfish colours, and I like to varnish the head white with a band of red around it, an attraction for deep water where light is diminished. I doubt I would need any other lure, for that one is a cracker. Would Helen Shaw let me name this the 'Green Ghost'? But the genius of this streamer is all hers, its clever appearance and sinuous fish-like movement in the water. It slaughters silly rainbows.

I guess the majority of *ferox* taken from the bank are accidental catches when the beasts are following migrations of baitfish in the shallows. We know about the movements of char; less about that of whitefish, powan, schelly, gwyniad and the like. Some *ferox* are hooked when the mayfly is up. My old friend, Mike Robinson has probably hooked and lost three on Cow Green, myself probably two more. I didn't see 'em!

I have added this section deliberately, as I respect specimen hunters, and working with a trolling rod and fly is, and should be, legitimate for such a deliberate target. The fish remains a mystery to me, and in my mind's eye I see a quarry the specialised feeding of which is the very first step along that process of natural selection discovered by Darwin. How long would it be before a *ferox* produced a baby *ferox*?

I put in no longer the patient hours for specimen fish, it is a younger man's game. Here are my conclusions. It is a distinct fish with a specialised feeding habit, but the diet change is not complete, the balance of this

[1]Author of *The Monarch of the Thames*.

has changed, by competitive pressure as it grew older, and in changing, it has also changed some of the physical characteristics of the fish, but it still remains a brown trout. I would hunt it in those clear lakes which have a numerous population of small trout. I have no qualms with the term *ferox* to distinguish it from fish of a good average weight from richer waters, with more catholic tastes.

Yet, why, oh why does it prefer to spend so much of its time in such deep water? Undoubtedly we know it does and my fanciful explanation is that this is a trick of nature, for were these monsters to roam regularly amongst the smaller fish the danger would be imprinted. The sudden rush amongst them, the unrecognised danger from beyond, that gives the predator an edge. For eat they must, 'the intestine rules the World'. In short, the depths become an embuscade.

Is this the answer? I wish I knew. Last year I saw that ferocious sally at dusk, an unbelievable commotion across a lake which before was at peace with itself, calm and still. The sinking sun glowed against a great bronze flank as a fountain of water rose into the air some fifty yards out. I was chatting to a young Cow Green regular, our jaws dropped open 'in wild surmise'.

To sum up on how to hunt the *ferox*, from the sparse information we have – sparse because few specimen hunters interest themselves in the quarry – there are four lines of attack.

The first, and most rewarding is deep trolling from a boat, which I would prefer to row. When I did this, I used a powerful rod with a very fast sinking head which allowed me to pay out a long line, over fifty yards being necessary to get the lure down into the deepest troughs of a lake. I only used my version of the Grey Ghost streamer as it proved to be the best imitation of a small fish. When I trolled I preferred to be alone in the boat with a single rod over the stern, and it was necessary to tighten up the reel drag, for when a 'take' occurs the fish usually hooks itself. It is quite usual to find the lure right in the back of the trout's mouth, and the take is one hell of a bang. I confess that when using a cheaper reel I simply put one foot on the drum to lock it.

Where boat fishing is either impractical or not allowed, the alternative is to cast a long line from the bank into the deepest water, which may be from a dam wall. At Cow Green, for example, at the far end where the Tees runs into the lake there is a deepish channel where a companion hooked and lost an unseen monster. The tackle is much the same, a very fast-sinking shooting head and the double-haul method will throw out a long line, for depth.

The third method is confined mainly to the autumn when *ferox* mix with the ordinary trout in a lake, the sex drive overcomes all other inhibitions, and they collect together in the bays into which streams, becks and sikes fall, ready for the fish to run up when the first floods allow them to do so. Again at Cow Green I lost one of my own hooked predators. It was a September afternoon and I had tied on a large water-beetle imitation, my

'Jack Ketch'. Where a sike, known as 'White Spot', entered the lake there was a typical deep channel. I threw the fly up into this, letting it sink. When I started the retrieve the fly was taken savagely, the rod being pulled down with tremendous force, then a second or two later, the rod tip bounced back as the hook-hold gave way.

The fourth way is what I call 'accidental' because it happens when fishing normally, towards the end of May and early June. Some *ferox* come inshore by day, perhaps to take mayfly, perhaps to follow smaller fish. This is when I took my own specimen, as depicted, on a small Williams' Favourite, and I lost another. This also was at Cow Green which is a notable water for these fish.

I wish that dedicated specimen hunters would seek out the *ferox* if only to allow us to understand more of its mysterious ways. We must not confuse them with 'ordinary' big trout from nutrient-rich waters. This distinctive race comes from the waters which are poor in food supply, where there is a stunted population of trout. They are old fish, but by no means always ugly, I have seen some splendid specimens.

I doubt that a wide choice of lure is necessary, I stick to my own favourite, but at one time I was persuaded by theoreticians that in very deep water, blue, or fluo blue is the most visible colour – and so it would be for the human eye. The hey-day of the Queen Mother specimen hunters proved the success of a very simple, though enormous lure they called 'the Blackbird'. Black lures certainly work. I have confidence in the streamer pattern I have described simply because it looks and acts so much like a small fish.

Generally, I am against the use of sonar in normal fishing. I prefer to use observation and intelligence, but proper specimen hunting involves an element of research and can justify its use. There are lightweight and compact models available for small boats. Of one thing I am certain, where land was flooded over a river course is a typical place to find your quarry, perhaps because the flow carries more dissolved oxygen into the deeps, who knows. I would not rely on the small sonar to find a solitary big trout, but rather to reveal the features of the lake floor.

I have said that *ferox* are found in rivers on rare occasions. Such a fish, over seven pounds, was found dead in a grating in Upper Teesdale, and my friend, Roland Stockdale, a gifted amateur taxidermist, showed me one from the Wear which he glass-cased. They are rarer than the lake *ferox*, which is where I sought them in my specimen hunting days. You may seek out your own typical waters, you know what to look for, but there will always be a local legend of great fish being seen, or hooked and lost, and if others scoff because these are known as 'small fish' waters, those are places to explore.

This is a plea to any reader who has a scientific mind, to see if we can add to our knowledge of this mysterious fish, for we know beyond dispute that it occupies the cold-water layer in a lake, in summer, known as the hyperlimnion. We do not know why. It is true that in the nutrient-poor lakes there is probably no layer of vegetable debris to take up all of the oxygen in the depths as would be the case in a rich lake. All the same, it is a harsh environment. It would be fascinating to learn more of the habits of the *ferox*. I was first interested in them by tales of Loch Awe, where, in days gone by, there was regular hunting for them, and from whence, I believe, this particular name for them was popularised.

I recall research from Calder loch finding that during the first four years of life, the growth rate of the trout was small, but then it accelerated. I think this is probably the first stage of *feroxism*, when the balance of the feeding habit changes. The researchers took no *ferox*, but some have been taken by anglers from that vast lake. It would be high on my list if I were intent on catching one.

I have some thoughts on specimen hunting as a philosophy, for unhappily it has changed. Some thirty years ago it was marriage between angling and science. The late Peter Tombleson FZS arranged a bi-annual coarse fishing conference at Liverpool University, and this was attended by the dedicated specimen hunters of the time. Most of these fishermen were not dedicated to a single species, though some were. I recollect that a successful angler, Peter Butler, hunted the huge roach from London reservoirs which, I guess from following his example, occupied the same man-hours as going after *ferox*. The target fish were naturally bred, naturally fed.

Fashions change, and a degree of artificiality came in with the carp fever, such huge quantities of high-protein bait being put into the water that these fish became grotesque and were caught so frequently that they acquired pet-names, and their mouths were a mass of scar tissues. A certain great pike or barbel would also be caught and recorded many times until it succumbed. This was encouraged by a sensation-seeking media and the temptation for reputation-building. The old spirit departed, the new age of 'instant success' dawned.

I think the *ferox* represents the division between the two, because there are also large brown trout growing naturally in eutrophic fisheries. There are also very big ones being planted out in commercial 'put-and-take' fisheries, though this is more commonly done with rainbow trout. This is a difficulty for me, for although I recognise the necessity of this latter type of fishery and, being a democrat, I would not wish to protest against it, it is simply not the type of fishing I enjoy. I have the choice not to do it. I mention this, because in this chapter about *ferox* hunting I hark back to a philosophy which must be alien to many modern anglers. It is strange that in its hey-day, the true specimen hunting supported what was probably the best technical fishing journal ever produced, called simply '*Fishing*'. It was edited by Roy Eaton, a highly competent angler who I was honoured to call a friend. Fishing is a fashion sport. The fashion changed, and the competition for bigger and bigger fish, artificially raised to unnatural weights, coupled to reputation-making, meant the death of the old ways. The new fashion invaded fly fishing, competitions came in, the rush and stress of modern life was part of it. Simplification was the order of the day, carp anglers snoring in their bivvies, fly-fishing flotillas drifting over recently stocked rainbow trout.

Yes, the long, lonely hunt for the entirely wild *ferox* divides these two worlds.

Two beauties from the Cross Lochs in Sutherland.

Trolling Lures

Here is my version of the Grey Ghost streamer. A long-shanked lure hook shank is lapped with a thin layer of hot orange floss, ribbed with flat silver tinsel. An underwing is tied in at the throat, of white bucktail, extending at least to the bend of the hook, and, underneath the hook three strands of bronze peacock herl with a hot orange hackle in front. The streamer wings are two pairs of dark olive or dark green cock hackles, extending just beyond the hook bend. Then a pair of barred black and white cheeks are centralised at the front, extending to not more than half-way down the hook. These are usually from a Lady Amherst or Silver Pheasant, but if unobtainable, then two teal or pintail flank feathers will serve. A pair of jungle cock cheeks are added in the usual position on the outside of these wings. Two long golden pheasant toppings are then tied on, one over the wing, the other to shroud the hackle under the throat, and they form a complete ellipse around the whole dressing. The head of the fly is given enough layers of clear varnish to make a smooth, glassy head, then white varnish is floated over this. When dry, with a dubbing needle I add a thin band of bright red varnish in the centre of this head. The effect of this streamer to resemble small baitfish is remarkable, especially of small trout and char. I rate this streamer as the most effective pattern of all of them. It is time-consuming to make, but well worthwhile.

Some years ago I invented my Beastie and Voodoo lures, the bases of which were long, whole-plumes of marabou. These were not trolling lures. On the contrary, although they were made with weighted heads and fished with sinking lines, they were deliberately structured to attack surface feeding fish, for the bulky feathers were intended to hold the fly on the surface whilst the line sank below the lure, which then dived in front of the approaching fish. You can see this was eminently a tactic for cruising rainbow trout, and it was most effective, also for stripping over sunken weed beds. I did not prefer it as a deep trolling lure. My Beastie-type lures were tremendously successful for rainbow trout, and, strangely for mullet in Christchurch harbour.

The above mentioned streamers and lures always outscored the simpler Dognobblers in my own fishing, but admittedly, they are more time consuming to make. A 'normal' large brown trout rarely chases a lure whereas a rainbow can often be seen furrowing the water for two or three yards in pursuit of either a surface lure or a wake fly. Brown trout cer-

120

tainly take these lures, but usually in a sudden upwards crash. Although the deep-lying *ferox* isn't seen, my feeling is that another change of habit is that like most fish-eating predators, it will dash after its prey. I add the cautionary word, that all fish break all the rules we make for them.

The once-famous Blackbird lure, as used at the Queen Mother reservoir was simply an enormous black lure dressed on three hooked mounts, tied tandem style to a length of six inches or so. The structure is very simple, versions being possible with cock hackles, bucktail or squirrel or marabou plumes.

Although I found that the normal streamer was effective, when I wished to experiment with a fast sinking line and a semi-bouyant trolling lure, rising above the bottom, then there is a range of standard Booby lures to choose from, the buoyancy being obtained from a pair of polystyrene eyes lashed on to the lure at its head. Success has been claimed for these, I'm sure with truth, as this lure travels over the heads of deep-lying fish.

I discount the use of tinsel-bodied flies for deep trolling for the attraction of tinsel is to reflect light which is weak at such depths. The aim should be for opaque silhouettes, mobility, especially of sinuosity, and also because I believe that vibration is a trigger to all fish predation. Here, a field of experimentation which I have not tried, is a linkage between two hooks as in tandem 'Terror' type sea trout lures. If I were trolling again today I would experiment by making a flexible hook by adding a small Waddington mount to the eye of a normal trout hook in such a way as to give side to side movement in the water. I'm sure this was a success factor in those famous Blackbird lures. I add that I fished my trolling lures on leaders of about twelve feet, and I did not use additional droppers for fear of catching up on the lake floor.

Where there is debris, the once-popular 'brush-off' system can be used. This is simply a loop of light nylon taken under the hook to form a protective shield around the bend and point of the hook. It is attached at the bend and then in front of the hook before the hackle is added. It's original purpose, in which I had a hand, was to protect salmon flies from fouling on sunken leaves in the autumn, but I see no reason why it shouldn't be used for deep trolling.

In an earlier book of mine[1] I mentioned experiments with lures mounted on tubes, using trebles, but I later abandoned this style of fly. It was in the times when the first trout-reservoir explosion was just beginning, and I quickly developed some ethical doubts. I also found there was no particular advantage in catch-rates. The general rule (sometimes broken!) is that trout hit lures hard, and having taken so many fish when lure fishing, I have noticed that, unlike normal small flies, the lure is often found right in the back of the throat. With small trebles this poses obvious problems, especially when fishing 'no kill'. For example, when having to kill fish by the rules, the fish-bag would have a spoonful or so of blood at the end of

[1]*Fly Fishing Tactics on Still Water.*

the day, and bleeding fish should always be killed as there is, I believe, no clotting agent in their blood to arrest a haemorrhage. They simply bleed to death. Lip-hooked trout do not bleed, there is no blood supply there, but this is not true of the 'deep throat' hooking. Trebles bounce around on their flukes and can tear tissue instead of achieving a straightforward puncture-hold.

If you put together the distance casting information given earlier, with the tactics on searching deep water from the bank, it is obvious that a bulky fly meets air-resistance to minimise the range. There is no reason why the lure should not be scaled down. I have often used a mini-beastie from the bank and dam at Bewl Water. It is also possible, strange though it may seem, to overcome the problem by using a strong wind from the rear, and by making a high, strong punch, the breeze grabs the lure and dumps it far out on the water. Sounds crazy? Try it; it does work astonishingly well.

Mayfly and Large Floaters

There is that fascinating notion that we can plumb the depths of entomology, yet from a practical viewpoint, this is completely unnecessary. To start with, there are two species of mayfly in the British Isles, but although one predominates, is it of no practical consequence, for they resemble each other for the purposes of imitation. It is also an interesting experience of mine that whereas mayfly imitation on rivers is not at all critical, on still water it is even less so, which is a paradox, given that theoretically fish have longer time to study the fly. Purely as a matter of interest, the mayfly we have in the British mainland is *Ephemera danica*, and it has the same two year life cycle on still water as it does in streams. The fact that it mostly appears in June is simply due to the changing of the calendar in times gone by, when people rioted because they believed the Government had stolen eleven days from their own lives.

It is such an easy fly to recognise that I mention only its large size, its three tail whisks and the season of its appearance as a dun, mostly to be expected from late May, on into June. This varies slightly from place to place, usually being true to a local tradition, that it will be early on one fishery, later on another, of short duration in one place, but lasting well into mid summer, say on certain Irish loughs. A curiosity is that a single hatch may crop up unexpectedly at a time and place where previously it was unknown, such a happening was in the Pennine stocked reservoir of Grassholme one year. In mid summer, fleets of mayfly duns suddenly appeared, and those anglers who luckily carried an odd imitation in their fly boxes made a killing. This was reported to me by the bailiff, Jeff Sage, an experienced fisher and naturalist, so there was no doubt, the fly was not mistaken for the so-called summer mayfly, a completely different fly.

The distribution of the mayfly is universal in Britain, from, say Seddlescombe lake in the deep South to Hakel Loch as far North as you can go without falling into the ocean. This is a truism, but I mention it for southern anglers like myself who, growing up with the duffer's fly on chalk streams, mistakenly associate it with warm southern waters, and we might carelessly omit it on our first trips to the Flow Country.

There is also a colour phenomenon, perhaps a symptom of this spectrum shift in the trout's vision, and we have to bear in mind that each of us might see colour in slightly different ways, but to my eye, against a darkling water, the fly sometimes looks a buff colour, even whitish, but the killing colour of my own dun imitation on still water is definitely green. I hold up the mayfly as a superb example of presentation being the key factor, rather than colour, for I prefer to use a simple olive bumble pattern on lakes, which can be fished wet or dry when the duns appear. But also a plain brown straddlebug works effectively.

I would hate to count the number of mayfly hatches I have fished through on lake and river, and admittedly it is dangerous to generalise, but whilst on occasion I have seen river trout preoccupied with the hatching nymph as it struggles to emerge from the nymphal shuck – the technical term is eclosion – I have not yet found this to be an important feeding factor on still water, and for this reason, I have never needed to make a specific hatching nymph pattern. There is probably some physical reason for this, perhaps still water mayflies emerge from their jackets quickly but certainly the duns are readily taken. As with small dry flies, though, an effective emerger is readily fashioned by clipping short the body hackles of a normal floater.

It is foolish to make general rules, but there are some patterns which reoccur. I prefer to be upwind from the bank on a mayfly day, at least to start with, especially if there is a westerly wind blowing down a water, say a northern loch. Although the actual emergence seems to be fast, the take-off from the water can be quite slow, a strange contradiction, and this is true when the wind is cold, with little sun, as it takes longer for the wings to harden sufficiently for the fly to take off. It is this time lag which makes the flies so vulnerable. On really cold days I have seen duns drift for over a hundred yards before getting away. If you take an upwind shore, under the prevailing winds we meet in this island, there will be the silty areas from which the nymphs come to the surface. The ripple here will be at its gentlest, under the lee shore. Lee shores also hold the strongest weed beds around which silt collects. The opposite is true of windward shores which are constantly pounded by waves.

Of course there will be territorial fish here, taking the duns, but the important thing is to determine the drift lines of the flies. This will usually favour one bank or the other, the more so if the drift takes the flies into a wind lane.

I would then find the place where the wind lane forms a Vee, forking away from the bank, but allowing the line to be cast across it and this would often involve walking 'along the side of the wind' to coin a phrase. Happily, the rise forms to mayfly duns are dramatic. This is an ideal situation, but ideals are sometimes not achieved!

It comes down to such choices, for admittedly, I have had good fishing right under the lee bank, fishing out into the ripple, and the fish are so intoxicated by the hatches of these large duns that they take with abandon. My preference is for the 'stronger' water, because the turbulence disguises the bigger fly and it activates its hackles the more. As mentioned before, but especially for mayfly, the rougher water on each side of a wind lane is often more productive for reasons which I do not understand, but rise forms will confirm this.

These conditions are suitable for a single dry fly. Another choice is to fish an olive bumble on a top dropper, with a single wet fly on the point as an anchor man, but again, this bob fly is virtually a floater, for it should be well treated with a floatant.

Yes, I know it's great fun to make a multitude of mayfly patterns, they are pretty, but they are also unnecessary. All that is needed is the simple bumble dressed on a size 10 hook. My own favourite pattern has a bunch of tippets for the tail, a simple olive dubbing for the body, ribbed with gold and an olive cock's hackle at the throat. I like to wind in a soft game hackle in front of this, say olive-dyed French Partridge, Green Drake or Guinea Fowl, it doesn't matter provided that these tips extend beyond the cock hackle so that they bend into the surface film while the cock hackle points then support the body of the fly. This, too, is part of my philosophy of paying attention to the structure of the fly, more so than to colour, for this is a dodge, this soft hackle in front, which goes back a very long way, and it has stood the test of time.

Having chosen my shooting place, the casting is straightforward, to the area where fish are seen rising, and once again, even with drifting mayflies, it is amazing how brown trout in still water, especially wild fish, hold their station, unlike cruising rainbows. The fish simply take position where they know a particular wind drift will bring the mayfly duns to them from the hatching places. This is a pleasant habit, for we can pick off rising fish almost as if fishing a river.

As I have this opportunity of casting across the wind, into wind and scum lanes, it is axiomatic that the line will form a belly downwind, which will cause the fly both to drag and to become waterlogged. The former problem is easily delayed, if not cured by mending the line upwind, and it helps to stabilise the fly on the water if the rod is pushed well away from the body when this mend is performed, for often the fish is so eager on mayfly it takes it the moment it alights. On very windy days the upwind mend can be put into the line as it turns over in the air on the forward cast. This is quite easy to do, just a sideways flip of the rod puts in the curve to the line. Stillwater trout will take dragging flies, but the danger is of waterlogging. Waterlogging of the fly is mitigated by taking the fly off the water with the 'snake cast' and this lifts the fly straight up into the air from the surface. This is very useful as we tend to become excited during mayfly hatches, switching to different targets, and rapidly changing the distance and direction of the cast.

My preference is to use the olive bumble as the top dropper, part of a two fly team, during the early time of the hatch, and I change to the single dry fly as this hatch progresses. Trout being contrary critters, break all of the rules and confound our theories, but even so, it is better to fish to a plan than to cast about frantically like a headless chicken. I feel that fish will be feeding sub-surface until sufficient flies appear on the surface to create the preoccupied feeding pattern. I do not have any reason for fishing a Coch-y-bondhu as the point fly, it only has the virtue of being very successful for me at these times. It has no resemblance to the mayfly; it is intended as a beetle copy. It works for me in mayfly time, unreasonably perhaps.

For me the famous 'spent gnat' is controversial. This is, of course, the female spinner which returns to the water to lay eggs and then dies. It is so familiar on rivers and lakes where mayfly abound, that I need only say that it conforms in appearance to all of those aquatic upright-winged flies which have two adult stages, in that it is brighter in colour and more agile when alive, than the duns. Also, the dead gnat is easily identified, its wings, outstretched on the water, support the body which can be collected at leisure by the trout. If, for example, during the mayfly time, early in the morning, you row quietly out onto the bay of any Irish lough you will see myriads of spent gnats glued to the surface film, and here and there the stillness of the water will be disturbed by the rise of a trout. Mostly these rise forms will be gentle sippings, because the fly, being low in the water, and completely inert, needs only be sucked in with the minimum of water by the fish. As on rivers, the patient observer can tell from afar whether fish are taking duns or spent flies.

I take far more trouble in dressing a spent mayfly than I do with the dun imitation, because usually the early-morning water is still, the fly acceptance is not hurried and by the time the spinners appear, fish can be gorged, even these days! They are just plain fussy. My own pattern has a body of fluo white floss cross-ribbed with black thread and fine scarlet floss. Three tail whisks are taken from a Silver Pheasant tail, barred black and white fibres. Two pairs of black cock hackle-points are tied on flat for the wings, and a very sparse badger cock hackle is wound on at the throat. This is a simple Black Drake. I do not dunk this fly in floatant, the aim is to support it by its wings on the surface film. Surprisingly it has proved effective for me, and it is one occasion when it is necessary to copy closely the natural counterpart. I usually dress this on a lightweight size 12 mayfly hook.

During mayfly hatches I have noticed on streams that, as trout will become preoccupied with spent gnats, they can be gathered in without effort, but I have not noticed this on still water, and in a mixed hatch of duns and fall of spinners, I will always prefer the dun imitation. Yet, in early morning particularly, spent gnats will be in abundance before the dun hatches begin, and the same may be true late of an evening. The problem when fishing a spent gnat is that often the water is of a flat calm when the leader shows up like a coach harness. Fished dry, as it must, it is important to degrease the last few inches of the leader and coax it to go just under the surface film. This is important, for I have noticed on occasion that when my leader would simply not sink, no fish took the fly until a gentle wind-ripple sprang up.

I should discuss this thorny question of fish movement, for although

I have pointed out that brown trout hold station, unlike cruising rainbows, nothing in fishing is ever rigid. This is only a general indication, for of course they do move, according to light, temperature, wind and feeding conditions. I am making a comparison between the roving habit of rainbow packs and the more sedentary behaviour of brownies. Many a time I have sat in a boat at the head of a wind lane at Hanningfield, watching shoals of gulping rainbows coming upwind to my fly and often I would simply wait, rod raised until the target was in range. On distant lochs in Sutherland and Caithness, I have moved along a bank, searching out little bays and headlands from which I could cast my dry mayfly to a fish rising constantly in the same place.

It is true that mayfly time, on river or lake, is the best time of the season for catching fish. It is a good time for the beginner, but failure will not be due to the pattern, and hunting through the box will be futile. These simple patterns will work for you if you follow the common sense guidelines I have described, and these are relating observation to the way in which you show the fly to the fish; it's simple.

I add an apology in that I do not describe how to play and fight the fish, for mistakes are the best teachers. The classical writers always tell us to have that equally classic 'God save the Queen' pause between the take and the strike. If only it were that simple. Is there a belly in the line? Is the line partly sunk? Is the rod tip high or low? You take into account what you see, and the printed page can give no precise instruction. Sometimes a trout slashes at a fly from below. A large fly is sometimes dived on from a leaping fish, always very hard to hit. As for playing fish, I leave the fish to be the teacher, for when you've lost a few you develop subconsciously what the late Dick Walker called 'hands'. I would merely remind you that the mayfly may be on a bigger hook, it needs a good tug to set it, but as my rods have light tips, if I am not too indolent, I smarten the point, take down the barb. Indolence? I'm being unfair to myself. I would never let a fish go off with fly and leader, but if a fish comes short or bounces off on the strike, as I release so many, this doesn't bother me, I doff my hat and wish it good luck.

I expect you to remind me that I have already expressed a preference for light line fishing, the rods for which have lighter tips which are less efficient at setting larger hooks. Usually I know the time and place for mayfly fishing which allows me to use the ten-footer I described earlier. On other occasions, when I am fishing small flies and the need arises for a bigger pattern, say an unexpected fall of daddies from the bank, then for that tactic I use a large fly on a small hook, accomplished by tying a detached body onto the hook shank as part of the dressing. The easiest way is to buy the moulded plastic mayfly bodies, which are hollow. For mayfly use they have to be pierced at the tail-end and three fibres of cock pheasant tail are inserted and glued there, a tiny speck of superglue is sufficient. The same body will serve for the daddy, the fly being finished with two hackle point wings of brown cock, tied spent, six knotted legs from the cock pheasant tail, a few turns of light red game hackle. You have a superb copy which floats so well, due to the air bubble inside that hollow body.

Detached bodies can also be made by lashing long bucktail or deer hair fibres onto a needle, then sliding this off and trimming it to shape, you have a ready-made body which is also superbly buoyant. You can also experiment with different shades of hair, light in colour for the mayfly, darker for the daddy. I usually mount these detached bodies onto size 12 dry fly hooks with a normal size of shank. Of course, if you have a rod with a heavier tip then there's no reason why you shouldn't dress a daddy on a long-shanked mayfly hook.

There's the usual argument, is it necessary to go in for a close imitation when we know that simpler, hackled palmers like the Loch Ordie will probably be taken for daddies, moths and other large terrestrials which have been trapped in the surface film? I enter this controversy with some trepidation. My opinion, and it is only that, is that this is a question of water movement. When fishing in a good breeze from a boat when images are broken up by the waves, I wouldn't hesitate to favour a simple bumble type fly. A strange difference between river and lake trout is that whereas drag is anathema to the former it can be positively attractive to the latter. The reason is that the river-fly use the current but the lake fly, terrestrial or aquatic, has to use its own strength to escape from the surface film. In both cases the behaviour is imprinted into the consciousness of the fish.

Daddies are almost as important for lake trout as mayflies, the more so on waters which have no mayfly. Daddies seems to come onto the water at any time of the season, but their activity is most marked in the later summer and autumn. The females lay their eggs in soft earth by pushing their pointed rear-ends into the ground, after which they become 'spent' and are carried by the wind onto the lake. Especially in years when rainfall has been sparse, the soft ground they need is close to lake margins. The rise to the daddy is easy to spot because it is a mini-commotion. It may include hefty tail swipes to submerge the fly. And clearly it is another bonus for searching along the lee shore and for watching the activity of birds.

So here, when I may be fishing from the bank into the ripple where the wind first strikes the surface, that is when I would fish a more imitative fly. This is where there is yet another mild controversy, whether or not to move the fly? The spent daddy does not struggle and when fishing a floater from the shore, I rarely move it. Another thing about daddies, the trout often taken them in two stages, the first being either to swamp them or to take them under in a light lip-hold and then to gulp them down. The strike is therefore slightly delayed. I have missed fish by being too hurried in my reaction to the 'take'.

My best recollection of daddy fishing was on Hundland loch in Orkney. At the far end there are two small hills which funnel the wind from that direction. I was there in September, and being afloat at first, I soon saw a typical daddy rise which was best fished from an upwind bank position. Coming ashore, I went along the bank to that place and gently wafted down into the ripple-edge one of the patterns I have described . . . it would be too immodest to recount the subsequent events.

A curiosity of daddy fishing is the success of the sunk fly, and it does work. The natural spent flies would hardly sink on their own, they are too buoyant, though possibly daddy-debris might if the spent females are pounded and broken up along a windward shore. The explanation might be that the fish are imprinted as they drag them under, or as I suspect, on occasion trout find it hard to differentiate between floating and sub-surface flies. Who knows? It doesn't matter. It suffices to know that a daddy, deliberately dressed as a sunk fly and fished below the surface succeeds far too often to be discounted.

I fish two other types of large floater, the sedge and the moth. The sedge is the copy of the Great Red Sedge, the same as the famous Irish Murrough fly. Mostly I use this as a wake fly, and I fish my moth patterns the same way. I first described wake-fly fishing many years ago in my book *Fly fishing Tactics on Still Water*. I was gratified to learn that my favourite moth pattern, the Hoolet, became a firm favourite at Blagdon. I first discovered the large sedges at Coldingham loch when I saw their amazing whirling action when they first broke surface to hatch, followed by the fast scuttle towards the bank when they picked up their bearings. I love the old Irish term for this behaviour: 'furrocking'.

Fishing a wake fly is simplicity itself, you chuck it out, from the bank, from the boat, and you pull it back to make a deliberate wake. Rainbows tend to chase it, you see an exciting V-wave coming after the fly, followed by the angry swirl. Brownies usually come up for it from below, with no warning, as do sea trout. The danger is water-logging of the fly, but this is overcome by building in a buoyancy chamber, my own old dodge being to whip a sliver of cork to the hook shank before fashioning the body. The hackles do not support the fly as in a normal small floater, they are there to make the wake.

So, taking a large sedge as an example, my pattern is dressed on a long shanked hook, say size 8, the cork sliver is lashed on the underside of the shank, then covered by the body material, my preference being a rusty red dubbing. The wings are simply copied by a bunch of red-game cock's hackle fibres, followed by two hackles of the same colour at the throat. Perfectionists can add a pair of antennae made by stripping two hackle stalks from a Cree cock.

The Hoolet is also simple, the body being made of peacock herls, twisted together, and wound over the cork. The wings should be made by folding a strip of brown owl's primary feather, but that being protected, any soft, brown speckled wing feather will do. Two red-game cock hackles are then wound in. Again, if you wish to spice up this fly, especially for dusk-fishing, tie in a fluo-orange butt. It is also easy to fashion a plain, large white moth and although the late Richard Walker scored well with it, my own confidence was always in the darker patterns.

Tactically, fishing these flies is simplicity itself, you experiment with retrieves of different speeds and lengths, and you use your common sense where to fish them, from lee shores, or across wind and scum lanes. Persistence will guarantee success. I have to discount an oft-repeated tactic of repeatedly tapping or banging the rod butt to vibrate the floating fly, try it by all means, but it never worked for me.

As large floaters also are favoured for dapping, given a strong breeze, it is just possible to dap from the shore either directly into deep water, or by wading out far enough to catch the wind. I mention this as all tactical experiments are fun, but wake-fly fishing would be a much better bet, the effect is similar, the water you cover is more extensive, and it is more efficient at targeting individual rising fish.

I first used successfully a copy of the blue damsel fly at Two Lakes after I had seen trout leaping for them. I was sceptical because the damsel is such an agile, fast flyer, but the very first outing with my copy produced two fine brownies, so I have applied it ever since on waters where this beast is prolific. Funnily enough, it has always attracted fish when being left inert on the surface, contradicting my inclination to drag it quickly. My dressing is on a long-shanked mayfly hook, the body being made from bright blue lurex ribbed with black button thread. Two pairs of grizzle hackle point wings are tied in the spent fashion, a short, pale dun cock's hackle is wound sparsely at the throat, followed by a turn or two or black ostrich herl for the head. This is my fun-fly for those sun-hot mornings when the blue flies are hatching. On some lakes they are prolific.

The most unusual large-dry is undoubtedly the floating fry copy. Although I have had success with this for rainbow trout I have yet to find it attractive to brownies. I include it, bearing in mind the image of the huge cannibals attacking small surface-feeding trout at Cow Green. Of course, a greased-up muddler minnow would serve well enough. The popular pattern is tied on a normal lure hook, the body being made from a white fluo floss or chenille. The back is a strip of white ethafoam sheet, protruding and shaped at the tail, and the body is ribbed with a flat silver tinsel.

When I used this against reservoir rainbows I followed the instructions given in the book *Dressed to Kill* by Bob Carnhill and Kenneth Robson. The ingenious fly was invented by John Wadham for Rutland Water where it has taken enormous rainbows. It was fished to imitate a small dead fish, floating on the surface, and so it is a true dry fly! I found that the book's advice to fish the fly directly upwind was valid. I imagine that if I encounter cannibal browns attacking on the surface and within range, this fly would prove effective, which is why I mention it here. I was impressed with the original, tactical imagination which inspired the fly and its method of application, reminding me of the time when it was discovered that large pike would pick up dead herrings from the lake floor. I hope I shall have the opportunity of using it in the haunts of the *ferox* . My reservation is that, although fish do not read rule books, there's a trend for rainbow trout to hunt over wide areas, sometimes just below the surface of a lake, whereas the brown trout adopts a feeding territory. However, once, long ago, when I was afloat on Blagdon, my wife and I saw brown trout in what could be described as shoals, heading together in the direction of the dam, dozens of them going past us. All fish must follow their food or starve, but how they know to follow the migrations of their food is a mystery, as witness the description given by Tom Ivens in that classic book, *Still Water Fly Fishing*, of the big snail migrations he saw in Ravensthorpe reservoir. The plainest example is of the intelligent pike anglers in my Canterbury Club who understand where the roach shoals winter-up and around them are the great pike patrolling.

To recapitulate, the large floaters can be fished from boat or bank, and, again, in the latter instance, an anchor would be useful to position a boat in the area of a hatch or, more likely in a food-drift from the shore. When using my favourite ultra-light line rod I add a pattern or two dressed with a detached body on a smaller hook. If deliberately using large floaters, anticipating a hatch of mayfly or a fall of terrestrials, then I take along my ten footer, the heavy artillery to throw a size 4/5 line. The critical striking factor is the weight of the rod tip, and as the years go by, we learn of our personal strengths and weaknesses, and often I have had to curse myself as I am not a 'strong' striker, a legacy from my earliest days as a flick-of-the-wrist, river dry-fly man. Instincts are, alas, a matter of muscle memory which stays with you for life and emerges when you are relaxed and dreamy. In passing, this fault was brought home to me when I once used a rod made from a mixture of carbon and boron which, for some reason, softened up my striking reaction. I had to discard this rod as I simply failed to set hooks at long range when bank fishing on reservoirs. The new airopace carbons have largely overcome this problem, but one advantage of fishing in remote places is that I can shriek curses to the heavens without offending other ears.

In case you have read my much earlier book on still water tactics, written over thirty years ago, there is one method I have not discarded. This was a semi-dapping technique, using a very long leader with a butterfly of tissue paper tied in about a yard above the fly, to catch the wind. It was used especially for the daddy, in trying to match the way in which the wind skips and bounces them when first they fall onto the water. It is an experiment well worth trying and another aim was to avoid the nylon (thick and shiny in those days) from lying on the water. The new 'invisible' leader materials have persuaded me that I need no longer do this, but it took some notable fish in its time.

Still Water Nymphs

I must admit that in my green youth I was intoxicated with the near-perfect imitations displayed in the colour plates in that fine book on lake fly imitations by C. F. Walker[1]. The dust cover shows the natural nymphs side by side with his copies and a cursory glance reveals that it is hard to tell one from another. Until that book appeared there had been no systematic attempt to copy the insect life of still water.

It is necessary to reiterate that for the sake of convenience we anglers apply some scientific terms rather loosely. Insects are not all true insects and nymphs are not all true nymphs. Happily, we understand this and larvae, pupae, bugs, crustacea are all inclusive in these broad definitions.

It would be unfair to claim that my application of this author's philosophy was sterile. I recollect on one occasion his painstaking copy of the Lake Olive nymph scored well for me. It dawned on me that there was a dilemma, whether to dress and carry innumerable 'fussy' flies, or whether to rationalise them along the lines of Ivens? To be fair to Walker, he also took great pains to discover how each 'insect' moved and behaved, and again, for the first time in angling literature, he gave precise instructions as to how each one should be fished. This is the main lesson of this book.

Corixa

Of course experience moved me in to the direction of practicality, but each fly fisherman reaches his own balance between imitation and presentation, which must be so. There are certain food items which must be related imitatively to artificial counterparts. The water-boatman (corixa) is an example, for as I have described, in some lakes, notably Blagdon, a proportion of the brown trout become specialised feeders on hard-shelled fauna like snails, corixa and so on.

It has been assumed that 'shelled' creatures need alkaline water from which to make their shells, but this isn't entirely true, there is at least one water-boatman that thrives in quite acidic waters. It is easy enough to identify corixa in a lake, their profiles are distinct, whitish bodies, brown-shell backs and outstretched paddles. Every tiddler-hunting schoolboy knows them, and, of course, they will turn up when you spoon the stom-

[1]*Lake Flies and their Imitation.*

132

achs of trout from those fisheries. It is not unusual to discover an odd corixa or two in trout, but it is astonishing when you spoon or clean a specialist feeder for the tummy will be packed with them, as was the case with a magnificent specimen caught in the Cross Lochs in Sutherland by Jeff Sage. A similar story is found with snail-feeders, you can literally 'crunch' their stomachs when you handle them.

The corixa imitation is easy to make. The body is white or buff floss overlaid onto lead wire, as usually you fish this nymph deep on a long leader. You can add a brown button thread ribbing if you wish, and a silver tag also helps as this beast collects a little air bubble. I usually omit a normal hackle, but the paddles can be made from fibres of brown feather. If such a feather strip is taken over the back from the tail, the fibres can be separated after tying down at the head, and kept in that horizontal position by figure-of-eight tyings of thread. Some varnish gives the back a shiny look. I usually make these patterns on size 12 hooks, and the curved grub hook pattern is attractive.

I mention here that bank fishing is advantageous for the slow fishing of the deeply sunk nymph, preferably on a long leader to a floating line. It must be patient work, and again, Ivens was also right in insisting on very slow retrieves, timing some of his at two and a half minutes. To achieve a steady and continuously slow retrieve, the figure-of-eight method is best, and is well worth practising. The aim must be to allow the nymph to come to rest on the lake floor, and often the 'take' will come with the very first retrieve.

Perhaps it is finicky, but I have always preferred to find a bay with a sandy or silty floor as I have a belief, maybe irrational, that this is the preferred environment of the corixa, and that trout hunt for them there. In passing, and as a matter of curiosity, some observers believe that the corixa is chameleon-like in being able to suit its colouring to its background, as a protection technique, and this is the basis of my own choice of fishing place when fishing a 'corixa lake'. Such a lake would be one in an alkaline environment, and even on peat moors the marl pits are good examples of such fisheries. As a general rule, if you see snails and shrimp, corixa should also abound.

Shrimp

I mention this as a distinctive copy is necessary, though it is not a favourite of mine as even when I have persisted with it I have taken very few fish on still water, though the contrary is true with my stream fishing. However, it is an alternative tactic to try on dour days. My choice would be to fish it close to weed beds, but I must admit that over four decades of fishing on still water I cannot recall seeing trout beat up weed beds for shrimp. On chalk streams in particular this is not an uncommon sight, typically the tails of the trout come through the surface film as they burrow, head down in the weeds. The nymphs, being flushed out, are then eagerly seized.

133

The curved grub hook is the one of choice, a pale olive dubbing is ribbed with a fine gold tinsel. Perfectionists palmer a light olive hackle down the hook and trim off the top fibres but I content myself with a normal throat hackle pulled down below the shank in the usual way. A strip of light olive raffine is taken over the back, from tail to head and varnished. The fly can be lightly weighted with an under-layer of fine lead wire. Naturally, this self-same fly doubles up for stream work.

I take this opportunity to dismiss a former favourite of mine, the Hoglouse; a pattern for which C. F. Walker described in his book. I was captivated by this nymph as one day it gave me a good catch, but persistence with it on subsequent occasions failed so dismally to live up to the initial promise that it has been evicted from my fly box.

Sedge nymphs

For convenience, I group together the larvae and pupae of sedges. With these flies the angling entomologist has a field day. Many years ago when fishing at Two Lakes, that skilled angler, the late David Jacques, made a point of identifying the individual sedges of the fishery, and copying them in their various life-cycle stages, even to the extent of farming them in tanks in his house. Simply to remain sane we must rationalise this vast army down to manageable proportions.

The larvae live on the lake floor, some are free swimming, some encase themselves in small items of debris. I have known perfectionists go to the trouble of sticking with superglue tiny stones, pieces of stick or vegetable matter to the bodies of their artificials which is plainly nonsense. To be brutally frank, a well-sunk Hare's Ear nymph will serve far better. It gives excellent results fished very slowly close to the bottom of the lake. The same is true of the Cove style long-shanked Pheasant Tail nymph. These patterns can be weighted then fished on rather long leaders either from the bank, or from an anchored boat.

It does no harm to identify the principal sedges in a favourite fishery, but it is also sensible to classify them roughly in terms of colour and size for practical fishing purposes. Thus there will probably be a choice between the Great Red Sedge, medium cinnamon coloured ones, the darker brown silverhorns with their barred antennae and speckled wings, and the one which captivates me, the magpie-coloured marble sedge, common in the far North. Persistent fishing with Pheasant Tails, Stick Flies and Hare's Ear nymphs certainly scores when fishing for trout feeding close to the lake floor on larvae, it has paid off for me handsomely. The pupa, though is a more fruitful source.

This is when the life cycle progresses to the final adult stage, the fly has to come ashore, to couple, to return to the water to lay eggs. Again, nature decrees different ways of doing things, some species come to the surface of the water, emerge from the pupal jacket, dry off and fly away. Others swim to the nearby shore or vegetation to crawl up into the air.

134

Some years ago I was fishing with a companion on Bewl Water when sedges were hatching, and being unable to take fish on my favourite Invicta, usually deadly medicine on these occasions, my companion opined that the fish were taking swimming pupae at mid-water, and that he had an unfailing remedy which he kept proving to me. He handed me one. 'This never fails,' he exclaimed. 'That's good news,' I replied on having an immediate offer, and from thence this nymph was nicknamed 'the Good News'. It is simplicity itself, as all the best flies are.

A long-shanked hook has lead wire lapped along only its bottom half. This is vital to get the correct swimming action and angle. The body is merely a mixture of three or four dubbings, the colours being to personal choice, whim even. Say you use blue, red, green and black. The fibres are mixed together, but must be straggly without chopping up in a blender. The mixture is dubbed onto the hook shank and picked out with a needle, ribbed with a fine flat gold tinsel and the nymph is finished off with a head of peacock herl. There is no hackle. It is amazing that such a simple pattern will kill so well when sedges are hatching, but I have lost count of the number of good trout I have taken on this, from Shetland to my own south-east corner of England.

Unusually, this is a fly made to fish mid-water. I remain convinced that when the trout are taking hatching sedges, then the Invicta is your best assassin, but occasionally, when sedges are seen to hatch prodigiously without surface rises, then a mid-water retrieve with the Good News will probably be the answer. So I take off my hat to Bill Robbins for introducing me to his secret weapon.

I was so taken with this nymph that I went in for combinations of body fur, getting overall colour effects of light buff down to an almost deep claret. It didn't seem to matter, and it brought home to me again that it depends very much on what the fish expect to see in terms of behaviour. I did turn up a few old notes and I accept that I was tending towards an overall colour effect of a deep orange-brown. I add this to those of you who believe that colour is the most important factor. Now, when I glance in my nymph box I see rows of various colour effects from white, through to olive, green, orange, claret and black. The effect is achieved by simply taking a larger pinch of the colour of dubbing fur you wish to predominate. It drives home the lesson of simplicity; this fly proves that your twenty minutes' toil on a woven body is a waste of time. Just pull the Good News through the water, it seems to send off sparks of fire, especially if you can still get seal's fur, a material which nothing surpasses – the secret, for God's sake avoid neatness! Get that body fur well picked out and straggly.

Snails, beetles and tadpoles

I class these together as yet another example of intelligent rationalisation pattern-wise. I have my own pattern to copy all three, I describe it later.

I recollect that it was Tom Ivens who described the migration of snails. He had seen it on occasion. Seemingly it was a wind drift migration, the parties of snails drifting along just below the surface. I admit I have never seen this, but snails are a part of brown trout diet, and another book on fishery management emphasises the importance of farming snails in little areas of the fishery, using shelters made of half-circular tiles.

Ivens was satisfied with his Black & Peacock spider as an imitation, both for snails and beetles alike. It is a practical and successful fly, I have taken numerous fish on it. It is one fly concept I decided to improve. This was the result of climbing out along a branch over my fishery at Sundridge in order to watch feeding trout. I spotted a large water beetle periodically popping up to the surface to collect an air bubble which glistened at its rear end when it filled its tanks again to dive. I guess this was probably that ferocious beast, the Great Diving Beetle, *Ditiscus marginalis*. It impressed on me the value of adding a silver tag to copy that air bubble, a concession I make to the imitationists.

I have always been impressed with the technique of mixing together different and contrasting colours of dubbing, and not wishing merely to embellish Ivens's spider, I made my new beetle pattern by mixing three colours of fur together, black predominating. These were wound over an underbody of lead wire and floss to make that plump beetle shape. A tag of silver tinsel was tied in at the hook-bend and finally two turns only of a long black hen's hackle was wound in at the head. I always try to find an undyed hackle with that sheeny green hue.

As with many of my nymphs, I prefer when possible to fish them from a floating double taper line from a fixed position: the bank or anchored boat. The preference for the floating line is that sometimes the nymph is taken rather questioningly by the fish. This is strange, for surface fishing with wet fly or dry, the brownie is usually a snatch-artist, on or off, but deep down, although one still gets the sudden take, there is also on occasion a subtle tightening of the line which is seen on the surface. I think it a mistake to fish for brown trout with the rod pointing down at the water, a normal practice for catching recently stocked rainbows which take slowly and come time and time again if they miss the first time round. For brown trout, as a rule it is sensible to have the rod tip higher so that the fast takes can be hit smartly. I have seen many frustrated rainbow fishers missing takes when they first come to wild brown trout waters.

There's no reason why you shouldn't fashion a tadpole shaped nymph. It's easy enough, a bulbous body of black floss on the hook and a tail of marabou herl. It is effective. Tadpole fishing, too is indicated when you see the little fellows in the water in early spring. Trout love them. It is also plain common sense to fish the fly in the area where the tadpoles are seen and the trout are seen to be feeding on them. It is probably one of the easiest ways to suit tactics to observation. If you come onto this situation unexpectedly, without a 'perfect imitation', then my invention or Ivens's Black & Peacock will serve adequately, as I know from experience.

As for my beetle copy, I baptised it after the famous hangman of yester-year, Jack Ketch.

The Damsel and Mayfly nymphs

The Damsel has been one of the most successful nymphs in recent years. It copies the larval form of the damsel flies we see hovering over the lakes in summer. The predominate colour of the adult flies are either an electric blue or a shiny olive, but the ubiquitous colour of the larva is a drab olive. Unlike some of the insects we have seen before, the distribution of the damsel larvae is more universal which explains why it succeeds in all parts and depths of a fishery. This makes it a good prospecting pattern, fished either close to the surface, at mid-water or deep down.

Modern dressings abound, but most have a tail of olive marabou feather, a tapered abdomen of olive dubbing, ribbed with gold, a thorax of similar material with a wing case of olive feather. Sometimes an olive hackle is tied in as a throat-beard and some dressers whip on a gold bead for the head. Perfectionists apply a tiny red-eye at the head. The best hook is one of the longer patterns made for nymphs. For deep fishing, again I prefer to use a long leader from a floating line.

Undoubtedly, the Mayfly nymph is second in popularity on British still water fisheries today, and the curiosity of both of these patterns is that they catch fish also where the natural counterparts do not exist. I discussed Mayfly tactics earlier, but here I add that the nymph can be tied onto a longer nymph hook, and it should be lapped with a loading of lead wire as the naturals are silt-dwellers. The tail is usually made from tying in two white or honey cock hackle points, or goose biots. The tapered body is a white or light buff fur ribbed with brown button thread. The thorax is usually a dubbing of the same material, dressed plumper, though I prefer to achieve a two tone effect in all of my nymphs, so I would choose a contrasting colour, perhaps pale olive or very light brown. A strip of brown feather is taken over the thorax, and a beard hackle is applied if necessary, though I consider it best left out. Variations on this theme are numerous, please take your pick, but this one works well.

Summation

The above patterns are the specialised ones I carry for those defined tactics. In addition I also carry standard patterns, notably the Pheasant Tail and the Hare's Ear as these suffice for the nymphs of pond and lake olives as well as sedge larvae. The buzzers are dealt with separately. Both the Hare's Ear and Pheasant Tails have contrasting thoraces to achieve two tone effect, and the thoraces should be of a darker herl or dubbing. To weight these two patterns I add copper or lead wire under the thoracic material.

Occasionally some local, rarer flies hatch and they can bring about preoccupied feeding. The Sepia Dun is a case in point, it was a particular feature of Two Lakes in April, the only fishery where I met it in significant numbers, so much so that fish would look at nothing else when it appeared. Then the Pheasant Tail is dark enough to fool the trout. I met an angler at Tongue whose favourite loch was peopled by another rarity, the Claret Dun, a problem which he had not solved, though I referred him to a weighted Welsh Partridge fly. Occasionally at Cow Green we find a corner favouring the summer Mayfly, and so it goes on. Dear old C. F. Walker patiently applied his brilliant mind and dexterity to offering us copies of all of these beasties in their various stages, nymph, dun, spinner. But imagine the size of fly box you would need if you had the patience to dress them all.

We do need to pay attention to simulation, but it is sensible to do this in broad brush terms, just to remain sane. I offer above my own rationalisation which works for me, there are few situations I cannot meet with an appropriate response. What we are talking about is balance, the equilibrium between these two factors, imitation, presentation. My claim is that once you understand what you see in terms of the trout's feeding behaviour, then you enhance your chances. The problems are when there is no surface activity – for most intelligent anglers can interpret that – then you have to make informed guesses at what is happening in the depths.

Again, there are some simplicities. For example, the lake of Loweswater is renowned for producing enormous hatches of mayfly and sedge which are not taken on the surface. This is a well recorded phenomenon, I have heard it time and time again. It follows that here the trout are accustomed to intercepting the nymphs at a lower level, catching them when they are ascending. Now, seeing the surface flies, it's tempting to fish imitations on or close to the surface, but another friend who did the sensible thing, fished a nymph mid-water, nearly lost his rod with a savage take, for there are fine wild brownies in that water.

It was once alleged that the editor of a popular tabloid newspaper thought 'erudite' was a form of glue. There is a danger of erudition, I must avoid it, for the happy truth is that the most successful fly fishers stick to the basic simplicities. Once you have decided where and how to fish a nymph on still water, persistence brings its reward. In a sense it can be the most frustrating exercise, like an author, lacking inspiration, staring at a blank sheet of paper. Many is the time I have stared at the blank surface of the water, retrieving the line over and over again, and longing to get back to the more exciting tactics of surface fishing. That is nymph fishing. It may seem as if the fish return is the poorer because it can be such slow and patient work, 'like watching grass grow'. The secret is to fit it into your tactical life and do not be discouraged when fishing in waters which are traditional to other methods, as in the far North and Islands.

And remember this simplicity. You have to find brown trout. They will not find you. This is the one huge difference between nymph fishing on a stocked southern rainbow water and a natural brown trout loch or lake in a remoter area. Here, in the 'fat' South we are used to picking our spot, hoping that cruising fish will pass by. On the brown trout water it's not like that, you must prospect. And that's good, for it means you are forced to read the water, to weigh up weed-beds, wind direction, nature of the lake floor and so on. So much rainbow trout fishing has become a mindless routine, chuck out a lure, drag it back.

This change in habit doesn't make you a member of Mensa. Once you solve a riddle you'll be astonished at how simple is the answer, and never be shy to ask a regular angler to your strange water. The same flies have been hatching in the same place for years and years, their history is known, the copies of those flies are known, the way the fish take them is known. It can be as simple as that.

Standard Dry Fly

Although I have already dealt with tactics for fishing the large floaters, it is useful to discuss what might be described as 'normal' dry fly fishing. This means copying the flies of average size, sedges, olives, buzzers and various terrestrials.

In my very early days of still water fly fishing I caught my trout entirely by this method, and I must explain this accident, for that is what it was. Although I related my personal fly fishing history in a previous book[1], I will briefly recapitulate. Towards the end of the last war I was hurt in the bombing and recuperated on a farm in the Weald of Kent. Seeking permission to fish on a nearby stream the farmer insisted that he only allowed dry fly fishers to make use of the fishery, and on expressing my ignorance, he gave me my very first instruction so that I became a purist, quite unwittingly. When the Weirwood reservoir opened before 1958 my very first visits were 'dry fly only' but quite successful, for I managed to take some 'limit bags' even though the annual stocking in those days of light fishing was a fraction of today's. If memory serves me aright, I think some three thousand trout – mostly browns – were introduced in the first year, and Authority mistakenly assumed that these would breed a wild stock to save them costs in subsequent seasons. Fishing was extremely hard the following year. To be kind to Authority, there was little previous experience of still water stocking, and as rod pressure was very low, at first anyway, the ratio of fish per angler was reasonable. Weekdays found just two or three bank anglers to some 120 acres of water.

My tactic was to arrive before sun-up. Again, this was also in the days of light bailiffing and in the absence of a permit dispenser I had to tramp through the deserted pumping station, 'hollering'. Eventually an employee would be persuaded to unlock the hut and sell me the ticket, and then in the dark, I would walk about a mile along the bank to where some weed beds stretched out from the margins, for at dawn trout would be seen to take small gnats there. My stream 'Grey Duster' served well for these fish, brown trout of about a pound-and-a-half.

It was exciting stuff. The first thing to do was to stretch the silk line along a fence, rub it clean, and then work mucilin thoroughly into it with the fingers. My first rod was an old Gold Medal which had a soft wet-fly

[1]*To Meet the First March Brown.*

140

action, a rod which I had acquired cheaply, but it was not entirely satisfactory for the work, being rather slow in setting the hook.

The Grey Duster proved to be an excellent fly to cope with all manner of tiny gnats and sand flies. I recollect it also provoked the first friendly debate I had with an angling entomologist as I claimed it to be valuable when the caenis hatched at Weirwood. These broad-winged, three tailed flies are distinctive, but of course they have white bodies, not grey. Retrospectively, I should have known that the 'behaviour' factor accounted for the success of the fly, for the caenis were seen by the trout with their bodies in shadow, darkened down by the view against the mirror-like surface. All I knew was that a small Grey Duster scored for me in caenis hatches. The Grey Duster still is a superb general purpose fly when trout are seen to be taking those small gnat-like flies which are too difficult to distinguish.

In those days Weirwood was rich in sedges. They collected in droves on the reed beds and the tufts of coarse grass along the margins. Perhaps it was unfair, but some crashing about in waders through this vegetation often sent some weary sedges out onto the water, sometimes to excite a rise. The agreeable aspect of still water sedges is that two copies suit nearly all of them, a Cinnamon Sedge for the vast army of brown ones and a Dark Silverhorn for the grouse tails.

To this day I prefer the age-old tyings. The Cinnamon, for instance, I used to make with a body of brown turkey herl, palmered hackle of red game cock held down with a gold wire rib, and a wing slip of brown hen, folded and tied flat. There was a final red game throat hackle to finish off this fly. Size 12 hook is about right. The important thing is to dress the wing properly. Taking a wing slip, about an inch of feather, I roll it over once, and then once again to make three layers. It is vital to lay this on top of the hook shank in a flat position so that it splits and makes a roof to the fly. This is the 'pent' wing style as possessed by the natural fly. The red hen feather is now hard to come by thanks to the wet-stripping of the modern poultry industry, but my favourite feather is the brown tail feather of the partridge which I frequently find mixed in with the more numerous speckled ones.

The Brown Silverhorn needs a separate pattern, for it is both distinctive and prolific on many still water fisheries. The dressing style is the same, but I make the body with a waxed olive tying thread, the body and throat hackles are a dark Furnace cock, the body one being trapped by a gold wire rib. The wing is also folded as before but taken from a sepia-coloured speckled tail feather of the Grouse. I am not falling into the 'precise imitation' trap, but experience proves that Silverhorns need a distinctive separate pattern.

Grey Dusters probably serve the buzzer hatches, and I also winged my Footballer nymphs for the same purpose. To refresh your memory, the Grey Duster has a body of blue rabbit underfur spun onto brown tying thread with a badger cock hackle for the legs and tail, simplicity itself, but do not fear to use it on very small sizes. If it is dressed on the curved grub-style of hook the wide gape compensates for the smaller sizes, down to 18, or even 20 if you have the eyes for it, though my general use was in the size 16 range.

Buzzer hatches are probably the most fruitful times for still water fly fishers, and the technique of wind-drifting tiny muddlers (and nymphs) is deadly. There is one specialised buzzer which has also killed well for me on occasion, and I call it the 'skimmer'. It is tiny, with a bright green body and as its name implies, it skims very quickly close to the water. There is an old favourite pattern, the Arrow Fly, which is in with a shout. The fly is also simple to make, for a stiff white hackle is palmered over a bright green body, choice of material being wool, herl, fluo or otherwise. The tactic is to retrieve this fly smartly.

The Pond and Lake Olive Duns resemble each other closely, both can be served by the Greenwell, and although my perfectionist tutor insisted on upright split wings, I long since replaced them with a second hackle. The trick is to follow my river practice, dress on a grub hook for its wide gape, and make the traditional body a gold-wire ribbed yellow thread. A hefty bunch of furnace cock whisks are tied downwards on the bend so that they hit the water to help flotation. The normal furnace cock hackle is wound at the throat, and a blue dun cock feather is reversed through it to splay the legs, again for buoyancy and visibility. Of course, an option is to make all floaters as palmers or dress them as bivisibles with a hackle at both the throat and hook bend. I prefer my style, and I hope the smoky, blue dun shadow wound through the furnace gives a winged effect.

Whilst I emphasise the importance of presentation, it must be married sensibly to 'the proper fly' as that great water bailiff, William Lunn pointed out – *'the proper fly, fished in the proper way usually brings the proper result . . .'* to paraphrase his wisdom. We discover particular natural flies on particular waters. Thus I would have been caught out at Two Lakes in my first year as I had never before, nor since, encountered the Sepia Duns and I raided the fly box of the late Oliver Kite. A dark brown herl with a dark brown hackle saved the day. I have only once seen a reasonable fall of small spent gnats, the red variety of the olive duns, and this was at Peckham's Copse where a Lunn's Particular from my chalk-stream box came to hand. One dry fly is vital, that is a simple black gnat. I doubt it matters which combination of materials you use. My preference is the Williams dressing, whisks and legs of black cock, the body of black – herl or floss – with a silver rib. It was such a fly that tempted my own favourite capture, not the best, but the Cow Green beauty.

It might even be an entomologist's nightmare to identity all of the black naturals which excite still water brown trout. Pride of place goes to the buzzer. The hawthorn fly may be blown onto the margins, given the right trees nearby, and this in early season, April and May. Above the heather line, on the moors, August will bring the spent heather beetles, and although a plain black fly deceives well enough you may add a dash of red to imitate the scarlet legs of this little beast. There are other candidates, but the black gnat is a fail-me-never fly when, as even honest experts will admit, you simply do not know what flies the fish are taking.

I admit to carrying one other pattern, a Heather Moth, for in high moorlands, moths are active by day. My pattern is a light blue dun cock hackle palmered over a pheasant-tail body ribbed with fine gold wire.

It's lucky that the 'purism' of days gone by has disappeared, for otherwise we might be embroiled in a discussion as to what exactly is a dry fly, for I sometimes read of competition winners claiming that they had been victorious with the floating fly when it was, perhaps an emerger. It matters not from a tactical viewpoint, the surface film is a food-trap from which trout profit. The simplest emerger, when 'caught short' is made by clipping the dry-fly hackle back to a very short stubble, then greasing it well. It signifies, too, that a top-dropper, similarly anointed, is fishing as a dry fly.

I have also read a theory that when the flat calm descends, this is the time for the dry fly, the angler being excited by the feeding-rings of the trout as far as the eye can see. It is about the hardest time to use a floater. I would then choose a sub-surface nymph. The reason is obvious, that the leader stands out like a cart-rope on the surface film, and even using the 'invisible' modern leader materials, copolymer or fluo-carbon, it is very hard to tempt the fish. The perfectionist will advise that the last few inches of the leader should be degreased, but then it is almost impossible to prevent the fly-floatant from creeping on to the leader.

For me, the ripple is almost essential. I have seen trout feeding many times all round my floating fly in a calm, only to snaffle it as soon as a breeze started up to break the surface film. If I had to choose an ideal, this would be fishing along a bank, a gentle wind behind, with no great light, say of an evening or early morning. The ideal would be to cast the line across the intervening calm, to put the floater a yard or two onto the ripple, fifteen to twenty yards out would be perfect. For reasons I do not understand, trout love to catch their surface food at that place.

If I were a fresh-water biologist I expect I could explain why some still waters produce a population of free surface rising fish where it's fun to fish the floating fly. I know of other lakes which produce masses of surface fly which do not excite the trout to any extent, just an occasional rise, far out. Would I be unkind as citing Loweswater as one of this latter type? Or perhaps the Cross Lochs in Sutherland? Clearly, the trout either prefer to feed below the surface, or, as I suspect, they harvest nymphs so quickly that they become satiated. One of the unresolved mysteries of trout behaviour is their feeding rate. When fishing Two Lakes, the owner, Alex Behrends, could tell by the intensity, or otherwise, of the feeding reaction to the food he scattered in his feeding pens what sort of a day it would be for the anglers on his lakes.

This is not conjecture on my part, for happily, the lakes which are good for dry fly fishing are known, and it is pleasurable to visit them with the floating fly, even to discipline oneself to taking only the dry fly box along. Having said that, I prefer to use the floater as a tactical option to suit appropriate conditions.

Most fly fishers may be familiar with the 'snake roll' which I use to take a dry fly from the surface of the water without drowning it when I need to make a sudden change of distance and direction. I add some notes for those who may be fearful of making a powerful circular movement of the rod as a variation of the 'back cast'.

The rod is raised to about sixty degrees. Then a vigorous and wide circular movement of the rod is made *towards the body* to sweep a wide loop along the line. The fly shoots almost vertically into the air. It is important to complete a full circle with the rod so that the casting hand finishes level with or even above the head, where it is 'stopped' and no further lay-back should be made as flexion will be lost. The line goes back and high, the fly being taken safely away from the body, and after the normal pause the forward cast is made to the new target.

It is understood that this is a variation of the back cast, and a problem with some new casters is that they are fearful of applying appropriate power to the casting action. I also mention that it is far easier to accomplish with a double taper fly line than with a line of a different profile.

You will discover the snake roll for taking a fly smartly off the water without drowning it. It is also a useful way of making swift changes of distance and direction. Occasionally there is a feeding frenzy when I switch between a number of targets within casting range, having a refusal, or pricking a fish, then going for another. This is when the snake roll comes into its own, it saves time in avoiding frequent mopping of soggy flies and reanointing them with floatant.

My own ultra-light line rod is a boon when fishing smaller floaters on fine leader points. Large fish can be handled with patience, those, the weights of which are far in excess of the leader's resistance, for axiomatically, small flies require fine leader points. Given the correct test-curve of the rod and a goodly area of water, even double figure fish can be mastered, as two monsters caught by acquaintances prove, namely a ten pound plus from Dever Springs and one over eleven pounds from Loch Leven. In fact a powerful, stiff rod is more likely to break off a fine leader point. Of course, the new leader materials mitigate this problem, but even so we should never equate the claimed breaking strength of leader material with the pressure which it will withstand from a sudden impact, the sudden surface 'take' for example.

I have separated what was once termed 'true' dry fly fishing from other surface tactics, the use of large floaters, wake flies, dapping, hatching nymphs (emergers) and even the working of a top dropper in the surface film, as it is a distinct tactical choice.

There is yet a controversy, often discussed in the angling press, as to whether to work the fly or not. We have to go back to Pooh Sticks! Watch! A dragging fly is not refused on a lake as it is on a stream (please don't quote freshly stocked stream rainbows as exceptions). Trout in still waters will gladly accept floating flies which are both retrieved, or wind-drifted. Often trial and error will provide the guide. Observation will indicate the direction of drift. Sometimes hatching flies are active in getting away in warm airs which dry their new wings quickly. A cold surface slows them down, and even in sunny conditions the breeze on the surface may be chilly. An overcast muggy day with little wind also slows down hatching, the surface film grows sticky and fish are seen picking off emerging flies in a leisurely way. The way in which the fish takes the fly gives clues to the careful observer.

Easier to spot is the way in which trout anticipate the fall of terrestrial flies off a lee shore. The strength of the wind, quantity of the fly, dictate within a few yards where the rise will be. This is one of simplest of tactical choices, as well as one of the most successful. It embarrasses me to write these words, it is the egg-sucking Grandma syndrome. I well recollect an August day at Cow Green, sunny with broken cloud and the season when the Heather Beetles were blown onto the water in large numbers. Though spent, they float well, they can be seen drifting far out. Plain common sense, to find a place with heather behind, the wind from that direction, and throwing a black floater into the ripple in front. In my fishing life I have profited from such a simple situation with various floaters, Daddies at Hundland loch in Orkney, moths at Blagdon, winged black ants at Darwell, and red ones at Two Lakes. These are samples of remembered times from many. Terrestrials are very important, the wind drift onto the lee margins can provide good bags and the floating fly is the primary choice, it is what the trout expect to see.

Of course, tackle make-up falls within the orbits of budget and preference. I use my 9.6-foot ultra-light *Brightwater* rod with a d.t 3 floating line. For dry fly work I prefer a tapered knotless leader of 12 feet, dulled nylon if I can get it. Given a choice, I like a mahogany colour. True dry fly work is the single fly, but why not have a nymph on the point and a floater on a dropper? I confess I am using sections of fluo carbon material, I am somewhat cautious about its impact strength, but the test curve of my rod design gives a shock absorber effect. It is too early to compare catches with regular nylons, but the 'invisibility' is a seduction isn't it?

Snake rolls will cut down on fly drying, but I admit that a simple paper tissue beats medicinal compounds and Ghink is my preferred unguent for the fly.

I stress again the value of my neo-Ritz high-line, high speed cast simply because it delivers the fly more accurately and more swiftly than old-fashioned elbow casting. It is a boon for targeting fish with the dry fly.

I must add a word on striking, for that, too has its controversy, the oft-advised 'God save the Queen' pause. On still water there's often a slackness between rod and fly, so I always hit a rise immediately with the smaller floaters. I do not use the modern fly line with absolutely no stretch, I prefer a cushioning effect in my tackle system, but that, again is choice. In casting, perhaps a weight-forward line will give slightly greater distance to some anglers but it lacks the versatility in the rolling off and snake rolling of the double taper. A small point, the popular hollow-braided nylon tippets for fly lines are anathema for dry fly work as they sink the line tip too much, giving a loss of contact in striking. I simply strip the plastic coating from the line, doubling back the core to whip down to a slender loop. This is best for all ultra-fine fly lines with fine tips.

Now, if you have discovered a change of emphasis in this section, a move towards imitation, then you are right. Is it hypocrisy? Hypocrisy may be an underrated quality without which political and social life would fall apart, but I plead not guilty. In fishing flies below the surface we are involved far more in activity, everything is moving and the fish are keyed to that in their search for food. The floating natural fly usually allows fish to examine more closely. In those early days at Weirwood I sometimes saw a trout come up under a fly literally to examine it. I was hypnotised by seeing the eye of the fish shining under the fly for a short moment, sometimes taking it, sometimes refusing it. So, yes, I think the dry fly man does need a somewhat larger armoury, related more closely to the natural counterparts. Consider this. We know from experience that in the rough and tumble of a northern stream that when March Browns are hatching the fish will gladly accept a simple Partridge & Orange spider tumbling in the current, but if you were going after the same trout on the surface, then experience tells you that you must make a different sort of a fly with more attention to detail. It is still another aspect of behaviour, isn't it? The golden rule, we must anticipate how the fish expects to see the fly; get it right, success.

A (above)

B (left)

Photograph (A) shows the arm and wrist position at the start of the cast with the rod tip pointing low to the water, the wrist is cocked forwards (closed position) with the rod butt touching the forearm. Note – the arm is comfortably bent at the elbow.

Photograph (B) shows the rod and arm position at the summit of the back cast when the rod has been 'stopped' by thumb pressure. The rod butt is not more than three inches from the forearm (open wrist position). This results in a high, fast line with a 'narrow loop'. It gives great accuracy with a fine line, even in adverse wind.

*The rod is thrown in an upwards arc from the shoulder, **not** backwards from the elbow.*

The rod is held as described with the tip pointing low to the water.

The arm is then raised smartly from the shoulder so that the comes high, level with, or above the head.

The sequences:

BOTTOM RIGHT:
After the pause to allow the line to extend behind into the back-c the rod is then punched smartly forward from the shoulder and wrist also snaps smartly forward, sending the line-turnover narrow loop above the water. The line unrolls, and as it falls straight, accurate direction it is followed down by the rod tip. forward-cast action is much like a boxer's short arm jab from shoulder.

elbow does not flex further during this lifting action. The wrist *s* to open **immediately** *the rod starts to move into the back-*, *but not more than three inches. This is a sharp, fast action.*

When the rod is stopped it should be firmly locked by thumb pressure. The timing of the wrist action is vital, earlier than in the traditional 'elbow' cast. It is a mistake to open the wrist later and wider as this gives a slow, low line with a wide loop. With practice, a progressive acceleration can be achieved to avoid an inelegant 'snatch off' the surface of the water.

THE KITE DRY FLIES

From top, left to right

Imperial, dark version for later and early season
Purple thread body – heron herl, redoubled at thorax, author prefers a darker blue dun herl from pigeon secondary wing feather.
Hackle and tail whisks – dark blue dun cock.

Imperial, lighter version for summer
Purple thread body – lighter grey heron herl, redoubled at thorax as above.
Hackle and tail whisks – pale blue dun cock.

Pale Water Dun
Body – white goose herl, but author prefers a very pale olive, style as above.
Hackles and whisks – white cock, but author prefers a honey or very pale ginger.

Ditch Dun
Body – medium olive dyed goose herl, Kite style.
Hackle and whisks – medium blue dun cock.

Sepia Dun
Body – dyed sepia (dark brown) goose herl.
Hackle and whisks – dyed sepia cock.

Apricot Spinner
Body – goose herl dyed apricot, Kite style.
Hackle and whisks – honey dun cock, or ginger.

Hawthorn Fly
Body – any good black herl, goose, crow etc, Kite style.
Hackle and whisks – black cock.
Note: this fly doubles up for all black gnats.

Pheasant Tail Red Spinner
Tail whisks – white cock.
Body – Bright red tying thread, widely ribbed with cock pheasant tail herl, doubled up at thorax.
Hackle – rich foxy-red game cock.

GEOFFREY BUCKNALL'S FAST WATER DRY FLIES

From top, left to right

Fast Water March Brown
Hook – Curved grub or Yorkshire sedge style.
*Tail whisks, hefty bunch of red game cock fibres tied on bend
to slope down to touch the water.*
*Body – thin strip of underbark from birch tree, ribbed
brown button thread.*
Hackles – (1) white cock, (2) longer brown partridge in front.

Bronze Spinner
Hook – as above.
Whisks – red game cock.
*Body – strip of bark from Tibetan Cherry tree wound over
yellow tying thread, ribbed fine copper wire.*
*Hackles – red game cock with blue dun cock hackle reversed
and counter-wound through it to splay the legs.*

Greenwell Variant
Hook – as above.
Whisks – Greenwell cock hackle.
Body – fluo yellow floss, ribbed fine round gold tinsel.
*Hackles – Greenwell cock hackle with blue dun cock hackle
reversed and counter-wound.*

Ginger Quill
Hook – as left.
Whisks – ginger cock hackles as above.
Body – stripped peacock herl quill, ribbed white tying thread.
*Hackles – ginger cock hackle with blue dun cock hackle
reversed and counter-wound.*

Leckford Professor (Cow's Arse)
Hook – as left.
*Hackles – red game cock at rear of hook, white cock hackle
wound in front.*
Body – rabbit's fur, ribbed fine silver oval tinsel.

Note: the important aspect of these flies is the style, and you may dress your own favourite dry flies in a similar
style for fishing fast water.

GEOFFREY BUCKNALL'S DRIFT FLIES

These flies, usually dressed small on normal dry fly hooks, are virtually simplified and miniaturised muddlers. The colours are chosen to copy the appropriate hatching buzzers on still water, and they drift with the wind. The bodies are made either from fluo, red green, olive orange etc., or black floss or a dubbed hare's ear, all suitably ribbed with fine round tinsel. It is important to use a hollow fine bucktail which is spun round the hook shank at the head then clipped short. These flies copy the buzzer pupae as they are hatching in the surface film.

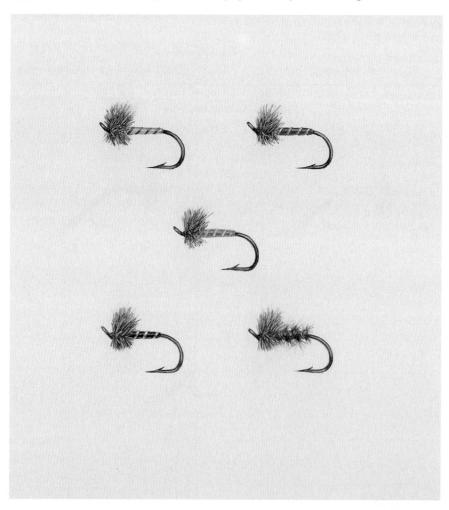

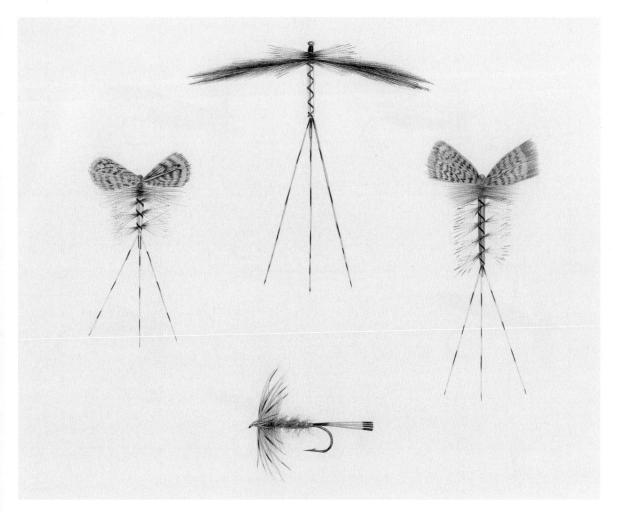

TAYLOR MAYFLIES

From top, left to right

Taylor's Yellow Champion
Hook – standard dry mayfly hook 10 to 12.
Tail whisks – three strands from golden pheasant tail.
Body – bright yellow floss, ribbed black button thread.
Body hackle – badger cock, short.
Throat hackle – yellow cock.
*Wings – brown partridge hackles dyed yellow drake tied
forward with narrow splay.*

Taylor's Green Champion
Top, far right
Hook – as above.
Tail whisks – as above.
Body – apple green floss, ribbed black button thread.
Body hackle – as above.
Throat hackle – olive cock.
Wings – as above but dyed green drake.
Note: a further shorter badger cock can be tightly
wound at the throat before the dyed cock hackle if
extra buoyancy is needed, say in fast water.

Taylor's Spent Black Drake
Top, central
Hook – as left
Tail whisks – as left
*Body – Fluo white floss, ribbed fine scarlet fluo floss but
counter wound with black button thread.*
Hackle – lightly wound badger cock.
Wings – two pairs of black cock hackle points tied spent.

Olive (Mayfly) Bumble
Hook – long shanked d/e 12 to 8.
Tail – bunch GP tippet.
Body – olive dubbing, ribbed fine gold oval tinsel.
*Hackles – one or two dyed olive cock with French partridge
dyed golden olive in front, longer.*
Note: a general purpose mayfly for a big wave!

GEOFFREY BUCKNALL'S WAKE FLIES

From top, left to right

Light Orange Underwing Moth
Hook – long-shanked lure hook, size 8.
Body – six twisted strands bronze peacock herl over a sliver
of cork, orange fluo floss at tail end of hook.
Hackles – two long-fibred red game cock.
Wing – a broad strip of any light browny-grey feather, tied
flat.

Dark Version of above
This is an optional version dressed exactly the same but
with a wing of a darker feather.

White Moth
Hook – as above.
Fluo orange butt – as above.
Body – white suede chenille.
Hackles – two white cock hackles.
Wing – white duck or goose dressed as above.

Hammond's Adopted
Hook – as above.
Body – white suede chenille.
Hackle and wings – as for Orange Underwings and Hoolet.

Great Red Sedge (Murrough)
Hook – as left.
Body – rusty-brown suede chenille or dubbing with fluo
orange floss butt.
Wings – a thick bunch of red game cock fibres, long and
dressed flat.
Hackles – two long red game cock hackles.
Note: the bottom fly is the normal, standard Hoolet
without the fluo butts of the two Orange Underwings.
Patterns with chenille bodies do not need cork
underbodies, which would make them too bulky, but
the chenille can be treated with a floatant or mucilin
when the fly is made.

Sticklebackers

It is a common error in the mind of many fly fishers to identify lure fishing as the same thing as catching trout which are feeding on fry. This is not the case. Fry feeding is a definite, preoccupied feeding pattern of behaviour and it needs an appropriate tactic. Lure fishing, by contrast, is a straightforward provocation.

An example of this difference was demonstrated many years ago when Blagdon was stocked with a higher ratio of brown trout, and I was fishing in the early hours before sun-up. In those days there were far fewer anglers on the bank. It is noticeable, when fishing very early, that trout come close in to the tranquil margins, but move out as soon as the boats go out and the majority of late-rising anglers arrive.

In early summer the fry have grown to a reasonable size, say an inch or so, and these fish hover in dark clouds around weed fronds. It was always an exciting experience to see the arrowing furrows of the charging trout terminating in angry swirls as they turned on the scattering shoals. The trout drive the fry against barriers, usually weed-bed walls, but I have seen trout chasing the fry against the banks even to the extent that the dorsals and backs of the pursuers came through the surface, nearly beaching the trout. The fry would scatter in all directions, breaking the surface in their anxiety to escape. It was, and still is, plain common sense to profit from this activity, either from the shore, or from the boat when weed beds are further out as in extensive, shallower bays.

As a matter of interest, marine biologists have studied the behaviour of shoals of smaller fish being attacked by larger predators such as shark. The activity I have described is typical when the shoals are attacked either close to the surface or in shallow water, the fish scatter, and they break the surface. When the shoals are attacked in deep water the behaviour pattern is different, the fish compress themselves together into a tight mass, presenting an image much like the shield wall of foot soldiers in ancient times. Then it is only the stray individualist which is picked off. There has been too little research done in freshwater to know if this also happens in our lakes and reservoirs, but it would not be an unlikely scenario.

If it is accepted that fry feeding is a distinctive feeding behaviour then it follows that although a standard lure will provoke a trout dashing at a shoal of tiddlers, a more accurate copy of the prey will be more successful, so much so that this is one of the occasions when success is almost guaranteed because the predator is in a feeding frenzy.

There have been several attempts to copy the stickleback[1] which have had variable success rates. Post-war, the most popular was Ivens's Jersey Herd. This had a minnow-shaped body, achieved by wrapping a floss underbody along the shank and covering it with the coppery tinsel from the bottle top of the Jersey Herd milk. This made sense for this tinsel was only moderately garish in comparison to the commercially applied lurex and metallic tinsel which soon replaced it. I always regarded the Jersey Herd as a lure rather than as a fry imitation simply because nature disguises the tiddlers with drab colouring to hide them against weed beds and the like.

Ken Sinfoil, a bailiff at the Weirwood reservoir, and later at Bewl water, recognised this with his own fry imitation, close in appearance to the stickleback. The basis of his invention was a body of clear polythene with a tuft of barred teal feather as a wing. The late Richard Walker took this a stage further with his intelligent Polystickle, a prodigious trout slayer in its day which probably fell out of favour for two reasons. The first was simply that unthinking anglers did not separate in their minds the provocative lure like the Dognobbler from a true copy of small fish. The second reason was that the automatic routine of stripping sunk lures, hour after hour, produced rainbow trout from the increasingly higher stocked fisheries. This lure stripping is entirely different to the tactic of searching out the sticklebacking brown trout and attacking it with a true imitation.

The Polystickle also had a body of clear plastic overlaying the hook shank, and a silver or gold hook would enhance the effect. At the throat there would be an underlay of a fluo red floss which shone through the plastic. This was to copy the colouration which the male stickleback assumes as its breeding finery in spring. The back of the Polystickle was made from raffine, a man-made raffia substitute for gardeners available in a choice of colours, black, brown, green etc. The trick was to moisten the raffine before tying it down from head to tail, varnishing it to make it glisten, and to shape it into a tail beyond the hook bend. A beard of orange or red cock hackle completed this simple, but effective fry-copy. The result was an effective copy of those 'redthroats' which excited us when young on our jam jar forays to village ponds.

I first became impressed with the need for a rather drab stickleback imitation when fishing one morning along the banks of Chew reservoir, coming across a number of brownies beating up a weed bed for fry. This activity is usually ferocious, the intent of the predators being to stun one or two tiddlers on each charge. The trout plunge in, grab a meal or two, then circle around in the deeper water to allow things to settle down again before they make another charge. It is simplicity itself to intercept the attacker, and as I have remarked, it is unusual not to do well.

[1]The term stickleback is used loosely in my text to describe all small bait-fish.

On this occasion I had neither lure nor fry imitation in my box. Wading quietly out towards the area of activity, I looked into the clear water and noting the drab appearance of the prey I chose an Ivens's Green & Brown nymph as being the closest copy. The short of it was that within half an hour or so I had landed a limit bag of good brownies.

Thinking about this later at my fly dressing bench it struck me as sensible to take the Green & Brown colouration and put it into a minnowy shape, none better than the profile of the Jersey Herd. This is how I made it: I first lapped a lure hook with an underbody of brown floss, shaping it like a small fish. Over this I wound alternate strands of green and brown ostrich herl, ribbed with a fine gold tinsel. I had tied on a bunch of bronze peacock herl, six or eight strands at the tail, leaving them to protrude, and I carried them over the back of the fly. I doubled a dark olive hackle and wound it at the head as in Ivens's own Jersey Herd, and finished off with a few turns of peacock herl in front for the head.

For many years I used the two Jersey variations, the standard copper-bodied one for fry-fishing in bright sunlight when the rays would light up the small fish and shallows, and under dull skies, my green and brown pattern would be more effective. My friends unkindly labelled this latter version the Jersey Turd. Nevertheless it proved to be a deadly killer, especially at first light along the banks before the boats go out.

Of course, fry fishing is a tactic suited to bank and boat alike. The strategy is simple, a normal leader is used, and I prefer the single fly. It is not sensible to strip quickly as in popular lure fishing, for although tiddlers shoot away when charged, the trout grab ones which are dazed by the impact of the assault, they are the prey they are looking for. Often I had only to move the fly a foot or two slowly to produce 'a take'. In spring and early summer the floating line suits as the shoals are usually in the shallows which are sheltered by weed growth, though as the season progresses and the tiddlers grow, naturally they scatter and migrate to deeper water. So I stress that I am discussing a planned, imitative tactic, not the routine and tedious lure stripping monotony one sees performed by anglers standing in boats on reservoirs.

There remain some less-important debating points to consider. Is it worth making more precise imitations of certain fry, say perch or roach? Personally I doubt it, though Sinfoil's fry was aimed at copying the perch fry which predominated in Weirwood reservoir when he managed it. My belief, once again, is that it is the behaviour pattern of the food-form which is the key to success.

The second query is whether or not this tactic overlaps for *ferox* trout? This I do not know for certain as I have no record of taking a distinctive *ferox* when using this tactic, my captures have always been the run-of-the-mill brown trout of the fisheries. The reason is probably that the major successes for me were in stocked reservoirs when brown trout were favoured more than the rainbow, obviously some years ago. Rainbows, too, are sticklebackers, I took my share. The *ferox* trout is rather a feature of wild brown trout lakes with a population of numerous, stunted trout. Whether or not stocked brownies in reservoirs go on to produce a minority of fish which could be termed as *ferox* is something I have not discovered. The *ferox* seems to be a lonesome individual, sticklebackers are often, and untypically, in packs, working in concert. *Ferox* migrate into shallows, characteristically when char come out of the depths into shallow water to spawn, and they hunt individually, driving up from the depths to trap surface feeding fish, perhaps in the evening rise. This is when we see those amazing fountains of water shooting upwards. So, my opinion is that the sticklebacking trout is one of the normal stock, being an opportunist, whereas the *ferox* has established a definite way of life.

A final word for those purist souls who might take me to task. A lure and a true fry imitation are simply wet flies writ large and I have no twinges of conscience in using them. My criticism of routine lure stripping is that it is unintelligent and boring, but occasionally, believe it or not, it can be a tactic of choice. I recount here an instance, when I was a syndicate member at Hanningfield reservoir before it became a ticket water. In summer time there would appear for a fortnight or so a layer of grass-green algae which used to occupy the top few feet of the water, below which the water was clear. The effect was to make the fish sluggish and dour, probably because this phytoplankton de-oxygenated the water. The only chance of a fish was to strip a lure on a sinking line below the algae layer. There was not, and could not be any chance of taking a fish on a floating line with 'normal' fly. The fish were too apathetic to come to a sunk nymph, but a brightly coloured lure would provoke the odd fish lying near to the lake floor. Now, that was an intelligent choice of tactic.

Criticism is too strong a word to apply to my preference for tactical fishing as against, say routine lure stripping simply because it adds a savour to our sport. This is why I prefer proper trout fishing to salmon fishing because the latter is entirely mechanical. Tactical trout fishing brings an intellectual element into the sport. In the end, though, a tolerant and democratic attitude must prevail, for the essence of fishing is to give pleasure, however sadly it is taken. Once a trout man starts to think about his fishing, this implies observation and it widens the pleasure when a thought-out tactic succeeds. Lures and fry imitations have their place in my armoury.

Buzzers

I would guess that there is one scientific term with which every still water fly fisher is familiar, that is *Chironomid*, though we colloquially refer to these insects as buzzers. It is probable that taken on average throughout the fishing season they form the largest part of insect protein ingested by the trout. Buzzers are in reality non-stinging gnats, and there are over 500 distinct species of them in British still waters, so many that I expect some of them remain to be classified. Their importance deserves a chapter of its own.

It is a happy coincidence to know that they survive in different conditions of lake floor, even unfriendly sand, for example. Silt, though, is one of their favourite habitats, and the larval forms can happily exist in tunnels below water of greater depth than would suit other forms of trout food. This explains why I can catch fish when casting from the shore line at Scarhouse, out across water which plunges down to a great depth. There are several reservoirs like this, gashes torn into deep valleys where the buzzer is a saving grace. In passing, the buzzer larvae are more resistant to sewage pollution than other insect forms.

The coarse angler recognises the buzzer larvae as the bloodworm bait, and this colouration is due to the fact that it contains haemoglobin which gives our own blood its redness. A glance into a water butt, especially an old one, shows you how they move by wriggling and lashing their bodies, a very difficult motion to copy, though some inventive fly dressers attach long tails of scarlet plastic or feather to their imitations. I did this in the past, and I had some modest success when fishing at Hanningfield reservoir over a plateau of silt deposited in front of the entrance of the River Chelmer. Trout taken there had their lips smothered in the red jelly much like a small boy raiding the strawberry jam in the larder. It is one of the rare occasions when I have known trout to rummage like a bream or tench to suck the bloodworms out of their burrows, and, in common with those coarse fish, tell-tale bubbles burst on the surface of the water, a give-away.

Reverting to Scarhouse, the importance of the buzzer in trout diet also reveals the tolerance to conditions which are low in temperature and light, for a notice warning visitors not to bathe also tells us that the water will never rise above 12 degrees, even in the height of summer. If this is coupled to the evidence that on the beds of many lakes the buzzer larvae constitute up to 75% of the insect life, then the importance of this to anglers is self evident. In passing, they also figure in the food chains of rivers, and I was once embarrassed to be told at a meeting of a chalk stream syndicate of which I was a member, that another rod was to be disciplined as he had been successfully fishing with my Footballer nymph, contrary to the 'dry fly only rule' operating at that time.

Strangely, there is not a great wealth of scientific research and information about buzzers even though their clogging of filters in pumping stations at reservoirs was one of the motivations for trout stocking, but a cursory observation seems to indicate that the larval burrowers come in two main colours, the spectacular scarlet livery, or an amber hue. We are lucky in that we can copy each life cycle stage of the creature, and even though the 'bloodworm' is probably the least successful, it can be simulated. A simple pattern has a transparent, red plastic material wrapped around a hook shank with a trailing tail of scarlet feather or plastic. A small head of red herl is added and patient, deep fishing with this results in captures.

The famous buzzer hatches are caused when the pupae, which are already mature, rise to the surface to hatch into the familiar adult midges. This is where the imitationist encounters a huge problem, for the colour and size range is enormous. Happily, most lakes have identifiable species. A few examples: I met a bright red buzzer at Darwell, in Sussex, but Blagdon presented me with a gingery brown one. Hanningfield was host to the small green and olive varieties. The most widespread two varieties are firstly the black adult, it turns up almost everywhere and is common on moorland lakes and lochs, and secondly, the orange-silver variety is widespread. Then there is a size variation, from tiny pinheads to the large ones, locally called 'Racehorses' at Chew.

The pupae can be fished at any depth, they are preyed on from the lake floor to the surface, but the typical and profitable buzzer rise is when the pupae are caught in the surface film, waiting for their shucks to break open which they achieve by pumping in air. They then have to dry off, gather strength to break free from the clinging surface film. Of course, given wind, sun and broken water, they get away reasonably quickly, but when the surface is flat and sticky, then the escape is slow. This latter demonstrates the typical evening buzzer rise, the unhurried humping of the fish through the surface film.

It is ironically amusing to read of the frustration of Blagdon fishers in days long gone, for the evening 'boil' was frequently described and rarely fulfilled its promise. Those early writers failed to identify the cause, and even on my first visits to Blagdon in the late fifties I heard nearby anglers declaiming that the reasons for their failure was attributed to a rise to caenis, the so-called 'angler's curse'. When the buzzer was identified, the first copies were inexact, being fashioned from layers of olive silk ribbed with flat gold tinsel.

I believe my Footballer was probably the first accurate buzzer nymph copy to be used at Blagdon, and if I relate the story, it's not merely an exercise in oneupmanship, it describes the way in which an understanding of the buzzer can lead to success. Briefly, fishing with a friend who was a good amateur photographer, we spooned a Blagdon fish to discover it packed with pupae. We photographed some specimens and enlarged the result. This showed us a distinctively hook-shaped abdomen of black and white striations, a dark thorax and head. In retrospect I realise that the original colour of the pupae may have been bleached by digestive juice, but no matter. The copy was made by winding black and white horsehair along the shank, side by side, and from well round the hook bend. The abdomen was simply a pinch of mole's fur, topped off with a head of bronze peacock herl. On its very first outing in a buzzer rise at the lake, four nice brownies were landed fairly quickly which some kind soul reported in an angling journal.

It was not long before imitations included tufts of fine white floss for the breathing tubes and tail filaments, but, strangely they were not successful on my Footballer. I guess the reason was that we were targeting rising fish, literally throwing the nymph into the widening ring of the rise, and this was dependent on a fast entry to present it immediately below the surface film. I believe this was the key to my Footballer and again, perhaps unwittingly at first, ' behaviour' took precedence over colour. I did introduce varieties the abdomens of which were made by overlaying a clear horsehair over fluo colours of floss, red, yellow, orange, and green, as well as an all black version. To this day I see little reason to vary this dressing, for modern counterparts are very similar in structure.

Fishing the Footballer became a definitive tactic for a particular condition. The concession to the hatch was in size, and on some waters even the 18 did execution, dressing the pattern on a wide-gaped hook. Having made an accurate cast close to the fish, in the excitement, the trick was to steel oneself to making a very gentle retrieve, for if the 'take' came, it was almost straightaway. It was pretty fishing.

Although the Footballer worked well within its intended tactic, a hatching version, with a badger hackle clipped short, was not successful, and in retrospect I believe that it was simply too neat to copy the tangled impression of the adult fly struggling free from its pupal jacket and a modern copy like Shipman's emerger, with a straggly, picked out dubbing, is a much better attraction. Also, although a Footballer floater, with glassy hackle and laid-back hackle point wings did excite interest, it was usually from smaller fish with their splashy rises. But used at the right time and in the right way, the Footballer has caught me innumerable trout, even holding the record at Grafham at one time.

To recapitulate, the precise Footballer tactic was to intercept the rising fish with a very accurate cast, anticipating the direction of its rise, which probably will be upwind, but the typical humping rise brings the dorsal through the surface film showing the way the fish is going. In flat calms brown trout harvesting buzzers may well move in tight circles.

In more recent times anglers have fished buzzer nymph at mid-water and closer to the bottom, using very slim, streamlined copies, for the pupa tucks away its appendages for quick ascent – it is very vulnerable. Such a fly should be finely dressed, and a coat of a varnish-type makes it glisten. The modern text books give several excellent dressings for this tactic.

The importation of the muddler minnow from America gave me an idea for dealing with buzzers hatching swiftly in a strong wind. I made very simple and very small muddlers, using body floss, ribbing and tight deer-hair heads on size 12 or 14 hooks. These were made with different coloured bodies, based on local information or experience, and the tactic was to cast across a side-on wind, making a downwind belly by mending the line. This gives a deliberate drag to the flies, which may be fished in a team. No other retrieve action is necessary, the wind fished the flies. This is a deadly way of fishing if you find drifts of hatching buzzers being carried along the shore line within casting range, or it is effective from an anchored boat. If the hair is of good quality, tightly packed and clipped, it is unnecessary to grease these flies, they are superbly buoyant.

Undoubtedly traditional wet flies are taken in buzzer hatches. The good old Grouse & Claret is a favourite of mine when black buzzers are hatching. The buzzy-black flies used as top droppers, patterns to choice like Kate McClaren, Black Pennell, and so on, they, too are accepted as hatching buzzers, so the question arises, are the more precise imitations necessary? I expect this question would be asked frequently by those who drift-fish on lochs. It is hard to give a definitive answer, but the nearest to it would be to think about wind and water. The wind-drift is all about movement, 'bringing fish up' being the standard formula with a well-worked top dropper. I am more than happy to fish this way, it has succeeded for hundreds of years.

Sometimes, though, more precise tactics are needed, especially when bank fishing gives you a wider tactical choice as against the limitations of short-lining from a wind-driven boat on a drift. This wider tactical choice is the one advantage the bank fisher has against the greater water coverage of the boat man. It may explain in part my preference for the shore.

Dapping

I classify this unhesitatingly in the specimen hunting category, for undoubtedly this tactic has the ability to bring up large brown trout. I have described how big brown trout come in two types, the *ferox*, which develops an almost cannibal feeding habit after its fourth year, typical of still waters which have a large, stunted population. It is important to separate these big predators from what I describe as 'normal' large trout. It is to be expected that these latter are the products of richer fisheries from a food supply point of view, for they can attain good body weights within a normal life span, four to five years or so. The reasons for this are still a mystery, but trout farmers will identify some fish of the same year which grow faster than their fellows, supposedly because of their more competitive nature when it comes to feeding. It is an aspect of almost all husbandry, dog-breeders know it, though they are more concerned with the other extreme, the ne'er do well runt of the litter. Television addicts of wildlife programmes will also have this shown to them in families of all creatures where there is a dominant offspring and probably a weakling which usually fails and dies.

There is also an overlap between what I describe as a 'normal' large trout, growing faster and more successfully than the fellows in the same age group, and the true *ferox* which is much older and which can be identified by its physical characteristics to the practised eye, or later by a scale reading. I know of one or two lochs in the far North where this overlap occurs, waters which contain both the 'normal' big trout as well as the older *ferox*. I would expect to find both types of fish in, say the Badenloch system.

One of the Pennine lakes which I have known for many years, because I am attracted by its loneliness and moorland scenery as much as its fish, is Cow Green. Here I know there to be *ferox*. I have seen them in action, I have known them to be caught and sometimes hooked and lost. The land was flooded long since. In the early years the native trout coming in from the Tees and sikes grew at a grand rate as is common with newly flooded land. I must diverge here to explain that the raising and lowering of water levels, common to reservoirs, does not have the same beneficial effect. On the contrary, food supply diminishes on these occasions. In those early years, though, trout averaging over the pound were common, it was glorious fishing for those appreciative of entirely wild fish. Of course, the average weights fell as the initial rich food supply fell, and today a half pounder is a reasonable fish, quite good fun on light gear and superb eating. I did bring back some of these small fish to be used as dead bait for pike by an angling friend. On enquiring as to his success with them he shamefacedly admitted to having eaten all of them, for on sampling just one as a test of its palatability, he was so enchanted by the taste that he promptly cooked and scoffed the lot.

The fact is that as I make a pilgrimage to Cow Green every year, simply because I love the place. Now and again I take a trout which is decidedly not *ferox* but which is bigger than the run of the mill stock. Not so long ago a companion took a fish of a pound-and-three-quarters and I landed one of half-a-pound lighter, and these are bigger than the average fun-trout we expect to take here. This is why I am sceptical of those who scorn to fish 'small trout waters'. You never know.

Another strange water is Rimsdale, the farthest of the three lochs of the Badenloch system of three interconnected stillwaters. This loch has a very large population of smallish trout. Usually I fish it from the shore, and on its day a fish will come to the fly at practically every other cast. I can return over one hundred fish in a half-day's fishing. Of the three lochs Rimsdale is said to hold the largest fish. There is a small number of big-trout hunters who go there for the bigger specimens which they catch by dapping. The water is open, so wide that the conifer forestry around it gives little lee shelter. Then there is only heather moorland to the distant mountains which are still snow covered in summer. The distinction I give between *ferox* trout and normally large ones is both controversial and indistinct, because all trout from a young age feed on small fish, but they are omnivorous and do not lay up in very deep water for much of the day.

These bigger Rimsdale fish which I know are often from about six to ten pounds in weight. My friend Joe Tingle hooked one in the channel between Rimsdale and its neighbouring loch, a favourite spot for the big ones. The rod was nearly snatched from his hand, the more unexpected as we had both been twitching out pretty half-pounders. Given the wind, the wide expanse of water, dapping is an excellent tactic for bringing up the bigger fish some of which are caught this way in most seasons. You will see them in the Garvault hotel.

The tackle system is simple enough. Most dappers prefer a stiff rod simply because the fish usually hooks itself against the tight line as it dives with its fly. As with my ultra-light line system, dapping is so specialised that few rod makers provide a suitable blank, Bruce & Walker being an exception. It is true that a cheap, telescopic, holiday coarse fishing rod serves very well for the purpose, it seems to be the most popular tool for the job. When first I started to dap for sea trout I bought a twelve foot blank which was favoured by competition fly fishers. It was in three sections and I was able to find a fourth butt piece to extend this by three feet or so. The trouble was that it was a soft rod and although I had some great fun on Loch Maree for what we call 'peal' in the South, I also failed to set the hook on occasion due to its suppleness.

Although special 'blow-lines' can be bought, the best is probably normal nylon carpet yarn bought from haberdasheries, a drab green colour serving well. I tie an overhand granny knot about every yard to prevent fraying, and the fishing length is about 24 feet. The backing line is normal monofilament, say 15 lb breaking strain and these two are wound onto a normal drum-reel, the bigger the better. The leader is some eight feet of monofilament, I use 10 lb breaking strain. This all blows nicely before the wind.

The fly set-up is simple enough. Whilst some anglers knot on a wet fly at the point with the dapping fly on a dropper, I prefer to have the single floater on the point. It matters little, it is personal choice. My reason for the single fly is that you never know what's going to take hold. On sea trout lochs it might be a salmon, and these fish, with big sea trout do run into the Badenloch system from the Helmsdale river. A dropper means a knot and knots are a weaker link in the chain.

As with all flies intended for bigger fish I use a hook knot I found safe when carp fishing. It is the normal tucked blood through the eye, but the nylon is passed twice through that hook eye before the knot is finished. This is wonderfully strong. So are big carp! And it held them.

I differentiate between dapping flies I intend for migratory fish and those for big brownies. I do not know why a Maree sea trout comes to an enormous Black Pennell, but it does. There's nothing in nature it resembles. Also, I described[1] how I accidentally fashioned a buzzy, dapping version of the Teal Blue and Silver and this accounted for numerous sea trout and salmon in Wester Ross, so much so that fish charged it from yards away. I believe, though, that native brown trout prefer artificials which resemble large terrestrial flies, daddies and moths, and mayflies in season. This explains the success of Loch Ordies and KeHes on Orcadian lochs, for instance.

The mayfly bumble is described earlier. I make it bigger and buzzier for dapping. The 'big daddy' is simply a great brown bumble two hackle points of which are tied off upright to catch the wind, they act as sails, useful in light airs. These are all that is necessary, but there's no reason why you shouldn't experiment, many anglers favour the combination of red-game and white hackles, the white one being to the fore of the hook.

It makes sense to work some mucilin type of floating grease into the body of the fly when you are making it up, and a suede chenille makes an excellent body material.

The dapping technique is simplicity itself; you need a good wind to carry the fly well in front of the boat, and you dibble the fly on the wave-tops. It does require a strong arm and a steady hand to keep it on station. Many is the time I have moved the fly to one side only to see a frustrated

---

[1]See *To Meet The First March Brown.*

fish making an angry boil in the place it was a second before. Where rainbows are stocked I have noticed that they are really poor marksmen in catching a dapped fly, they sometimes miss it by a yard or more. Sea trout are best, they rarely miss, and instead of plunging like a big brownie, they run straight up the line, making me bat the centre-pin like hell to keep in touch before swivelling round to pass the line under the boat to play the fish on the other side. I usually know when I've hooked a large brownie as it dives deep, the line sings in the water.

The bugbear is the light wind, especially on those days when it falls away. The blow line falls limply, the fly doesn't work. If the boat is of ample size it makes sense to carry a made-up wet-fly rod for these occasions. Dapping is one occasion when I prefer to have a boatman, it does make the management job so much easier.

When fish are coming to the fly it gets soggy, changing it is necessary, and the hat is a good place to dry out the waterlogged failures. Happily, the carpet yarn blow line dries out very quickly indeed.

Given a strong wind, a longish normal fly rod can be adapted if there's a frustrating rise to daddy or mayfly. A very long leader will blow before the wind, if a butterfly of tissue paper is folded into it a yard or so above the fly. This helps to sail it out. I have caught well when improvising in this way. The aim in dapping is to hide the leader directly above the fly, and to move it in an attractive way on the wave tops. The fly works well directly down wind with a boatman keeping the boat side-on in a wind lane or where there is a drift of natural fly. It is easy fishing, and probably the best way of sorting out a big fish or two from lochs such as I have described.

It is easy to get into a debate about the nature of the big trout which come to the dapped fly. I cannot rule out *ferox*. One my friend Colin North took on Maree definitely had those characteristics, but in the main it seems to attract bigger fish of the 'normal' type.

Whilst I am being controversial, I do know those who prefer to impale natural flies on their hooks, mayflies, daddies, murroughs and the like. Of course they work, but in the main, artificials seem to score as well, when I've been fishing anyway, and I'm happy that this proves my dictum, that behaviour is the key.

I return to this question of dapping from the bank. It is both possible and productive, given a strong breeze from a lee shore and the ability perhaps to wade out a fair way. I have succeeded with this tactic. In autumn, for example, female daddies push their pointed abdomens into soft ground near to the shore line, lay their eggs, then in weakened condition the wind carries them onto the margin of the lake where they are eagerly snapped up. Bold fish come in quite close, given no alarm signals, and a fifteen foot rod will dap a fly up to twenty feet out.

Dapping, though, is for the big waters. Follow the lesson of this book, simplicity itself, watch or surmise where the food-drift is. The keys are the obvious ones, wind and scum lines, mayflies hatching from silt beds under lee shores, daddies being swept off grass and heather, swifts and swallows dipping the surface, or competing gulls squawking and circling, or, believe it or not, rising fish! Pocket binoculars are a boon.

Dappers love to discuss striking, earlier or later, whether to do so, or not. With my first soft rod I had to do it early and strongly, but one legend I believe to be true is that you need a stiff rod for this work, my jelly-stick lost me many a fish, and when I had a more rigid one, then, yes, the fish hooked themselves against the tight line, it was just necessary to hold 'em. I also resist the temptation to raise myself up on a boat seat, the height advantage would increase visibility. I've known this to kill a sea-trout rise stone dead. And as in all boat fishing, to stand to fish is plain folly as well as dangerous.

Where does dapping fit into my life? It isn't a first preference, but when a water has the reputation of bigger fish coming to the dap – and the Badenloch complex is a prime example – then it's worthwhile. I often fish no-kill, I am not a glass-case man, but I do have an artist friend who will turn a poor photograph into a painted marvel – true to size, I kid you not.

I add just one note, try to find a 'sea kindly' wooden boat, for a light plastic or glass craft which skates before the wind is anathema. If you really want a big fish, persist in dapping, sooner or later, you'll get your reward and some biceps of which to be proud.

The tactics discussed in this book are those which I do, or have done. There is one exception, that is the modern use of the float tube. I have no experience of this, nor do I anticipate having any in future. It is a useful tool for the modern angler and therefore deserves a place in this book. Rather than adopting a journalistic practice of rehashing material from other writers, which is certainly not my style, I asked an expert exponent of float tubing to contribute the following section, based on her own experience of fishing from such a 'personal' craft on her native lochs in Caithness and Sutherland.

Mrs Crawford is a highly experienced brown trout fly fisher, and living within shouting distance of dozens of wild brown trout lochs, she has been able to build up a business aimed at helping anglers to this fascinating area. Her experience has also been encapsulated in the guide books she has written for visiting anglers and, like myself, she is a firm believer in writing only what she does and knows, every loch she describes she has fished herself.

GB

Float Tubing for Trout Anglers

Lesley Crawford

*'Float tubing is about as close as
you can get to living with the fish'*
LCC

The first time I saw someone using a float tube I thought my loch had been invaded by a very large green toad complete with flippers and a rubber ring. On the bank this alien creature seemed dreadfully clumsy, staggering around under all his paraphernalia. However once afloat he took on an entirely different perspective. As the angler stealthily manoeuvred himself over the best trout holds, creeping up on the edges of those 'just out of reach' weed beds, I began to see definite attractions in the 'tube'. Here was the quiet, comparatively light alternative to that awkward heavy boat I had been looking for all these years. Something relatively portable and easy to use, capable of reaching those difficult inaccessible corners of the loch margins where my bank-cast fly never quite reaches. Despite the tube's odd appearance, a convert was made that day and anyway, looking silly has never bothered me before!

Ever since the first 'tube' bobbed its way on to our still waters in the early 1990s, float tubing has had a small but growing band of devotees. If you are thinking of giving it a try, and I suggest you do because it's great fun, you will need the following basic equipment. First the tube or 'belly bag' itself which will set you back £150 upward. Tubes come in various designs, the classic is of course, the round rubber ring, but there are also ones which are U shaped and these are said to allow greater freedom of leg movement. Whether circular or U shaped, choose one with a good firm high back as you will need to lean hard into this to propel yourself about. Also ensure the tube has at least two 'inner tubes' so that if one outer skin is punctured the other one remains afloat long enough for you to get ashore. Also ensure the tube has a bright orange fluorescent back because on very busy reservoirs it is easy to be hit by a fast boat if you are not very visible.

Next you require flippers or 'fins' and my diving friends inform me that the longer the fin, the less strokes required to move about. I would qualify this advice however by adding that short legged persons find long fins hard work on the calf muscles, so its swings and roundabouts on the size of fins! Most UK freshwaters are far from pleasantly temperate zones and you will also need high backed neoprene chest waders with boots or stockings attached to keep yourself dry and warm. This you wear akin to a wet suit with the flippers strapped to your feet. For safety you should also wear an adequate flotation device, preferably one of those jobs which keep arm restriction to a minimum, because initially you feel trussed up like a chicken in all this gear! Other essentials include a long rod as your centre of gravity is much lower than normal and you will need a high back cast to lengthen line. Working top droppers can be difficult when sitting so low in the water but with a 10ft plus rod you can execute this loch style technique reasonably well. I do recommend using your less treasured equipment to begin with when learning the intricacies of float tubing. It is possible to break rather a lot of equipment when first clad in tube and flippers! Also make sure your essentials like nylon and scissors are secured about your person as it's easy to lose things over the side of the tube. A floating fly box is also recommended.

Having appropriately equipped yourself it's time for your first tentative steps into the float tubing world. If you are a complete novice to this art I would recommend you take time to familiarise yourself with the techniques involved in manoeuvring the tube without taking the rod afloat, it's not as easy as it looks. One of the most difficult aspects I found was the actual getting in and out of the water. Obviously you must be able to set off and land safely so choose a shallow gently sloping shore, making sure flippers are well secured around the heel and then step into the middle of the ring. Walk down backwards into the water (you cannot walk forwards in flippers!), do up the seat straps and then simply sit down in your oversized rubbery armchair. Lean back into the tube and flip your flippers to move offshore. Next practise maintaining a 'drift' with the wind behind and how to move sideways. Different leg actions are involved in these manoeuvres and until you get the hang of them it's easy to spin round like the proverbial cork.

Once you feel confident in working the tube it's time to give the rod an airing. Make sure everything is assembled together i.e. rod, nylon, line and flies are made up before you go afloat. It can be desperately fiddly at first trying to tie knots etc. with water sloshing all around you, but you do get used to it. Being so close to the lake gives you a very different and more exciting perspective on the trout's world. Float tubing is about as close as you can get to living with the fish. In the tube you become integrated into their habitat (in fact it is said that to trout you appear to be a very fat duck) and this is the aspect of tubing I find the most unique. I don't propose now to tell you how to fish for your trout, Geoffrey will have covered this amply elsewhere, however do note techniques from a float tube vary slightly from the norm.

I mentioned that you need a long rod because you sit so low in the water and with this I would recommend using a floating line in order to be able to airialise line quickly. If you are using 'sinkers' it seems to take a lot of time and effort to draw line up to the surface and then cast it out again. This happens anyway whether you are in a boat or on the bank, however in a tube it always seems much harder on the arm muscles. Fly selection will of course be to suit the conditions, but fishing a single dry like an Elk Hair Sedge or a Stimulator, when you yourself are inches from the surface film is extraordinarily exciting. You see the trout come up and take the dry almost right under your nose and in this aspect a float tube wins hands down over conventional boat or bank fishing. In addition, you can suss out rapidly any changes in the fishes' element, especially the coming and going of a hatch. If, like me, you fish on lakes or lochs with a mayfly hatch, sitting inches from great trout gulping down the fat nymphs or exploding the water surface to snatch these upwinged flies, has got to be the best thing since fly fishing began.

When in the tube it is worthwhile trying some traditional 'loch style' with a team of wet flies. Though many devotees of 'loch style' fish a three fly cast, I prefer only two spaced 6ft apart so as not to appear related in any way. From the tube it is not necessary to try for long distance casting, a short line is perfectly adequate. Cast out and allow the tail fly to sink then draw the flies back towards you with rod parallel to the water. Just before lifting off, raise the rod tip and dibble the dropper fly along the surface. Sometimes you will get a follow and an almighty thump on the fly and, because of your close proximity to everything, a strong nerve and a steady hand is required; however that's all part of the fun. Good wet flies from the tube in my highland neck of the woods include the Silver Invicta or Grouse & Claret for the point and a Zulu or Kate McLaren on the bob.

Used properly, float tubes are a grand alternative to both the ancient leak-riddled boat or a too light fibre glass boat which cannot hold a drift. The tube's low centre of gravity makes it much less likely to tip and actually much more comfortable to sit in when compared with the hard boards of a boat which always numb the posterior no matter how many cushions! Use 'tubes' to get to those trout just out of your casting range and/or to drift on to reefs and islands of waters where there is no boat available. You can at a pinch take them up hills and out to remote normally inaccessible lakes/lochs but you need to be pretty tough for that game.

Float tubes are not for everyone but for the fit, adventurous, slightly mad water lover they are the greatest of fun. Give them a try!

Standard Lure Fishing

I was tempted to omit this part of my book, but, on reflection I realised that tactically I resorted to lure fishing on occasion. The problem is that what I term 'standard lure fishing' must overlap previous, precise methods of using imitations of fry and bait fish or deep trolling, for *ferox* and for sticklebackers. There is, though a definite lure tactic, an example I give here.

This is a development of that drift-fisher's use of a bright or attractive fly on the top dropper, and he will explain that this is 'to bring the fish up', meaning that when a trout takes the middle dropper or point fly below, it's first temptation has been to come to the bob-fly. It's to take this further that I have on occasion fished a lure on the point with a basic insect imitation above. This is to give the impression of a predatory 'lure' chasing a small food item to set up a competitive reaction by the trout, to grab one or the other. It has worked well when I haven't been able to think of anything else, say one of those 'blank' looking days on a lake or loch, no rise, no fly.

It gives rise to an interesting discussion on the question of 'why' a trout takes a fly. This has preoccupied angling writers from the past. I recollect that the great Mr Skues analysed three or four feeding patterns, hunger, irritation, aggression and so on. Of course this is the basis of our enjoyable fly dressing hobby when we try to make a fly to satisfy one of these criteria, and sometimes it tilts our fly dressing too much in the direction of 'perfect imitation', which is encouraged by fly making competitions judged for display success. This is a very human way of looking at animal behaviour. We translate it into human terms, which is known as 'anthropomorphism'. You often hear anglers comparing 'the intelligence' of - different species (I sometimes indulge myself). Objectively, the feeding behaviour of fish is more accurately understood in terms of conditioned reflexes as researched by the famous Russian physiologist, Pavlov.

We do not need to go far into this! Sufficient is it to know that there are no complex reasoning processes going on in the mind of the trout, and if I may join that army of speculators, I divide their feeding behaviour into two categories. These are *random feeding* and *preoccupied feeding*. There is a cross over between the two, for instance when an angler believes his black lure to have been taken for a horse leech, but on spooning a trout you rarely find it to have been stuffed with a hatch of black lures, do you?

164

Random feeding is simply a predatory response to movement, vibration and colour. That is lure fishing, pure and simple.

It does expose the colourists' fallacy. An extreme example is common in America where fishermen for pike tell you that the best plug bait has a white body and a bright scarlet head, which I found effective when I joined the winter pike cull on Bewl Water. Such plugs resemble no fish prey of the pike. The choice of lure colour should rather be based on the prevailing light conditions, choosing a tinsel-bodied one for reflecting bright sunlight, a drab, mobile pattern for dull skies and, perhaps garish colours such as orange or yellow for deep work in coloured water. Having said that, the precise choice is personal, you can do no better than obtaining that excellent book of patterns, *Dressed to Kill* by Robson and Carnhill.

This is good place briefly to discuss preoccupied feeding behaviour, which is simply the 'impressing' process which animal rescuers know when they keep an injured creature so long that it identifies itself with its carers. The basis of this is food supply, but the animal cannot be released again into the wild once it has been 'impressed' for, in simplistic terms it believes itself to be a human being. It cannot distinguish the difference. This conditioning process is simply brought about by repetition, the creature receives the same amount of food at the same time. When regular hatches of insects come along seasonally the trout then sees the same fly repeatedly so that the image is impressed, and that was, and still is, the basis of 'exact imitation'. The error was in supposing that the trout saw, and sees the fly in the same colour spectrum as ourselves, but countless exceptions, previously described, prove this to be wrong.

This is a simpler division of trout feeding behaviour that satisfies myself and it explains why I never rule out standard lure fishing. Unfortunately the image of the routine lure fisherman is poor. It is of a man standing in a boat on a rainbow reservoir, hour after hour, throwing out a sinking line with lure attached, and stripping it back, often at high speed.

The prejudice against this is unfair, for a lure is simply a wet fly writ large. Nor need they be monsters on size 6 long-shanked hooks. My favourite lures of choice are dressed on standard shanks, from 12 down to 8, and a lure family I carry could be called 'Sweeney Variants' as they are versions of the renowned Sweeney Todd, the main difference being that I carry patterns with different colours of thorax with matching hackles, magenta, hot orange, bright green, scarlet and so on. One reason for using the mini-lures is that, having less air resistance, I can chuck them a very long way with a shooting head from the shore of a loch.

Yes, overlapping lures with fish imitations is a human problem. My Beastie lures, with their mobile, long tails are intended to copy small bait fish, as is my Green Ghost, but this is my intention, not the trout's, and who knows exactly what motivates the trout to take them? Nor does it matter!

Basically, I need two types of lure, the Sweeney Variants for silhouettes in dull conditions or for low angles of sunlight, and a tinselled one for the bright days. The most success I have enjoyed with the latter has simply been a normal Dunkeld tied to appropriate size. When water is very coloured, after heavy rain, then a really garish red, orange or yellow lure is the only chance of success. Fishing along a windswept shore at Hanningfield one day, when the inshore water was a muddy slick, the scarlet and yellow Chief Needabeeh saved my day.

There's little more to say, for I confess that I resort to plain lure fishing rarely. This will be a time when I simply cannot think of what else to do, almost a desperation ploy for dour conditions. Those few patterns hide in one corner of my fly box. It is almost a limbo-land in tactical choice, and whilst it is distinct from making a deliberate attack on fry-feeding trout, it is difficult to determine when and to what extent it overlaps. In the fly dressing books we do not separate small-fish imitations from frankly provocative lures, we cannot do so. The separation exists in my own mind when I choose how to fish. I know when I'm after a fish-eating cannibal, or a trout on a fry-eating binge – or when I'm just searching 'blank' water hopefully, but even then, as described at the beginning of this chapter, some intelligence can be applied to the otherwise boring line-stripping process. There can be some pleasure in mastering distance casting technique which normally accompanies lure fishing, for it is a water-searching affair, the more water you search, the better.

I should repeat one truism, which like many such, has its exceptions. Most experienced anglers recognise that lures are usually retrieved at too fast a speed. The tactical choices of lure fishing are plain enough, trying different speeds and different depths. Strangely, when bank fishing from reservoirs, an old roach fishing tactic scored for me. We called this 'corner fishing'. It was down at the great London Metropolitan reservoirs. It was assumed that such corners were food traps into which big roach would collect, and the trick was to sit on one side of the corner and cast the bait towards the other, the depth being at least twelve feet in those concrete bowls. The same seemed to be true for trout, and it was successful to draw a lure from one corner wall to the other, for it is known that when still waters are stocked with both rainbow and brown trout, the latter are driven into small pockets by their more aggressive cousins, and the brown trout, being territorial, tend to remain there. Some such fisheries have their known 'brownie corner' for example. This is equally true of rainbow-stocked reservoirs with native wild brown trout populations, as in the North Pennines.

The problem with this tactical section is that, contrary to some opinions, rainbow and brown trout neither feed nor take their food in the same way. This is an aspect seen in the regular fisher of stocked waters, for the rainbow trout usually takes slowly, and it will often come again and again after a lure if it misses the first time. Knowing this, you see the habitual lure stripper holding his rod tip low, pointing downwards to the water. In many cases, eventually the rainbow hooks itself. When deliberately fishing for brown trout, even on a mixed fishery, I would never hold the rod in this way, the brown trout is a fast grabber, it has to be hit from a higher rod tip and with a quick reaction. It rarely comes twice.

There you are, I do not discount the standard lure, it has saved many a blank day, but I admit it is hard to fit it in to a tactical range of choices. Of course it overlaps with more precise attacks on fry-predators. It has its place, and it is right to accept it alongside the use of provocative wet flies, like the Butcher, Alexandra and Peter Ross, and it is patently absurd to accept the one and condemn the other. It is a paradox that in seeking the wild brown trout the most popular fly fishing method on still water occupies the smallest place in this book simply because when you think tactically you realise that what most anglers would describe as 'lure' fishing is refined to dealing with a feeding pattern on small fish. The remaining 'desperation ploy' leaves experimental fishing at various depths and speeds, with the colour of fly body suited to the light conditions. It cannot, alas, be more than that.

It is nevertheless not to be discounted, and it can be both testing and pleasurable on occasion to fish a lure from the bank of a vast water, using a shooting head and double haul, to brush up that long lost art of distance casting. Who knows, you might bump into a real specimen fish that way.

Restocking a Kentish stream, River Teise.

Part Four
Snapshots of Memory

The enigmatic lake of Loweswater.

This is a collection of experiences and locations where I have fished. For a thorough guide you need to consult a book like the comprehensive *Where to Fish* which comes out every two years.

I always begin my trout season on the Monteviot beat of the Teviot, near to Jedburgh. On and off, this has been a regular expedition for more than thirty years. The fishery is a beat of some two miles or more, mostly double bank and with one or two companions, we rent the fishing with a well-maintained estate cottage. I had this river in mind when I chose the title for my recent book, *To Meet the First March Brown*.

Although the Teviot is a tributary of the mighty Tweed, and the beat is some eight miles or so from the famous Junction pool at Kelso where the twins meet, even at Jedburgh it is still a considerable river. High on a hill above our cottage at Nisbet stands a monument commemorating the Duke of Wellington and from this spot you have a wonderful vista of the river valley. More than that, the rich farmland rolls away below you, and whilst this freshly ploughed earth delights the farmer, it gives the angler a problem, for if rain falls higher up the valley towards Teviothead, then the river quickly becomes too cloudy to fish.

When choosing a fishing holiday situation it makes sense to take into account conditions which might prevent you from fishing, and to have alternatives to hand. Thus it is in the far North, when gales stir up the shallow marl pits you need to know where there are other lochs with stony floors which remain clear, for suspended silt in river or lake causes fish to become too sluggish to feed. Happily, the Scottish border country is a veritable heaven for fly fishers, there are lochs in abundance and other day-permit streams, like the Whiteadder and Blackadder may well be clear when the Teviot is unfishable.

That apart, the Monteviot water is as near perfect a stream to my mind as I could find. Unusually, the stock of wild trout grow well in spite of a considerable run of sea trout. It is generally believed that sea trout rivers have poor stocks of stunted brown trout. Indeed, some authorities believe this to be the cause of the migratory habit. Happily there are exceptions, rivers like the Don, Tay and Deveron where the two species flourish side by side, and the Teviot is such a stream. In autumn there is a run of salmon from the Junction Pool. A smaller run comes through in 'spring' and during the summer there is often a grilse or two in our beat. My guess is that the Teviot probably holds the largest grayling in Britain, but that is beyond the scope of this book.

Historically these border rivers have changed. If we could have stood by the stream two hundred years ago, when there was a period of rain we would have watched the level of flood water fall gradually, day by day. The sudden rush of dirty water would have been less. This is due to many developments, the furrowing of forestry land, the laying of concrete and so on. The difference was described by Stewart as rainfall on a thatched roof, dripping off slowly as against a slate roof where it poured off quickly as it fell. This is a most apt simile.

I have never found a statistical analysis of fly life between today and yesteryear. Clearly the use of insecticide must have made a difference, for we know this, working through the food chain, has had a dramatic effect on both birds and mammals like otters. Realistically, even on sporting estates, agriculture must take precedence so that toxic substances leach into the water. Our stretch of the Teviot still produced good hatches in April which may have been one benefit from the fast run-offs of water, flushing out the river. As I write, genetically modified crops are being developed which will tolerate higher concentrations of insecticide and weed-killer. The effects on aquatic fly life are as yet incalculable.

That previous book title of mine, *To Meet the First March Brown*, was a quotation from a poem written by an earlier angling writer, but it struck a note inside my own consciousness, for as the drear winter months dragged by I would sit by the fire, glass in hand, conjuring up the scene which would, hopefully meet my eyes when I walked the river, with my companions on the Sunday afternoon of our arrival. This would be the second week in April. Our climate is so variable I never knew how I would find it, what mood it would be in. On occasion there would be a heat wave so that we would sit at noon in our shirtsleeves outside the fishing hut, cursing the bright, hot sun. An opposite extreme was the snow covered banks with flurries stinging in our eyes and the rod handles too cold to hold. One thing was certain, come rain, come shine, the March Browns would still sail down the current around noon, usually mixed in with their cousins, the Large Dark Olives. The two other flies we would expect to see at that time would be the Iron Blue and an early caddis for which the river was famous, the Sandy Sedge. If the weather was unnaturally warm this would fool a few Medium Olives into believing that summer had arrived.

I imagine that the trout are as eager to see these hatches. It must have been a lean winter for them. This is why the April fishing was so captivating, the trout came to the fly so boldly.

April weather in the borders can be severe. Usually the wind is constant, from the North-west, blowing straight downstream, making upstream work impossible. Although many fishermen will associate dry fly work with warmer weather, northern anglers know that trout take from the surface even on the coldest of days. The reason is that the duns take longer to dry off and harden their wings, remaining vulnerable on the surface for some time. It was fascinating to watch the flotillas of flies coming down towards me, being hit on the surface, but also I was unable to cast a floater upstream into the strong Nor'wester. This is no lack of skill, we were all good casters, but not only was the prevailing wind strong, the high banks funnelled its power, and at that time of year it might well blow the whole week.

Of course, when writing a fishing log the temptation is to dwell on one's victories and consign the frustrations to the dustbin of memory, but that would be untrue to a discussion of tactics. Coming from a southern chalk stream to a typical border river, I was struck by the sheer length of the beat. On the Test I was confined to just a few hundred yards of highly stocked river. The custom there was to perch on a bankside bench to watch for a rise. Given more than two miles of mixed pools, weirs and runs on the Teviot it was no great trick to guess where the flies would hatch, for as we split up between different, widely separated pools, one of us would be smothered in flies around noon at one end of the water whilst another would scarcely see a fly at the other. A day or two later this situation would be reversed. This is one reason why I always carried a small pair of binoculars, knowing that sea gulls would give the game away, swooping over the surface as soon as the hatches started. When researching the *Fishing Gazettes* for my recent anthology I smiled at the wise advice being given by its Honorary Chaplain in the last century, that once a fisherman had located the hatching places for March Browns, then he should return there at the same time next day, the flies would certainly meet both himself and the fish. If only it were that easy. It also amuses me when I read one of those accounts of a river visited for a day or two by a journalist who becomes the instant expert with all the secrets revealed. It is true, a picture does emerge, but only after many years, that even though the river still catches you out, you begin to anticipate when and where the flies will hatch. You begin to learn about the regular stony hatching places for those flies.

The capricious feeding behaviour of the Teviot trout always amazed me, for often it could not be fathomed. There would be a year when the March Brown hatch was mixed in with Large Dark Olives, and although I could see the former fly being snaffled by the trout, on the mixed team, only the Blue Dun would be taken. I doubt this had anything to do with 'imitation', it would be *how* my fly was seen by the fish, probably its position on the leader being the most important factor. There would be things I could not know. The March Browns might be hatching from a rocky bed higher up than the silty home of the Blue Duns further downstream. Anglers over generations have remarked on the frustration of a March Brown hatch when fish are taken at the start of it, but as it progresses, the artificial fly fails, even though naturals are being knocked off all around. This is when the artificial fly is questioned, it's not quite colour-perfect, but that is nonsense. It is not so much what the trout sees, it is how it is seen.

The richness of the food-life in 'our' stretch of the Teviot can be gathered from the fact that from time to time one would catch fish of some three pounds or so, powerful wild brownies we labelled 'Teviot Expresses'. I finish this short account of the river in April with my favourite fish-memory, one amongst many, but not my largest fish. We had invited the late George Aitken to have a day with us. He was a former salmon fly casting champion. It was decidedly chilly, and we elected to fish the top of the beat where high banks afforded some shelter. The wind was still strong, downstream, and I had to wade out in my 'chesties' to cast to the opposite bank, for the March Browns were tucked up against that far bank. A small eddy was curling some flies behind a heap of floating branch-debris. A trout had tucked itself into the slack there and it was knocking off the duns at its leisure. I had as a point fly a Partridge & Orange which, according to ancient lore, I fondly believed, copied the female March Brown, and knowing that George's critical eye was upon me, I had to avoid the barbed wire fence behind and drop the fly within the inch or two of water between the branch and the trout. As luck would have it the fly fell perfectly, the trout hit it firmly and I presented George with a pound-and-three-quarter breakfast, to which he added a twin minutes later.

I believe that a day on the Whiteadder is going back to school for a fly fisher. This is another favourite border stream, joining the Tweed at Berwick. I fished this for the first time forty years ago, and it still draws me back on occasion. In summer it is crystal clear. By day, when you can see every pebble for yards away, you would say it had no fish, but as dusk falls and you wait patiently on the bank, there, on the far side, in the deepening shade of the trees, you hear the gentlest of plops as a fish sucks down a fly. You have to be a good fly fisher to succeed on the Whiteadder. I doff my hat to its regular anglers because the greater part of the river is divided between two Associations which, as I write, will sell you a visitor's ticket. The clarity of the water and the democracy of the fishing tests skill, especially by day.

So why do I love this stream? Simply because it has a quiet, lowland beauty, as well as being a challenge.

Not far from the monument where the Count de la Bastie was ambushed and killed by the murderous Homes in days gone by, there is a pool, said to be haunted by a red-haired lady who, unusually, walks by day. There is a whin-lined pool where, even under the sun a trout was sipping down flies. It scorned my floating Pheasant Tail, so I gave it close scrutiny. The nature of the rise was quiet, the surface of the water being little disturbed, just the merest ghost of a ring coming at regular intervals. Not having a proper emerger pattern, I chose a small Hare's Ear floater and clipped the hackle very short. This bogged down nicely in the surface film and that trout saw this fly in the way it expected to see it, and thus it was taught a lesson when I slipped it back in.

When I first fished the Whiteadder, few if any salmon could run the cauld at Berwick but today they have made the passage easier. Like its off-spring, the Blackadder, it exemplifies the enormous range of prime border trout fishing open to the visiting angler. Each year the tourist organisation produces a fine booklet with details of the many border trout streams, two examples of which I have given. If you catch a nice trout on the White-adder on a bright summer's day, buy yourself a wee dram in the local hostelry, you certainly deserve it, for my guess is that local experts come to the river at dusk. Of course, I know that a careless footfall spooks trout, but the Whiteadder fish are the spookiest I have encountered, the slightest movement would send them arrowing away to sanctuary.

Cow Green reservoir is the highest in England being situated in Upper Teesdale. I caught a trout there of which I am most proud, not because of its actual size, but simply because it gave me the greatest satisfaction. I was introduced to Cow Green when the fish were still enjoying the rich feeding binge which always happens when land is first flooded. Naturally it had to settle down, and to be brutally frank, today the average weight of the native trout is well below the pound. Like many of these unstocked reservoirs in the high country the regular visiting fishermen, though few in number, go there more for the solitude, and the wild scenery than the expectation of catching large trout. Providing that the tackle system is scaled down to match the smaller fish sport can be enjoyable, whilst there comes to the fly the occasional fish of above average size.

There are four English reservoirs which attract me for these reasons. As well as Cow Green, they are Selset, Balderhead and Scarhouse.

It was in 1982 when I caught my specimen fish from Cow Green. It was a day of early summer when I drove through thick mist from Langdon Beck along the three mile track to the fishing hut. I was dismayed to see the lake still shrouded, but as I used the self-service dispenser to buy my ticket the sun began to burn off the mist and a refreshing breeze sprang up.

The art of fishing these remote lakes is to keep moving. It is rarely necessary even to enter the water. My own method is to throw a line out into the ripple, then to take a couple of steps along the bank so that the fly will be retrieved along the curve of the line. It amuses me to see the odd visitor from a lowland stocked water plunge in to his wader tops, and, rooted to the spot, cast a heavy line as far as he can, only to wonder why the lake is so unproductive. I have discussed before the territoriality of the brown trout, you have to go to find them. You also need to guess where are the natural food traps in a lake.

I had fished along a mile or so of bank. The day had developed into perfect fishing weather, a reachable ripple offshore, a light breeze, broken cloud sending shadows scudding across the fells which surround the place. I have always felt hopeful where spits of land protrude into the water, and on reaching such a place I noticed that small black buzzers were hatching and a fish or two were rising within range. It's nice to know that unlike rainbow trout, these brownies would not cruise away upwind, so I had time to tie on a small Williams' Favourite, greasing it to make it float.

Almost immediately I hit a sizeable fish and to my chagrin the loop on the end of my line gave way. This was pure carelessness on my part, I hadn't examined it for some time. I hastily fixed on another leader, using the old-fashioned figure-of-eight knot, then fished with a similiar fly. A fish was still rising, and this one took boldly. The terrain at Cow Green is rugged. You have to walk either through wiry heather or along very rocky beaches, so I leave behind every unnecessary item, which includes the net! Knowing this, I played out the fish with care and when it began to show me its flank, I slipped it into the marginal shallows. I have no idea what it weighed. It was a long fish, healthy with a powerful propeller. I photographed it, and recently finding that this picture was fading, I asked my artist friend, Noel Messenger, to copy faithfully its photographic portrait.

I know from conversations with other anglers that the idea of fishing for small brown trout with the hope of a very rare bigger one would not bear comparison with the rainbow-stocked reservoirs nearby, Hury and Grassholme, and I pass their crowded banks when I am on my way to the wild fisheries. I sometimes meet an angler at 'the Big Cow' who has gone there by accident, and he usually expresses his disappointment in no uncertain Geordie terms. There's little need to explain further the difference between our two fishing philosophies. All I can say is that there's a magic to Cow Green, you either feel it or you don't.

I first went to Scarhouse reservoir when rain and wind were ruling the place. It was a dreadful day, but two Yorkshiremen were humouring me about my love of wilderness, saying that they could more than match Cow Green. We were all defeated that day. The past year as I write this I had returned to a favourite 'watering hole' of mine, the Buck Inn in the tiny hamlet of Thornton Watlass which offers its guests fishing on the local club stretch of the Ure. The river was swirling down in flood, the coffee in my flask was of similar colour. Not wishing to go to nearby rainbow reservoirs, Thornton Steward or Leighton, a glance at the map revealed a tortuous lane running between dry stone walls over the hills, to drop down into Niddedale at the head of which was Scarhouse.

It amazes me that they managed to tuck the village of Lofthouse into a fold of the hills above the lake. The postmaster smiled when I asked for my day ticket, grace of the Niddedale Angling Club. The wind was booming in the eves of his roof. 'You won't find it crowded', he smiled.

As I drove along the track to the reservoir, the trees were bending before the force of the near-gale. The track rises as the infant Nidd falls away into a gorge, and then the splendid dam rears up before the eyes, fortifications, turrets and battlements, for the northern reservoir builders created magnificent dams. The lake is some 120 acres, a long, deep slick of water impounded into a gash between high hills. There was no other car in the park which was so exposed and swept by the fierce wind that my rod bowed over as I threaded the line . . . but beyond the cream-topped waves and spin drift I could see some quieter bays under the lee of the hills, the wind wasn't gun-barrel straight down the valley.

The only sign of human activity was a string of tiny yellow and scarlet beads threading along the high fellside paths above my head, anoraked masochists like me, the hill walkers. Where else was I to find a sizeable lake to myself? And as I pushed my body through the wind, along the shore, I saw that the golden sands of the strand were free of footprint, no one had fished that way for a while. Two furious oyster catchers scolded me for invading their patch. A notice warned me not to bathe. The deep water never rose about 12 degrees. The water of such lakes has a deep golden colour, some would call it peaty, but the problem is one of depth, mostly it plunges down into darkness from not much further out than a rod's length.

I believe it was Halford of old who advised his followers to view the Red Spinner as the sheet anchor for an angler on an unknown water, his favoured chalk streams. But on these unstocked reservoirs any small black fly will succeed if the fish are in a taking mood. The ubiquitous black buzzer is the insect which always manages to thrive in the deepest and darkest places, the trout have a surface eye for it, so greasing up a small hackled Williams' or Pennell will excite their attention. It is not difficult to make a quantity catch at Scarhouse, the fish are hungry and eager. If you take a pounder you have an exceptional fish, but with scaled down tackle, if you go there for the pleasure of wandering like the knight at arms who was deserted by *la belle dame sans merci*, then you may discover that small fish are sweet.

For wild brown trout fishing the multitude of lochs in the far north, in Caithness and Sutherland, is a fly fisher's paradise. The possibilities range, according to personal choice, from very dour fisheries which yield specimens of high average weight to the patient angler, down to lochs with populations of stunted fish of a few ounces which come to the fly eagerly. Between these two extremes are fisheries where the trout may average around the pound and you might bag up to half-a-dozen on a reasonable day . . . The reason for these variations is the obvious one, relationship between spawning facilities and food supply. I omit the famous limestone lochs in the areas of Cape Wrath and Durness because I have not fished them, but I have a long and wide experience of the lochs in the eastern and central areas. These are mostly easily accessible on day tickets from either the good tackle shops in Wick and Thurso, or from local hotels in Tongue and Forsinard.

The Badenloch system can be fished from bank or boat by enquiry at a small fishing hut as you approach the lochs, but as this isn't intended to be a guide book, excellent and comprehensive information of the area is given in such books by local experts like Mrs Lesley Crawford and Bruce Sandison.

Choosing to mix some activity with reasonably sized fish, I took myself to what may well be the most spectacular loch, with the interesting name of Hakel. This is close to Tongue. The agreeable aspect is that it is of just the right size to fish round completely from the bank in a day. A photographer's delight, with banks of yellow gorse and the three mountain peaks of the 'Bens', frown down from the background, the eye is tempted to wander at the scenery just when the lightning take of a fish is missed.

I arrived in mayfly time. The weather was perfect, blue sky with puffy clouds scudding by, but just to remind me that it was highland country, a volley of passing hail rattled my Barbour coat as I was rodding up in one of the lay-bys above the loch. I chose the far right corner to start, for there a spit of pebble-beach gives a feeling of hope, and then a long strand runs up to an attractive bay with an island. The mayflies were hatching sporadically, exciting rises, but one of those conundrums, the Olive Bumble on the dropper was mostly ignored whereas an unlikely Coch-y-bondhu on the point was eagerly accepted.

Hakel is fairly popular for that remote place, being near to a resort as well as close to the road. Even so, the trout population holds up well, and I believe that the constant pruning of the stock keeps the average weights up to a good, takeable size. The water is pellucid, but what fascinates me is the changeability of the bank structure in such a small area. There will be flat, slaty beds of rock here, pebble strands there and bays of a clean, golden sand. Trout are slim, strong and although most northern loch trout take a sepia stain from the peat, Hakel fish are sometimes silver and blue with bright scarlet spots.

There are days which stick in the memory. This was one such, for everything was perfect. The fish came well to the fly, but not so easily as to remove the challenge. They still had to be fished for, and a day's hard work brought some dozen to hand, before being sent back to fight another day. Another benefit, Hakel is not quite so cursed with the dreaded midge, perhaps the hills and mountains funnel the wind to keep them at bay.

Afternoon finds me half way round the far bank. There is another island, easily reached across a shallow channel, and on the far side I wade out over rough ground, and casting a long line, the fly is taken boldly, the light line rod bows over into its fighting curve, and after a brisk fight a near pounder comes to hand. Then on I plod to my favourite place, a finger-shaped bay, a classic food trap where it is rare never to see a rising trout.

The evening, or what passes for one in the 'simmer dim' finds me on the home straight, a lengthy, pebbly strand with the mayfly finished and the trout taking a small, black midge, and just to prove that this loch isn't solely for beginners, they prove to be fussy. Never mind, the sun has dropped behind the three peaks which stand like sentinels against the quiet sky. The wind has dropped with the sun and the gentlest of ripples gives the trout a chance to be suspicious. A chill reminds me it's time to break down my rod, for I have the long drive back to the cottage near Wick. Yes, Hakel is not always a challenge, though it has its dour times, but truth to tell, that spectacular scenery draws me back time and time again. It tries hard not to be a lochan, but I think it manages it.

Our race of angling writers is often criticised, not without justice, for describing our successes and keeping an *omerta* about our failures. I thought I would tell you of the other extreme of the northern fishing, my ignominious failure on the Cross Lochs, so called, I told my companion, because after hours without an offer, I felt quite cross. This is the Specimen Hunter's sanctuary, a group of dark lochs found by driving for miles along a forestry track, then yomping a mile or so over a quaggy moor. I have a recollection of immense loneliness, the bleakest place I could imagine. I had been warned by a fellow angler I met, brooding over his glass in the bar of the Forsinard Hotel. He had spent a fruitless day there. His frustration was enhanced by the tremendous hatches of fly including those great, black and white marble veined sedges, but the mirror-like surface of the water was untroubled by any protruding neb of trout. 'They must feed deep on the larvae,' he opined. And I made him right.

I might well have given the Cross Lochs the proverbial elbow, but a patient companion, Jeff Sage, took up the challenge. He came back with that fabulous three pounder, the one which hitched on to his Teal & Green middle dropper. It had no similarity to the corixas stuffed into its tummy. 'Two takes, one fish,' he averred. But what a beauty. I weighed it up. I also checked with Bruce Sandison's guide book.[1] 'The most infuriating lochs in the North', Bruce tells me.

Why not go? I was staying for a month and could afford one day of tugging a poor offer through a rich larder of natural food. So booking a day ticket at the Forsinard Hotel, I bumped up that rough track, crossing a stream which would have tempted Richard Clapham of old, hill beck fisher supreme, until I came to the high fence with a tiny arrow pointing across the moor to the five lochs, the marly beds of which spoke volumes of chunky trout feeding selectively on plentiful food. I guessed the water would be alkaline, those corixas proved that, but my day was of chilly wind and lowering skies with only a passing eagle as a sign of life.

Yes, I failed, and failed without glory. The flies were cast, hour after hour, the natural flies hatched in abundance, the famous huge sedges were there, but no rise did I see all day, and the faintest tug of the fly on leader was absent. I had the feeling that I was at the end of the World, I wanted loneliness and wilderness, and this was it. So why trumpet a failure? I give you the extreme *par exemple* of a dour water, not the famed problem of the

[1]*Trout Lochs of Scotland.*

gin-clear limestone lochs to the West, but perhaps one where food is so rich and the spawning renewal so low that a small population of fastidious Bunter-like trout can be so selective. True, the odd nine pounder has succumbed, so if you are one of those very patient seekers after really big, wild fish, true brownies not of the *ferox* race, for my friend's fish was a Brummell of a trout, then Cross Lochs are for you . . . Oh, I will certainly return, please God as the Irish say. And, to rub it in, when giving a talk to a club the Chairman kindly described me as an expert trout fisher. Sourly I told him: 'I wish someone had told that to the fish in the Cross Lochs!'.

I was reading an account of that grand old ghillie of the last century, Donald Gunn. He looked after trout anglers fishing the Badenloch waters at Forsinard, and I mused about his reference to a fellow helper with 'his moor charger'. I know that some anglers profit from great wheeled vehicles with which a ghillie conveys them across the heathland to distant lochs, but dear old Donald lived before the internal combustion engine was invented. I imagine this must have been some sort of horse-drawn carriage, but to reach distant lochs my friends and I have to fall back on the art of yomping with map and compass. Such is the nature of the terrain, that going is uphill, and, happily, homeward bound with a happy heart and tired legs, is downhill. That is how it should be. In Shetland it always seemed to be the other way round.

My friend and I had chosen to yomp to a distant loch called Druim a Chliabhain, but we called it simply 'Drum' for short, for the Gaelic tongue sounds as if one should have a mouthful of rusty razor blades to speak it properly, but I always smile at the memory of a ghillie cursing Negley Farson[2] in Gaelic when he dropped a bottle of whisky. He couldn't do justice to the catastrophe in English, the language was too weak. This was a golden day, the uphill haul was said to be a couple of miles, it felt like more, and the track climbed up past the Garvault Hotel, said, and rightly so, to be the remotest in the land, and its white walls, shining in the sun, were a comfort in that stark landscape. At the summit of the second hill we reached the first loch, of Coire nam Lang, then following the connecting stream, we found ourselves at 'Drum', lying gloriously between two mountains, Ben Griams and Ben a'Mhadaidh. It is a fair sized loch, about two miles long with clear water, often over that golden sand one surprisingly finds on heather and peat moors.

Our one mistake was to make this a 'day trip', for the sun shone down onto a glinting ripple, and although we had booked the use of the boat, we elected to fish from the bank. Yet the fish came to the fly, averaging about three-quarters of a pound, though the loch is reputed to have its legendary monsters.

I closed my eyes in the heather and dreamed of dear old Donald Gunn. He was whipping up his horse with his 'moor charger' and there, sitting

[2]*Going Fishing.*

on the bench in the back, clutching his rod for dear life was the famous William Murdoch who always booked Donald when out from Forsinard, for Donald claimed he knew where the 'big troots' were. Many was the three pounder he got for his fishers, and many the not-so-wee drams they forced down his unwilling throat! These trout from these high-up lochs, they are of the pink flesh, so I'm told, but it wasn't the weight of my creel that made me return them, it seemed so shameful to deprive them of such a wonderful home.

I do remember the fly I favoured, that's no problem, for whenever I cross that great bridge at Inverness, in my mind's eye I am already fixing the Grouse & Claret to be my tail fly, and it stays there unless, and unusually it really fails. I did not see mayfly at Drum, too early or too high. I wouldn't know, but the book told me that standard loch flies would work well, the more so if I started at the North end of the West shore, and it proved its point, that magical fly scores so well. I must take a Halfordian dictum, and call it my sheet anchor on any unknown loch in distant parts. Until the trout prove me wrong, that is. And yet, given the long haul, and even with Donald's 'moor charger', it seems a shame to me that transport carries engines and lazy anglers to the high lochs, they lose something of their mystery, magic and challenge, and the spirit of 'instant trout' seems to be invading even the wilderness. Yomping should be part of this fishing, I think, but that's turning the clock back to a race of stronger men, and stronger ale.

A reservoir-fishing Southron like myself would feel at home on Calder Loch, for that is exactly what it is, a water supply reservoir, the deepest and largest in Caithness and over 100 feet deep at its best. This is the home of the *ferox* and the occasional monstrous cannibal is taken when it comes into the margins , following the spawning migrations of the char which also live habitually in the deep water. The patient troller afloat would find this a water of choice, but I enjoy the long eastern shore, starting at its southern end, mostly of typical grazing meadow. I keep a weather eye for bulls, but there are miles of bank fishing.

The western bank is notoriously dangerous. I have recounted the sad fate of an angler who drowned there. This is the favourite fishery of Mrs Lesley Crawford who introduced me to it on my first visit to Caithness, many years ago. The sheer vastness of the waterscape appears daunting at first, but trout are numerous and on their day they come to the fly eagerly enough, and as I have explained, there is this strange phenomenon for those of us who are used to throwing a very long line from the bank at Grafham or Rutland, to over-cast the fish. On a good day I can usually put out a whole double taper line, even with my ultra-light outfit, but until I hit on the reason, I couldn't understand why I retrieved about half of this length before a trout came to the fly. This is nice to know if you are a newcomer to our sport.

There is a hatch of mayfly at Calder and though I have been there in season, I have yet to see a prolific one. It seems mostly a scattering of the duns but the trout take them well enough. Curiously, I found many needle-fine stoneflies on the shore on my last visit, and having tied up some of the 'unknown' Tod flies which were made by that great wet-fly man of yester-year, I was rewarded with a good catch. Truth to tell, Calder was unkind to me on my first three visits, the fish were numerous, though small, and I nearly wrote it off in my mind as a 'stunted' trout fishery. This last year it bestowed its favours. I came with a companion just before the mayfly was up, in early June and the breeze was favourable from that eastern shore.

Calder was one of the lochs which were chosen by the research team from the Herriot-Watt University, and I remind you of the strange growth pattern they discovered, a rapid acceleration in weight after the fourth year, and this explains the occasional three pounder taken from the water. That same year a lady angler, fishing with Mrs Crawford who has her own wall-mounted Calder monster to her credit, landed a six pounder from the shore on a Blue Zulu fly, a considerable feat as, like many of us, she carried no net. The splendid specimen had to be beached.

I admit, too, that I was pleasantly astonished to take my first fish on the Tod Fly, for today it is completely unknown. In fact that famous family of needle flies, so lauded before the last War, is rarely tied as the imitation-fever has gone in for nymphy copies. It was the very first cast after I had tied it on as the tail fly that I had a rewarding pull and a sepia-coloured trout came to hand.

This great lake gives me the opportunity to philosophise on the advice given in guide books, that 'typical loch flies' will serve here, as on so many places, and that famous Blue Zulu is a mystery unless, like myself, you believe that blue simply appears to be black in the trout's vision. Given that, it's easy to fit in all sorts of explanations, that the fish took it for a black buzzer or any similarly coloured terrestrial fly blown onto the water. I think it to be a waste of time to tease this out, I prefer simply to know that some favourite patterns have caught fish for generations, and to equate the successful Wickhams and Butchers is unnecessary, unless you can show me a hatch of Soldier Palmers.

My personal preference when fishing along the bank of lochs like Calder is to use a two-fly team, the top buzzy dropper being high up the leader. The reason is clear, on windy days or with high banks of wiry tufts behind, three flies can get themselves into horrendous tangles, just when a rise is going strong. I would love to kid you that I rarely tangle, but, alas, this isn't true. I have my share. It also makes sense to use a tapered cast, for Calder's banks are exposed to winds which sweep along for miles and you need to put the leader across gusts, and straighten it.

I think of the famous remark by Neville Chamberlain. He was asked where he was going just before a reply to his ultimatum to Hitler had been delivered. He replied along the lines that he was going fly fishing on one of the remotest streams in this land, and who could blame him? I was invited to do some fly dressing demonstrations in the village hall at Dunnet and when asked where this was, I replied about as far north as you can go without falling into the sea. In this village you can purchase a day ticket at the Northern Sands hotel to fish the well-managed loch of St John's. This loch suits the southern eye as it lies in pasture land. The St John's Club manages it, and it is unusual in that it has its wild stock topped up from an efficient hatchery owned by the Club.

St John's is a shallow loch, one of those which does cloud-up for a day or two after a strong blow. The Chairman of the Club kindly offered me the use of his boat for the day before I gave my evening talk. It was a perfect day, the weather I love the best, mild, a gentle breeze to make a light ripple and puffy clouds breaking up the direct light. Fish seem to take as the clouds drift across the sun and shadow falls briefly onto the water. I remember this day because the wind kept boxing the compass, the boat was swinging with it, but, irritatingly, as it changed from bank to bank. Trout were rising on different wind-lanes and the hatching flies seemed to change species with alarming rapidity. One time I would take the boat upwind to start a drift across the loch from a lee shore, then a sudden swing of the breeze found me charging down the windward shore just a few yards away. St John's is one of the few lochs which I would always prefer to fish from a boat due to its marginal shallows of clear water when not stirred up by gales.

I was first attracted to Lake Vyrnwy by the reports of the wonderful sport given in the *Fishing Gazettes* in the early years after the reservoir was opened and stocked with the then famous silver Loch Leven strain of trout. A luxurious hotel was built, overlooking the lakes and the story of both this hotel and the fishing is related in a book, *Lake Vyrnwy, the Story of a Sporting Hotel* by John Baynes and George Westropp both of whom clearly love the place and the surrounding impressive scenery. It is not my intention to duplicate their fascinating story other than to conjure up the image of the Victorian maidservants hustling along the corridors with copper kettles of hot water for the morning ablutions of the guests. How things have changed.

Not only the facilities! The fishing, too has altered. In those early years the surrounding hills were bare of trees which allowed a goodly fall of terrestrial insects to augment the poverty of aquatic insects from a lake which is deep even close to the banks. These hills were planted with trees, many of them conifers, which reduced the food supply, so naturally the average weight of the fish declined, the more so after the first blossoming of trout over newly flooded land. Truth to tell, I find the atmosphere of the lake today to be dark and brooding, but spectacular for all that, and the fishing is well managed by the hotel, both for its guests as well as casual visitors. The lake has to be fished by boat unless the water level falls well below the two arches of the prominent tower pier. This is sensible because the close planting of trees to the shore otherwise makes bank fishing tricky.

183

If we have lost the trout treasures of yesteryear, the Levens have given way to the stocked rainbow trout, but my interest was in the population of dark, scarlet spotted wildies in the lake, even though I expected a three-quarter-of-a-pounder to be a respectable capture.

Now, Vyrnwy is a long lake, six miles long, and about three-quarters-of-a-mile wide at its broadest part. One thing to be said for the forestry is that in most directions of wind, there is a lee shelter, though the downside of that is the flat calms which fall across the water, as happened on my last visit with my companion, Joe Tingle. We had a day of lowering clouds, flat calm water and intermittent drizzle. The wonder of it was we caught fish. There are several boat stations around the lake. We elected to fish at the farthest end from the dam where we believed rightly that the shallows would harbour food and fish, and the scenery was agreeable, though occasional rancid odours from the stinkhorns in the marshy woodlands assailed the nostrils.

It is axiomatic, in a deep lake, that the best chances come from fishing the shallows close to the bank, but the only tactic which paid off was to scull the boat from place to place. When water is very calm one sees from afar the delicate rise-forms of fish, to be approached with care. The only fish which came to the fly were those rising rings into which we swiftly threw the flies, and so calm and clear was the water that the ultra-light line rods proved to be a boon.

There must be *ferox* in Vyrnwy, it has the typical characteristics of such a water, but whether anyone patiently tries for them I do not know. Being there for a day we contented ourselves with fishing for the average wild browns until Joe hooked a demented rainbow. I honestly forget what flies we used there, but I would imagine they would have been copies of the ubiquitous black buzzers which never let you down on waters too deep for many other flies. The trout are numerous, thanks to the breeding grounds in the various streams which tumble down into the lake from the high hills.

Truth to tell, I doubt that exactitude in fly choice is necessary at Vyrnwy, the fish are hungry, with the proviso that even in 'hungry' waters, all trout can be capricious. A small black fly is vital, somewhere on the leader, then you play about with other personal favourites. I'd take a bet the black one outplays the others.

I returned to Vyrnwy Hotel a year or so later, rodless, but with my wife to enjoy a walking and bird-watching holiday in that spectacular scenery. Yes, it is sombre, but that is personal taste, for whereas I love open heaths with wide sky vistas, my wife prefers a landscape encircled with many tall trees. And if you either pop in to hire a boat, or stay in the hotel for a fishing holiday, take the sheer impressive nature of the place into account. And pick up a copy of that book, it gives a thorough description of the contours of the lake, the best fishing places. If someone had told me it were possible to write an unputdownable book about the history of a single hotel I would have laughed in disbelief, until I read this one. It lured me to fish Vyrnwy, and those flat calms tested our skill to the utmost.

The next of my small snapshots of my favourite brown trout lakes confronts me again with the dilemma of what exactly is a wild brown trout, for undoubtedly the majority of the fish in Talyllyn lake in Gwynedd are stocked, but so well managed is the fishery that I am content to include them in my own definition of true trout fishing because the stocking policy allows that essential time and space for the trout to develop a natural feeding habit, and space to roam freely. It is a large lake beneath the frowning heights of Cader Idris.

I was invited to fish Talyllyn lake when the fishery manager, Chris Pettigrew had been impressed by an article I had written on ultra-light line fishing for brown trout, and he invited myself and my regular companion, Joe to stay in the comfortable Tyn-y-Cornel hotel and to fish the weekend, both free of charge. It is not the sin of pride which made me decline the offer to fish unless we paid our way, and, happily my brother had a cottage nearby where we stayed. The problem is that such invitations also imply an obligation to praise a fishery no matter what its quality. This is why invariably I refuse such kind offers, though I needn't have worried, we both enjoyed a day of splendid fishing. It is a brown trout fishery *par excellence*.

As described earlier, the lake in May produces the most rich hatches of still water olives, and I recollect that both the pond and lake olives were on the surface most of the day in a ripple of just the right height to disguise our wiles. We were, perhaps a mite too early to meet the sea trout and salmon which run into the lake from the river Dysinni, though my own first fish was a peal. It was that day when I found myself bereft of Greenwells or similar olive copies, and I resorted to a small Invicta, greased up to work on the surface, and this accounted for my own thirteen fish, none of which were below the pound in weight. Joe went native and scored nine with his Welsh Harry Thom.

We had both come to prove our ultra-light rods on still water fish above the average weights we had been catching on the Upper Pennine lakes. They had been expressly designed for upstream wet-spider fishing on northern rivers but it was important to establish their versatility, given fears expressed by 'the Heavy Brigade', that they couldn't handle bigger still water trout. I know I cannot convert the average British angler to very light line fishing, the old heavy tradition is too ingrained, but the rods performed as well as we'd hoped, teaching two lessons, that although the first few seconds after striking are 'exciting', the cushioning effect of the parabolic curve brings fish of good size quickly to heel. Secondly, we had to adjust to striking with a longer line without the strong current to help us such as we had on fast rivers. Yes, the striking did have to be a firm bang.

Given the pleasant ripple, the water was very clear and we felt that our fine lines, coupled with the equally fine leaders, had allowed us to make respectable catches, and the only trout killed was one bestowed on a bank angler, frustrated, as it was his first time ever with fly rod in hand, and he needed to justify his new sport to his sceptical wife who expected him home, fishless.

The following day Chris took us up to the 50 acres of the Bugeilyn lakes, which are entirely unstocked. These are remote, on the moors, and a special old banger was employed to transport anglers whose own cars would have been chipped by the loose stones flying from the wheels along the rough track. I was bemused to be lead to the chosen lake – there are two – as we followed Chris along a sunken causeway, about a foot below the surrounding swampy terrain. It reminded me of the legends of Hereward the Wake in his secret fastness in the fens.

On reaching the pulling boat we went afloat and again had a fruitful day, though at this height the flies were the universal black buzzers. The stock here is entirely wild, relatives of those we catch in the Upper Pennine Lakes and of a similar size. The strange thing was the variety of colours. One fish would be typically peat brown, another sea-trout silver whilst the third variety was blue backed and silver bellied with big red spots.

On the high moors, where the wind rules, I was anxious to lay to rest that other irrational fear, that with a very light line there can be no accuracy. It is a fallacy, not only because the fine line has less resistance in the air, but also because I had developed that neo-Ritz casting style which gave a narrow looped fast-line which cut through the cross winds. I could literally punch the line through the wind to cover a rise . . . Good on you, Charles!

One from the Emerald Isle to join this circuit of our Island group, and this was to Lough Conn at a time when we were escorted to the lake by the local police because of pickets who were striking against their Government's plan to introduce trout fishing rod licences. Many fisheries were simply closed, it being impossible to hire boats or find boatmen. Conn was an exception.

Being there for the week I had intended to take one day off when a large wet-fly contest was being fished. I am not a competition fisher, so I thought a day on the grassy bank by the old Abbey, with a good book and a packed lunch, would suit me well. Such a restful day was ruined when friendly Mike Tolan, who was running the affair, was let down by one of the fishers who was booked to go out in his boat. They prevailed on myself to fish my first – and last – competition. My boat partner was Dr Whittaker whose signature graced the famous 'punt' banknotes from the Bank of Ireland, but whose main claim to fame in my eyes was the magnificent home-cured ham which he offered me, for in keeping with their gentle lifestyle the Irish anglers sensibly took an hour off for lunch, when some boats were heading in the direction of the town bars. That's how competition fishing should be!

Funnily enough, the trout were somewhat dour that day and that is why I managed to win that leg of the match, thanks to playing a fish with my hat. The popular method is to fish a team of flies on the drift, using a short line and lift, typical loch style, but I opted for 'fishing on the pull' with two flies, a Silver Invicta on the point and an Olive Bumble as a high-up top dropper. I chose this as the wind was slight and I thought it sensible to throw the flies well away from the boat and to work them back. I caught four trout and thought I had little chance.

That hat came in useful as two fish were hooked, one on each fly, and they took off in different directions, one choosing to dive under the boat. The other fish broke free, so I swivelled round, and in so doing the line entangled itself in the flies in my hat. So, holding hat in one hand, rod in the other, I managed to bring the fish to net. It was astonishing that with some ninety competitors my four trout came out on top, but this didn't convert me to competition fishing, I still prefer the lonely lake and the sky.

'Quit while you're ahead,' they say.

Pride goes before a fall, for after two other legs had been fished, we went afloat for the final, myself fishing with the expert, Brendan Smith, a man of trout wisdom and courtesy, and although I had my rod nearly snatched from my hand by the most powerful 'take' I've ever had – and missed – I was overtaken. That day was one of great wind and the loch short-line style ruled supreme. Trout did take close to the boat and I picked the wrong option, that's my excuse, I'm sticking to it. So at the end, another Irish expert, Peter O'Reilly greeted me with his classical 'Jesus, Mary and Joseph', hailing me, very flattering, but 'just another loser', I replied.

Summing this up, I have chosen from the memory banks a selection at random of some fishing places and experiences in my quest for the brown trout. I'm afraid that these are for anglers, like myself, who are not mean but of average means. Those mouth-watering places of high renown and cost were never within my grasp, I do not miss them. Yet with these scenes there are options from small fish and frequent action, which I never scorn if the scenery is grand, to the middle range, which always satisfies, right up to the dark, lonely places where very dour fish of great size might – or might not – come once or twice to a patiently fished fly.

A good place to finish is at the starting line, that little Wealden stream where I first learned, and later forgot, to throw a dry fly. We have a Club there now, and the nature of the stream has changed since they built the mighty Bewl reservoir out of which the compensation water flows, giving us a depth and variation of current unknown in days long gone.

True, the wild fish are still breeding, one has to know where they live, but given a membership, we have to stock, even with some silly rainbows, which, happily just as quickly come out again. The banks are high, so much so that I carry a rope down which I abseil here and there, and just passing my seventieth year I wonder if that is wise? The great mayfly hatches of yesteryear have gone, but a few survivors cheer me, they are creeping back. Today we have the rapacious mink which idiotic animal rightists have released, causing havoc to native wildlife.

I fish it as I always did, waiting until the fish settle and begin to rise to the surface. I slide down the banks and wade quietly upstream with brook rod and nymph or dry fly. I've told you how I fish, but can I tell you of a magical evening when I can't remember if I caught or not?

It is the calm of summer, the sun has gone down behind the rim of the hills above the valley, and I see two church towers, Horsmonden to my right, an old plague church, and, facing it on the opposite hill, the square tower of Goudhurst. That evening I felt at absolute peace with the world, I would have asked to be in no other place in the universe. Between these twin towers flows the little Teise, a dead poet at each end, Siegfried Sassoon, who hunted these fields long ago, from Brenchley. At the Yalding end grew up the rural poet, Edmund Blunden. Both were cricketers, both anglers. Both fished this stream, and I know the place where Blunden must have seen the huge pike which scared the wits out of the miller when he opened his hatches at the old mill, now long gone.

This is where I see the little rise, above me in the stream, and I am perched precariously on the steep slope of the bank. The fish is under the overhanging willow branch, so the cast is made, sideways and low. The hackled Coachman drifts down, there is that most exciting moment in any sport, the water cleaves as the trout accepts the fly, but as is usual with my weaker left hand, the hook doesn't go home on the strike, and off it goes to fight another day.

So pause here. I have taken you to the farthest trout of this land, in Shetland, and west to Wales and Ireland, but here, within forty minutes of my home I can recall those days when I first cast a fly, near to my own roots in the Weald when we watched the bombers come, stretching from horizon to horizon. I would never have guessed then that I would still be hypnotised by the same scene, gazing from the bottom of the valley upwards to the two churches, and in bell ringing days, they talked to each other across the stream.

And, yes, we also stock the river, but still the wild trout, the chub and grayling are there, and this, the right side of the Medway, the fishers are 'Men of Kent' and on this clay and iron which stains the river, grows the best fruit. I trust that politicians will understand that hops and apples cannot thrive on concrete, and that the river will still flow, and the trout still rise when I am with the ages.

So, if I have roots, they are with the Bramleys and the hops in this Wealden clay, but it is not the pleasure of any narrow nationalism, for when I had to abandon tracing our family history, I realised that I came from mongrel stock, like my first dog, Chester, called Chester for short, due to his howling at the moon (Chester Song at Twilight). You see, I came across so many bar-sinisters and Gallic infusions into our ancestral blood stream, I was gladdened to belong to a sport where carrying a fly rod is a passport to almost any community of anglers, and it's a wonderful vaulting pole for class barriers, too. Rarely, unlike golf clubs, will you be requested to wear a tie in the bar of a true trout fishing pub. Yes, there's stratification, between the humble trout fishers and the seekers for salmon in the richest beats, but, happily, some of the best, budget trout fishing is in places where those tweedy types find it of little account, and permission is freely given, or is of reasonable cost. Only the force-fed, simple-minded rainbow is becoming expensive to find, but then it's a foreign visitor, isn't it?

I have excluded the Western Isles in these snapshots, not because they lack superb brown trout fishing, and names like 'Benbecula' have a magic ring to them. Farson's *Going Fishing*, showing him crossing the sea-covered path to the isles, clutching rod in hand and grimly perched in a horse-pulled cart, speaks of the choice of migratory fish, doesn't it? Friends of mine trail off to the Uists for the fabulous sea trout and salmon. My deliberate expeditions for brown trout took me to the Orkneys and to Shetland.

Although both Orcadians and Shetlanders might deny it, there's a tactical unity between their lochs and those in Caithness and Sutherland, and also the moorland lakes of England and Wales. It would be agreeable to describe an erudite adaptation to different conditions, but it would be a deception, the same trout take the same flies in the same way, though apart from some small burns running into the island lochs, it is still water that commands. The same strong winds drive the waters, perhaps more so.

Rather than analyse this similarity, I give an illustration of my friend, Colin North who was a most successful competition fisherman on the usual 'rainbow circuit'. He fished twice for his country. Wishing to widen his experience, he joined me on the wild trout lakes in the High Pennines and soon mastered the art of catching the swift-taking fish. When a 'Final International' was fished on Loch Harray, he applied those lessons and scored the top weight for his team.

Truth to tell, when I first went to Orkney I was seeking escape. Some years before I had started a small fishing tackle manufacturing business, little realising that it would snowball into a big, successful company, bringing with it a way of life I had never visualised. The personal affluence during those years was at a cost of health and family life, and I was seeking a refuge. Spotting a house for sale on the tiny island, Rousay, I packed my fishing gear and booked my passage, intending to stay for a few days on 'Mainland'. There is a mystery about the lochs on the islands. You have to discover which ones are 'fishing'; and which ones are 'off'. This is easy on Orkney, there seem to be more fishermen about, you meet them in the bar and you can ask. Not so easy in Shetland with its innumerable lochs, you can drive past dozens of them without seeing a soul. Often you take pot luck.

In previous years Shetland had earned the reputation of being a superb

189

location for sea trout, both in the lochs as well as in the voes, but perhaps due to the over-fishing of sand eels, the sea trout declined. Now, for myself, the excellent brown trout fishing is the attraction, though there is still the chance of a sea trout in some of the lochs.

I must confess that in both places the Grouse & Claret for a point fly with a Kate McClaren on the bob, rarely left my leader. An exception was to match a fall of crane fly on Hundland loch in Orkney. I have a recollection of my son climbing a Shetland hill when the loch bored him, only to be attacked furiously by a pair of 'bonxies'[3] whose territory he had invaded. I saw him waving his arms as the clacking beaks were working in front of his nose. I must add that as a visiting angler I like to put something back into the fisheries I visit by joining the local fishing associations and this also provides useful information about location of fisheries with the best bank places marked.

My memory also conjures up those words by Housman, 'the old wind in the old anger', for these islands are dominated by wind, so much so that trees are a rarity. This is something we must take into account when going there. The weather is changeable, a still morning 'haar' can, within hours, give way to strong wind and rain coming down sideways. A typical pleasant day in summer is relatively cool, with cotton-wool clouds drifting by and a nice ripple on the loch. Perhaps I have a preference for Shetland, the lochs are mostly those which you can fish round in a day, and for the most part you can choose one for yourself, alone.

There you are, this isn't a guide book, it would be impossible for me to name the hundreds of lochs, but my eye would sometimes be astonished to discover seaweed growing in one, whilst another would be an almost black hole, seemingly featureless until a circle far out descries the rising fish. No, these word-pictures are to be a meal in reverse, the appetiser comes at the end of this book.

How to sum up?

The attraction of tactical fishing for wild brown trout is that it uses both aspects of our being, the physical skills we must master, and the intellectual qualities of the mind to relate the way we choose to fish to the observed or assumed behaviour patterns of the quarry. This makes it far more exciting than salmon fishing which is entirely mechanical.

I am content to apply a liberal interpretation to my own definition of wild fish, for although this implies trout which have been spawned in a fishery for generations, I am happy to include intelligent stocking programmes which allow the fish time and space to develop wariness of enemies and a natural feeding habit. I am not interested in intensive 'put-and-take' fishing because it lacks the challenge. I have developed my own tackle and casting systems to allow me to use a much lighter line as most

[3]Local name for the Great Skua.

190

British flyfishers are overgunned for their quarry. Not only does this tradition deny finesse and pleasure, but it also brings about an unfair score of fish which are normally smaller than the gut-bucket rainbows introduced into fisheries in recent years. The fishing I enjoy most is for gourmets rather than gourmands.

I also reject the other extreme, the anthropomorphism which falsely gives trout exceptional gifts of eyesight and intelligence which can only be defeated by the closest attention to the exact anatomical imitation of the natural fly, for this is not the way in which trout take their food. The fly must be right, tactically, but there is also a balance between what we fish with, and how we fish it. Often this is out of perspective.

It would be easy to fall into a negative attitude, by criticising the tackle we use, the way we cast and dress flies for display and the way we resist change. Of course, new ideas have to replace those which are less efficient, and that implies criticism, but then that criticism has to be followed by a positive alternative idea-system. That has been the purpose of this book, and in strictly practical terms, that has been how my own fishing life has developed.

Finally, I know yet another school of thought, that to be over-absorbed with the techniques of fishing is to miss the essentials of our sport, which is the enjoyment of nature. I recollect that there was much criticism of the dedicated specimen hunters after coarse fish when that philosophy first entered our sport and the High Priest of technology could have been dubbed as that wonderful description of a dry politician as a 'dessicated adding machine'. I have much sympathy with this critique, for me the places I fish are more important than the fish I catch, I have a fondness for wide skyscapes over bleak moorlands with the lonely music of oyster-catchers and curlews. The frenzy of the competition fisher, the material-ism of the salmon-only man, are not for me, but the glory of the seeker of wild fish in wild places is the balance in the human spirit, and even so, I do go out to catch fish. I have told you how I do it.

Index